# AMERICA

# AMERICA

## A NARRATIVE HISTORY

VOLUME I

---

GEORGE BROWN TINDALL

SECOND EDITION

W · W · NORTON & COMPANY · NEW YORK · LONDON

Since this page cannot legibly accommodate all the copyright notices, the
Credits section beginning on page A44 constitutes an extension of this copyright page.

*The text of this book is composed in Caledonia, with display
type set in Torino Roman. Composition by New England
Typographic Service, Inc. Manufacturing by R. R. Donnelley.
Book design by Antonina Krass.*

**Library of Congress Cataloging-in-Publication Data**

Tindall, George Brown.
America: a narrative history/George Brown Tindall.—2nd ed.
p.    cm.
Bibliography: p. 000
Includes index.

ISBN 0-393-95604-0 Vol. I pa.

1. United States—History.    I. Title.
E178.1.T55    1988
973—dc19                    87-23174

W. W. Norton & Company, Inc., 500 Fifth Avenue, New York, N.Y. 10110

W. W. Norton & Company Ltd., 37 Great Russell Street, London WC1B 3NU

1   2   3   4   5   6   7   8   9   0

For Bruce and Susan
and For Blair

# CONTENTS

# MAPS

# PREFACE

The reception accorded the first edition of *America: A Narrative History* suggests that it met a demand for a new survey of American history, one written and produced as a book, attractive in design, yet affordable and light enough to carry about without inducing curvature of the spine.

The plan from the start was to produce a basic text written with what clarity and wit the author could muster. I set out to present the major themes of American history, but also to reach out to readers with a story featuring vivid characters and great events, as well as common folk and their lives of joy or quiet desperation. The purpose was to offer both a story of promise and achievement and, inevitably, a story of irony, tragedy, and unfulfilled ideals—and to avoid dogmatizing or proselytizing along the way.

I have tried to fashion the second edition of *America: A Narrative History* to be as useful to students as a text as it is pleasurable to read as a book. In so doing I have pared a good many names, dates, and details from the narrative without, I trust, sacrificing any of its richness or flavor. The result should be an equally compelling narrative that conveys more directly to students the major themes and events in American history. The revised narrative is now complemented by almost twice as many illustrations as appeared in the first edition.

In the attempt to bring the book more nearly up-to-date, the chapters covering the post-1945 period have been thoroughly revised and reorganized. The second edition features a new chapter on society and culture in the 1950s (Chapter 32), much new material on culture and politics in the 1960s (Chapter 35), and a more complete assessment of the Reagan years (Chapter

36). Earlier in the book, I have included new discussions of the ecology of colonial America, and on the social aspects of war.

Several years into drafting the first edition of this book, at a meeting of the American Historical Association, I heard one well-known historian hold forth on ways in which the field of history had proliferated in method, subject matter, and theory: quantification, oral history, women's history, black history, the "new" economic and social histories—these were the latest in the train of new histories that have had a run since Herodotus invented the craft in ancient Greece.

The field, this speaker reasoned, had become so complex that no one person could be on top of everything. The day of the broad survey by a single author had therefore passed. Alas, I was then too far committed to this project to back out, although I had to admit reluctantly my own limitations. But it quickly dawned on me that if it were too much for any one historian, it would surely be too much for any one freshman or sophomore, or any other finite human being, and always had been. History, conceived most broadly, encompasses all human knowledge, and more: everything that was ever thought or said or happened.

In a brief survey one can hope neither to exhaust the facts of history nor to bring readers abreast of every fashion of theory or interpretation, whether old or new. One can hope to offer a tour of the field, so to speak, an overview, point out many doors, stop to open a few, step inside some of them, and hope that readers will be drawn eventually to explore further what is behind those and others.

# ACKNOWLEDGMENTS

Once more, as in the first edition of this book, the single name on the title page neglects credit owed to many others, including those named in the previous volume. Among them, Joseph J. Ellis of Mount Holyoke College, advisory editor on the first edition, left a lasting mark, especially with his well-formulated suggestions on the final chapters. David E. Shi of Davidson College performed a like service in this edition, by sharing his knowledge of recent social and cultural history. Gary R. Freeze, former graduate assistant, put his mark on the bibliographies, which have now been refined and brought up-to-date by David B. Parker, who contributed other chores to both editions.

Having taken to processing words on computers, I no longer need harass typists with constant revisions, but I remain indebted to those who put up with them before I entered the age of high-tech.

At W. W. Norton & Company, James L. Mairs, vice-president, senior editor, and director of production, the "belly editor" who worked with me in devloping the book, then turned me over to "line editor" Steve Forman, an accomplished wordsmith who has a certain flourish at his disposal, and also knows where to put commas and how to find apt illustrations. Donald Lamm, the busy president of Norton, managed to pop up now and then with timely suggestions. Jean Tremblay, the cartographer who created the excellent map program in the first edition, has added new maps to this one. Fred Bidgood, copy editor for the second time, once more plowed through the manuscript with patience and efficiency, and Margie Brassil, proofreader, eliminated many glitches. Deborah Malmud and Lael Lowenstein looked after essential details at crucial times.

My old friend and colleague, J. Isaac Copeland, voluntarily and without my knowledge until he was well on the way, read through the entire book and supplied meticulous notes and suggestions much to my profit. Other readers to whom I am indebted are Sidney R. Bland (James Madison University), F. Nash Boney (University of Georgia), William Breitenbach (University of Puget Sound), Russell D. Buhite (University of Oklahoma), Leonard Dinnerstein (University of Arizona), Robert H. Ferrell (Indiana University), Robert L. Ganyard (State University of New York at Buffalo), Gerald F. Moran (University of Michigan), Paul Paskoff (Louisiana State University), and Stephen Strausberg (University of Arkansas).

This revision has benefited also, I hope, from reports specifying failures of omission or commission offered by readers too numerous to list. To any who may find that I neglected to act on well-considered advice, I can only offer apologies and heartfelt gratitude for the effort to set me straight.

George B. Tindall
Chapel Hill, North Carolina

# AMERICA

# 1

# THE COLLISION OF CULTURES

The earliest Americans are lost in the mists of time, where legends abound. Like people everywhere the Indians told myths of creation, which varied from tribe to tribe: some spoke of a habitation in the sky from which humans and animals had come; still others spoke of miraculous events, such as the union of the Sky Father and Earth Mother. In the Southwest the Pueblo people had a place of worship called the kiva, a stone pit in which a deeper opening symbolized Sipapu, a place of mystery in the north where people entered the world from underground.

Some romancers have had it that the American Indians came from the mythical lost continent of Atlantis; others, that they drifted across from Asia, Africa, or Europe. Their pedigree has been linked variously, but without proof, to the Japanese, Chinese, Hindus, Egyptians, Phoenicians, Moluccans, Polynesians, Scandinavians, black Africans, the ten "lost" tribes of Israel, or to the Welsh who followed a fabled prince in the twelfth century.

Chance contacts across the waters may have occurred. Ecuadorian pottery, dating from about 3000–2000 B.C., bears a striking resemblance to Japanese pottery of the time. The sweet potato, otherwise a peculiarly American plant, grew in Polynesia before modern times. Still, granting the odds that some cultural traits crossed the oceans, the likelihood—now almost a certainty —is that there was a real place in the north where Indian peoples entered the New World, not from underground but from Siberia to Alaska, either by island-hopping across the Bering Strait or over a broad land bridge (Beringia) from which the waters receded during the Ice Ages.

Beringia must have been the route by which the horse and camel, which apparently evolved first in America, crossed to the

Old World before they became extinct in the New, and by which the deer and the elephant (the extinct American mammoth) went the other way. There is no evidence to place the origin of *Homo sapiens* in the New World, nor in the Old World much earlier than 50,000 years ago. Given the advance and retreat of the ice sheets over North America, a crossing might have been possible 50,000–40,000 years ago, but the most likely time for the latest crossings would have been just after the last heavy ice coverage, 18,000–16,000 years ago, when people could still walk across and then filter southward toward warmth through passes in the melting ice.

Once the ice sheets melted and the sea rose again, these migrants to the New World were cut off from the rest of humanity (except for the short-lived Viking settlements on Greenland and Newfoundland) until Columbus came in 1492. For those long eons about the only written records are the relatively late pictographs of Middle America. Most of these writings, mainly Aztec and Mayan, remain untranslated, and some undeciphered. The story therefore remains in the realm of prehistory, the domain of archeologists and anthropologists who must salvage a record from the rubble of the past: stone tools and weapons, bones, pottery, figurines, ancient dwellings, burial places, scraps of textiles and basketry, and finally bits of oral tradition and the reports of early explorers, all pieced together with the adhesive of informed guesswork.

*Out of the mists of time, a carved jade head of the Olmec culture.*

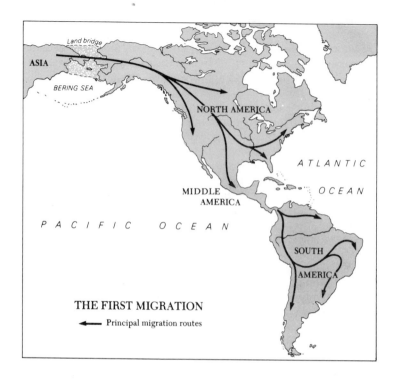

Land bridge

ASIA

BERING SEA

NORTH AMERICA

ATLANTIC

OCEAN

MIDDLE
AMERICA

PACIFIC          OCEAN

SOUTH

AMERICA

THE FIRST MIGRATION
◄—— Principal migration routes

## Pre-Columbian Indian Civilizations

Archeological digs add yearly to the fragments of knowledge about pre-Columbian America. The richest finds have been made on either side of the Isthmus of Panama, where Indian civilization peaked in the high altitudes of Mexico and Peru. Indeed it has been possible to reconstruct a remarkable sequence of events in Middle America, a story of peoples who built great empires and a monumental architecture, supported by large-scale agriculture and a far-flung commerce: the Olmecs, Mayas, Toltecs, Aztecs, Incas, and others.

EARLY CULTURAL STAGES   On either side of these peaks of civilization, Indian life dwindled into more primitive forms. By 1492 about 100–112 million people lived in the Western Hemisphere, about 10–12 million (or 10 percent) in what is now the United States. Their cultures ranged from those of Stone Age nomads to the life of settled communities which practiced agriculture, although none of them ever achieved the heights of the cultures to the south.

Remnants of stone choppers and scrapers suggest the presence of people in the Americas long before the development, by about 9500 B.C., of projectile points for use on spears, and later, on arrows. With the invention of projectiles early man entered the age of the big-game hunters, who ranged across most of the Americas, chasing down mammoths, bison, deer, and antelopes, driving them into traps or over cliffs.

As hunting and gathering became a way of life at around 5000B.C., diet became more varied. It included a number of small creatures such as racoons and opossums, along with fish and shellfish (hooks, nets, and weirs from this period have been found) and wild plants: nuts, greens, berries, and fruits in season. The Indians then began to settle down in permanent or semipermanent villages; they invented fiber snares, basketry, and mills for grinding nuts; they domesticated the dog and the turkey (or as some would have it, the dog, who knew a soft touch when he saw one, domesticated its master). In southern California, then as now relatively well-populated, tribes were able to specialize in sea animals, shellfish, and acorns.

A new cultural stage arrived with the introduction of farming and pottery. In these developments Middle Americans got the jump on the tribes farther north and became the center of innovation and cultural diffusion. By about 5000 B.C. Indians of the Mexican highlands were cultivating or gathering plant foods that became the staples of the New World: chiefly maize (Indian corn), beans, and squash, but also such plants as chili peppers, avocadoes, pumpkins, and many more. These evolved into the forms now familiar by cross-breeding, accidental in part, but believed to have been also the product of experiments by Indian horticulturists. Maize, for instance, began as an ancient Mexican grass which cross-bred with another grass to produce teosinte. Countless crosses of maize with teosinte over the centuries produced the types of Indian corn which the Europeans found later.

THE MAYAS, AZTECS, AND INCAS   By about 2000–1500 B.C. permanent towns dependent on farming had appeared in Mexico, and so had pottery, which possibly diffused northward from Ecuador. The more settled life in turn provided leisure for more complex cultures, for the cultivation of religion, crafts, art, science, administration—and warfare. A stratified social structure began to emerge. From about A.D. 300–900 Middle America reached the flowering of its Classic cultures, with great centers of religion, gigantic pyramids, temple complexes, and courts for ceremonial games, all supported by the surrounding peasant villages. Life centered in the cities of Teotihuacán and Monte Alban and

*The stone statue of a human figure found in Teotihuacán, once a great city of some 250,000 people.*

the Mayan culture of present-day Yucatán and Guatemala. The Mayas had developed enough mathematics (including a symbol for zero) and astronomy to devise a calendar more accurate than that the Europeans were using at the time of Columbus. Then, about A.D. 900, for reasons unknown the Classic cultures collapsed and the religious centers were abandoned. The Toltecs, a warlike people, conquered most of the region, but around A.D. 1200 they too withdrew, for reasons unknown.

During the time of troubles that followed, the Aztecs arrived from somewhere to the northwest, founded the city of Tenochtitlán (now Mexico City), traditionally in 1325, and gradually expanded their control over central Mexico. When the Spaniards arrived in 1519, the Aztec Empire under Montezuma II ruled over perhaps 5 million people—estimates range as high as 20 million. They were held in fairly loose subjugation for the sake of trade and tribute. They also furnished captives to sacrifice on the altars of their bloodthirsty sun god, Huitzilopochtli (symbolized by the hummingbird), to feed and strengthen him for his daily journey across the sky. Because their culture was heir to the technology, arts, and religions of previous peoples in Middle America, the Aztecs are sometimes compared to the ancient Romans, in contrast to the more creative Mayas, considered the Greeks of the New World.

Farther south, in what is now Colombia, the Chibchas built a similar empire on a smaller scale; still farther south the Quechua peoples (better known by the name of their ruler, the Inca) by the fifteenth century controlled an empire that stretched a thou-

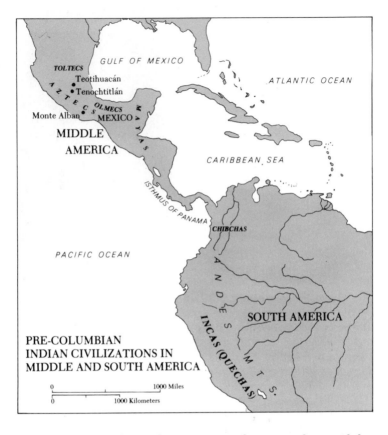

PRE-COLUMBIAN
INDIAN CIVILIZATIONS IN
MIDDLE AND SOUTH AMERICA

sand miles along the Andes Mountains from Ecuador to Chile, connected by an elaborate system of roads and organized under an autocratic government which dominated life fully.

INDIAN CULTURES OF NORTH AMERICA    The peoples of the present-day United States reached the stage of agricultural settlements only in the last thousand years before Christ. There were three identifiable cultural peaks: the Adena-Hopewell culture of the Northeast (800 B.C.–A.D. 600), the Mississippian of the Southeast (A.D. 600– 1500); and the Pueblo-Hohokam culture of the Southwest (400 B.C.–present). None of these ever reached the heights of the Classic cultures of Middle America, although they showed strong influences from the Mayas, Aztecs, and Incas.

The Adena culture, centered in the Ohio Valley, was older but overlapped the similar Hopewell in the same area. The Adena-Hopewell peoples left behind enormous, and to the early settlers mysterious, earthworks and burial mounds—sometimes elaborately shaped like great snakes, birds, or animals. Evidence found in the mounds suggests a developed social structure and a specialized division of labor. There were signs too of an elaborate trade network which spanned the continent. The Hopewellians made ceremonial blades from Rocky Mountain obsidian, bowls from sea shells of the Gulf and Atlantic, ornamental silhouettes of hands, claws, and animals from Appalachian mica, breastplates, gorgets, and ornaments from copper found near Lake Superior. The Northeastern Indians at the time of colonization were distant heirs to the Hopewellian culture after its decline.

The Mississippian culture of the Southeast, which centered in the central Mississippi Valley, probably derived its impulse from the Hopewellians, but reached its height later and under greater influence from Middle America—in its intensive agriculture, its pottery, its temple mounds (vaguely resembling pyramids), and its death cults, which involved human torture and sacrifice. The Mississippian culture peaked in the fourteenth and fifteenth centuries, and collapsed finally because of diseases transmitted from European contacts.

All the peoples of the Southeast, and far into the Midwest, were touched by the Mississippian culture, and as late as the

*A wooden carving of a mother carrying a child, found in a Hopewell burial mound in southern Ohio.*

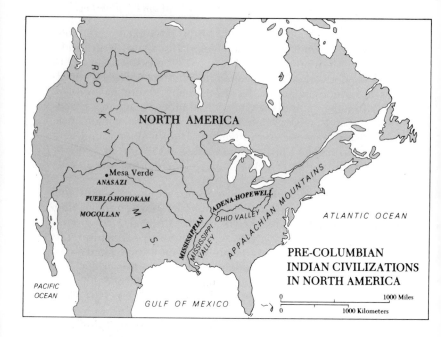

NORTH AMERICA

Mesa Verde
ANASAZI

PUEBLO-HOHOKAM

MOGOLLAN

ADENA-HOPEWELL
OHIO VALLEY

MISSISSIPPIAN
MISSISSIPPI
VALLEY

APPALACHIAN MOUNTAINS

ATLANTIC OCEAN

PRE-COLUMBIAN
INDIAN CIVILIZATIONS
IN NORTH AMERICA

PACIFIC
OCEAN

GULF OF MEXICO

0          1000 Miles

0          1000 Kilometers

eighteenth century tribes of the Southeast still practiced their annual busk, or green corn ceremony, a ritual of renewal in which pottery was smashed, dwellings cleaned out, all fires were quenched, and a new fire kindled in the temple.

The greatest capacity for survival in their homeland was displayed by the irrigation-based cultures of the arid Southwest, elements of which persist today and heirs of which (the Hopis, Zuñis, and others) still live in the adobe pueblos of their ancestors. The most widespread and best-known of the cultures, the Anasazi ("the ancient ones," in the Navaho language" centered around the "four corners" where the states of Arizona, New Mexico, Colorado, and Utah now meet.

The Anasazis never gave up their traditional patterns of hunting and gathering, eating small animals, rodents, reptiles, birds, and insects, along with seeds, mesquite beans, piñon nuts, yucca fruits, and berries. With the coming of agriculture they perfected techniques of "dry farming," using the traces of ground water and catching the runoff in garden terraces, or in some cases, extensive irrigation works. Housing evolved from pit houses, which suggested the later kivas where religious observances were held, and developed into the baked-mud adobe structures which grew four and five stories high and were sometimes located, as at Mesa Verde, Colorado, in canyons underneath protective cliffs.

In contrast to the Middle American and Mississippian cultures, Anasazi society lacked a rigid class structure. The religious leaders and warriors labored much as the rest of the people. In fact warfare was little pursued except in self-defense (Hopi means "the peaceful people") and there was little evidence of human sacrifice or human trophies. Toward the end of the thirteenth century a lengthy drought and the pressure of new arrivals from the north began to restrict the territory of the Anasazis. Into their peaceful world came the aggressive Navahos and Apaches, followed two centuries later by Spaniards marching up from the South.

Even the most developed Indian societies of the sixteenth century were ill-equipped to resist the dynamic European cultures invading their world. There were large and fatal gaps in Indian knowledge and technology. Southwestern Indians had invented etching, but the wheel was found in the New World only on a few toys. The Indians of Mexico had copper and bronze but no iron except a few specimens of meteorites. Messages were conveyed by patterns in beads in the Northeast and by knotted cords among the Incas, but there was no true writing save the hieroglyphs of Middle America. The aborigines had domesticated dogs,

*Ruins of Anasazi cliff dwellings at Mesa Verde, Colorado.*

turkeys, and llamas, but horses were unknown until the Spaniards came astride their enormous "dogs."

Disunity everywhere—civil disorders and rebellions plagued even the Aztecs, Mayas, and Incas—left the peoples of the New World open to division and conquest. North of Mexico, the nearest approach to organized government on a wide scale was the Iroquois League of the Five Nations in the Northeast, with weaker parallels like the Creek Confederacy of the Gulf Plains and the late–sixteenth-century Powhatan Confederacy of Virginia. But as it turned out the centralized societies to the south were as vulnerable as the scattered tribes farther north. The capture or death of their rulers (one usually followed the other) left them in disarray and subjection. The scattered tribes of North America made the Europeans pay more dearly for their conquest, but when open conflict erupted the bow and arrow were seldom a match for guns anywhere.

## EUROPEAN VISIONS OF AMERICA

Long before Columbus, America lived in the fantasies of Europeans. Seneca, the Roman philosopher, wrote in his *Medea:* "An age will come after many years when the Ocean will loose the chain of things, and a huge land lie revealed." Before Seneca the vast unknown beyond the sea had entered the mythology of ancient Greece. In the west, toward the sunset which marked the end of day and symbolically the end of life, was an earthly paradise. There the great Greek poet Homer put his Elysian Fields, the blessed abode of the dead, and Hesiod, a poet of the eighth century B.C. (a contemporary of the Olmecs and the North American mound builders), located distant islands which Father Zeus provided for a "godlike race of hero-men" who lived untouched by toil or sorrow. Whether called the Isles of the Blest, Avalon, or some other name (perhaps, some thought, it was the Garden of Eden), this happy land survived in myth throughout the Middle Ages, coloring the perceptions of explorers. When Sir Thomas More envisaged an ideal society in his book *Utopia* (1516), he placed it on an island in the New World.

Peter Martyr, the earliest European historian of the New World, said in the late fifteenth century that the Indians "seem to live in that golden world of which old writers speak so much: wherein men lived simply and innocently without enforcement of laws, without quarrelings, judges and libels, content only to satisfy nature, without further vexation for knowledge of things to come." This "Noble Savage" (as an English poet later called him) would haunt the imagination for centuries—his reputation still clings to the popular image of the Indians. And the vision of America as a place of rebirth, a New Eden freed from the historic sins of the Old World, still colors the self-image of the American people.

Fugitive myths of legendary lands and forgotten voyages gripped the medieval imagination and appeared on fanciful maps: St. Brendan's Isles, visited by Irish monks in the sixth century; Antilia, whence Christians had fled the Moors and built seven cities ruled by seven bishops; Brasil; Satanazes; and others —some of them perhaps confused reports of the Azores or Canaries, some even perhaps garbled accounts of real discoveries. Now and then curious bits of carved wood, even corpses that looked vaguely Chinese, washed up in the Azores—vagrant reminders, like meteorites from space, of worlds unknown.

## THE NORSE DISCOVERIES

Norse discoveries of the tenth and eleventh centuries are the earliest that can be verified, and even they dissolved into legend, in stories that no doubt grew in the telling before they were written down centuries later in *The Saga of Eric the Red* and the *Tale of the Greenlanders.* Like Eskimos crossing the Bering Strait to the east, the Norsemen went island-hopping across the North Atlantic to the west. Before A.D. 800 they had reached the Faeroes, and about A.D. 870 they conquered Iceland from Irish settlers while other Vikings terrorized the coasts of Europe. Around 985 an Icelander named Eric the Red colonized the west coast of an icebound island he deceptively called Greenland— Eric was the New World's first real-estate booster—and about a year later a trader missed Greenland and sighted land beyond. Knowing of this, Leif Ericsson, son of Eric the Red, sailed out from Greenland about A.D. 1001 and sighted the coasts of Helluland (Baffin Island), Markland (Labrador), and Vinland (Newfoundland), where he settled for the winter.

Three attempts to colonize Vinland followed over the next fifteen years, but they were all abandoned after fierce attacks by natives. The sagas then told no more of Vinland. Speculation had long placed Vinland as far south as Rhode Island or Chesapeake Bay, but in 1963 a Norwegian investigator uncovered the ruins of a number of Norse houses at L'Anse aux Meadows, on the northern coast of Newfoundland. This almost surely was the Vinland of the Sagas.

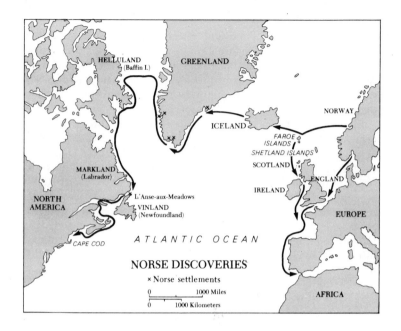

HELLULAND
(Baffin I.)

GREENLAND

NORWAY

ICELAND

FAROE
ISLANDS
SHETLAND ISLANDS

SCOTLAND

MARKLAND
(Labrador)

IRELAND

ENGLAND

NORTH
AMERICA

L'Anse-aux-Meadows

VINLAND
(Newfoundland)

EUROPE

CAPE COD

*ATLANTIC OCEAN*

NORSE DISCOVERIES

× Norse settlements

0        1000 Miles

0        1000 Kilometers

AFRICA

The Norse discoveries are fascinating, but they had no connection to later American history unless Columbus heard of them, which is doubtful. The Norsemen withdrew from North America in the face of hostile natives and the Greenland colonies vanished mysteriously in the fifteenth century. Nowhere in Europe had the forces yet developed which would impel men to colonize and subdue the New World.

### The Emergence of Europe

During the five centuries from Ericson to Columbus, Europe emerged slowly from the invasions, disorders, and weakness that had plagued it since the fall of Rome. In the twelfth century, a time often called the High Middle Ages, western Europe achieved comparative stability. The age of discovery, in turn, coincided with the opening of the modern period in European history. Indeed the burst of energy with which Europe spread its power and culture around the world was the epoch-making force of modern times. The expansion of Europe derived from, and in turn affected, the peculiar patterns and institutions which distinguished modern times from the medieval: the revival of learning and the rise of the inquiring spirit; the rise of trade, towns, and modern corporations; the decline of feudalism and the rise of national states; the Protestant Reformation and the Catholic Counter-Reformation; and on the darker side, some old sins—greed, conquest, exploitation, oppression, racism, and slavery—which quickly defiled the fancied innocence of the New Eden.

RENAISSANCE GEOGRAPHY  For more than two centuries before Columbus the mind of Europe quickened with the fledgling Renaissance: the rediscovery of ancient classics, the rebirth of secular learning, the spirit of inquiry, all of which spread the more rapidly after Johan Gutenberg's invention of movable type around 1440. Learned men of the fifteenth century held in almost reverential awe the authority of ancient learning. The most direct though by no means the only contribution of antiquity to the age of discovery was in geography. As early as the sixth century B.C. the Pythagoreans had taught the sphericity of the earth, and in the third century B.C. the earth's size was computed very nearly correctly. All this had been accepted in Renaissance universities on the word of Aristotle. The story that Columbus was trying to prove this theory is one of those durable falsehoods that will not disappear in the face of the evidence. No informed man of his time thought the earth was flat.

The foremost geographer of ancient times—and of the fifteenth century—was Claudius Ptolemy of Alexandria, whose *Guide to Geography* was compiled in the second century A.D., later preserved by Byzantine scholars, and printed in many Latin editions after 1475. Columbus knew the book and also the work of a leading geographer of his own time, Cardinal Pierre d'Ailly's *Imago Mundi* (*A Picture of the World*), written about 1410 and published in 1485—a copy survives with Columbus's marginal notes. Ptolemy made the earth too small and grossly overestimated the extent of Asia. Other writers favored by Columbus, especially the Florentine scholar Toscanelli, with whom he corresponded, brought the Asian coast even nearer to Portugal—to about where America actually was—and thus spurred the idea of sailing west to reach the East.

Progress in the art of navigation came with the revival of learning. The precise origin of the magnetic compass is unknown, but the principle was known by the twelfth century, and in the fifteenth century mariners took to using the astrolabe and crossstaff long used by landlocked astronomers to sight stars and find the latitude. Steering across the open sea, however, remained a matter of dead-reckoning. A ship's master set his course along a given latitude and calculated it as best he could from the angle of the North Star, or with less certainty the sun, estimating speed by the eye. Longitude remained a matter of guesswork, since accurate timepieces were needed to obtain it. Ship's clocks were too inaccurate until more precise chronometers were developed in the eighteenth century.

THE GROWTH OF TRADE, TOWNS, AND NATION-STATES   The forces which would invade and reshape the New World found their focus in the rising towns, the centers of a growing trade which slowly broadened the narrow horizons of feudal Europe. In its farthest reaches this trade, quickened by contacts made during the Crusades, moved either overland or through the eastern Mediterranean all the way to East Asia, whence Europeans imported spices, medicine, silks, precious stones, dye-woods, perfumes, and rugs in return for the wines, glassware, wool, and silver of Europe. The trade gave rise to a merchant class and they in turn gave a boost to the idea of corporations through which the risks and profits might be shared by many stockholders.

The trade was both chancy and costly. Goods commonly passed from hand to hand, from ships to pack trains and back to ships along the way, subject to levies by all sorts of princes and potentates, with each middleman pocketing whatever he could. The Muslim world, from Spain across North Africa into Central Asia, lay athwart all the more important routes and this added to the hazards. Little wonder, then, that Europeans should dream of an all-water route to the riches of East Asia and the Indies. Interest in the Orient had been further stirred by travelers' stories, of which the best known was the account by the Venetian Marco Polo, written in 1298–1299 and printed more than once in the fifteenth century. Christopher Columbus had a Latin version, with margins heavily annotated in his own hand.

Another spur to exploration was the rise of national states, with kings and queens who had the power and the means to sponsor the search. The growth of the merchant class went hand in hand with the growth of centralized power. Traders wanted uniform currencies, trade laws, and the elimination of trade barriers, and so became natural allies of the sovereigns who could meet their needs. In turn merchants and university-trained professionals supplied the monarchs with money, lawyers, and officials. The Crusades to capture the Holy Land (1095–1270) had also advanced the process. They had brought the West into contact with Eastern autocracy and had decimated the ranks of the feudal lords. And new means of warfare—the use of gunpowder

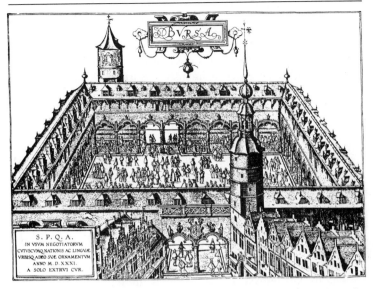

*The Antwerp Bourse, or Exchange, was erected in this Netherlands trade center for the use of merchants of every nation and language.*

and standing armies—further weakened the independence of the nobility. By 1492 the map of western Europe showed several united kingdoms: France, where in 1453 Louis XI had emerged from the Hundred Years' War as head of a unified state; England, where in 1485 Henry VII emerged victorious after thirty years of civil strife, the Wars of the Roses; Spain, where in 1469 Ferdinand of Aragon and Isabella of Castile united two great kingdoms in marriage; and Portugal, where even earlier, in 1384, John I had fought off the Castilians and assured national independence.

### The Voyages of Columbus

It was in Portugal, with the guidance of John's son, Prince Henry the Navigator, that exploration and discovery began in earnest. About 1418 Prince Henry set up an information service to collect charts and data on winds and currents. In 1422 he sent out his first expedition to map the coast of Africa. Driven partly by the hope of outflanking the Islamic world, partly by the hope of trade, the Portuguese by 1446 reached Cape Verde, then the equator, and by 1482 the Congo River. In 1488 Bartholomew Diaz rounded the Cape of Good Hope at Africa's southern tip, and in 1498 Vasco da Gama went on to Calicut in India.

Christopher Columbus meanwhile was learning his trade in the school of Portuguese seamanship. Born in 1451 the son of a weaver in Genoa, Italy, Columbus took to the sea at an early age, and made up for his lack of formal education by learning geography, navigation, and Latin (still the universal language of the learned). At the age of twenty-five he reached Portugal and went on voyages to Guinea, England, and Iceland, and during the 1480s hatched a scheme to reach the East by sailing west. But Portugal was by then too involved with African explorations. Christopher's brother, a professional mapmaker, hawked the idea in the courts of England and France, but they were busy with other matters. In 1486 Columbus turned to Spain's Queen Isabella, and after years of disappointment finally enlisted the support of King Ferdinand's advisor, Luis de Santangel, keeper of the privy purse. Santangel won the support of the Spanish monarchs and himself raised much of the money needed to finance the voyage. The legend that the queen had to hock the crown jewels is as spurious as the fable that Columbus had to prove the earth was round.

Columbus chartered one ship, the *Santa Maria*, and the city of Palos supplied two smaller caravels, the *Pinta* and *Niña*, exacted in punishment for some offense against the crown. From Palos Columbus sailed to the Canary Islands and by dead-reckoning westward. Early on October 12, 1492, after thirty-three days at

A 1493 woodcut depicting Columbus's discovery of America. At left is Spain's King Ferdinand, who with Queen Isabella authorized the expedition.

sea, a lookout sighted land. It was an island in the Bahamas, called Guanahaní (Iguana) by the natives and renamed San Salvador (Holy Savior) by Columbus—long assumed to be the present Watlings Island. More recently, a team sponsored by the National Geographic Society, using computers and other modern technology to retrace Columbus's voyage has named Samana Cay as the site of the first landfall. According to Columbus's own reckoning he was near Japan. He therefore continued to search through the Bahamian Cays down to Cuba, a place name which suggested Cipangu (Japan), and then eastward to the island he named Española (or Hispaniola) where he traded for some gold nose-plugs and bracelets with the people he insisted upon calling Indians. The friendly islanders of what Columbus thought an outpost of Asia belonged to the Arawak-language group who, pushed out of South America, had in turn pushed the Siboney Indians into western Cuba and western Hispaniola. Columbus learned of, but did not encounter until his second voyage, the fierce Caribs of the Lesser Antilles. Because of their location the name of the Caribbean Sea was derived from their name; because of their alleged bad habits the word "Cannibal" was derived from a Spanish version of their name (Canibal).

On the night before Christmas the *Santa Maria* ran aground off Hispaniola and Columbus decided to return home with the two caravels, leaving about forty men behind. On the way home he discovered the need to move north and out of the easterly trade winds, which had brought him westward. This course led him to the Azores and thence to Portugal. The Portuguese thus learned of the new lands first, and John II laid claim to the discoveries on the grounds that they probably lay near the Portuguese Azores.

When Columbus finally reached Palos, the news spread rapidly throughout Europe. Ferdinand and Isabella instructed him to prepare for the second voyage and immediately set about shoring up their legal claim. Pope Alexander VI, who was Spanish, issued a papal bull (after *bulla*, or seal), *Inter Caetera*, which drew an imaginary boundary line 100 leagues west of the Azores, and provided that the area beyond should be a Spanish sphere of exploration and possession. Alarmed, the Portuguese monarch dropped his claim but demanded a dividing line farther west. In the Treaty of Tordesillas (1494) Spain accepted a line 370 leagues west of the Cape Verde Islands. In 1500 Pedro Alvares Cabral, a Portuguese captain on his way around Africa, swung southwestward across the Atlantic and sighted the hump of Brazil, which lay within the Portuguese sphere.

Meanwhile Columbus returned in 1493 with seventeen ships

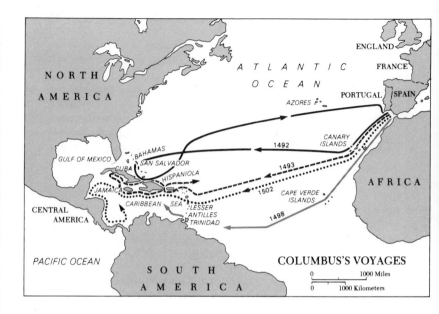

ENGLAND
FRANCE
NORTH
AMERICA
A T L A N T I C
O C E A N
PORTUGAL SPAIN
AZORES
CANARY
ISLANDS
1492
GULF OF MEXICO BAHAMAS
SAN SALVADOR
CUBA 1493
HISPANIOLA
JAMAICA 1502
AFRICA
CENTRAL CARIBBEAN SEA
AMERICA LESSER CAPE VERDE
ISLANDS
ANTILLES
TRINIDAD 1498
PACIFIC OCEAN COLUMBUS'S VOYAGES
SOUTH 0 1000 Miles
AMERICA 0 1000 Kilometers

and some 1,200 men, and planted the first Spanish colony on Hispaniola, where he learned that the men left behind on the first voyage had been killed. He found the Lesser Antilles, explored the coast of Cuba, discovered Jamaica, and finally returned to Spain in 1496, leaving his brother Bartholomew in the new colony to found the city of Santo Domingo. On a third voyage in 1498 Columbus found Trinidad and explored the northern coast of South America. Back in Hispaniola he displayed a disastrous vacillation about dealing with a rebellion, and was arrested and sent back to Spain in chains. But he regained enough favor to lead a fourth voyage in 1502, during which he sailed along the coast of Central America, still looking in vain for Asia. Marooned on Jamaica more than a year, he finally returned to Spain in 1504 and in 1506 he died at Valladolid.

To the end Columbus refused to believe that he had discovered anything other than outlying parts of the Orient. Soon after the first voyage Peter Martyr, a learned Italian at the Spanish court, wrote letters in which he spoke of a New World, and noted that the size of the globe suggested something other than India, but even he did not find this New World inconsistent with the Indies. Full awareness that a great land mass lay between Europe and Asia dawned on Europeans very slowly. By one of history's greatest ironies, this led the New World to be named not for its discoverer but, in what one writer has called a comedy of errors, for another Italian, Amerigo Vespucci.

Vespucci was a Florentine merchant and navigator sent to Spain as an agent of the ruling de Medici family. He knew Columbus, may have been among those who welcomed him back from the first voyage, and certainly helped outfit his ships for the second and third. Later, by his own accounts, Vespucci himself made four voyages to the New World, although there is firm evidence for only three. He did not command any of them, but his letters, which inflated his role, circulated widely in print.   Both he and Columbus used the expression "New World," but an Italian printer pulled it out of a Vespucci letter to his patron, Lorenzo de Medici, and used it as the title of a Latin translation, *Mundus Novus*. Then, in 1507, the young geographer Martin Waldseemüller published a new Latin edition of Ptolemy's *Cosmography*. Out to make a name for himself, Waldseemüller appended another Vespucci letter which, either by design or by a printer's error, credited Vespucci with having reached South America in 1497, one year before Columbus did. For that reason Waldseemüller suggested that the new continent, "the fourth part of the world," along with Europe, Asia, and Africa, be named "America" in his honor.

Actually Amerigo Vespucci's first voyage began in 1499, and there is no firm evidence that he, any more than Columbus, ever believed he had touched anything more than a part of East Asia —or perhaps a continent to its southeast. So many writers and mapmakers followed Waldseemüller's idea, however, that the name was entrenched before Vespucci's right to the honor was questioned.

## THE GREAT BIOLOGICAL EXCHANGE

The first European contacts with this New World began a diffusion of cultures, an exchange of such magnitude and pace as humanity had never known before and will never know again short of contact with extraterrestrial life. It was in fact more than a diffusion of cultures: it was a diffusion of distinctive biological systems. If anything, the plants and animals of the two worlds were more different than the people and their ways of life. Europeans, for instance, had never seen such creatures as the fearsome (if harmless) iguana, flying squirrels, fish with whiskers like cats, snakes that rattled "castanets," or anything quite like several other species: bison, cougars, armadillos, opossums, sloths, tapirs, anacondas, electric eels, vampire bats, toucans, Andean condors, or hummingbirds. Among the few domesticated ani-

*An iguana, drawn by John White, one of the earliest English settlers in America.*

mals, they could recognize the dog and the duck, but turkeys, guinea pigs, llamas, vicuñas, alpacas, and guanacos were all new. Nor did the Indians know of horses, cattle, pigs, sheep, goats, and (maybe) chickens, which soon arrived in abundance. Within a half century, for instance, whole islands of the Caribbean were overrun by pigs, whose ancestors were bred in Spain.

The exchange of plant life worked an even greater change, a revolution in the diets of both hemispheres. Before the Discovery three main staples of the modern diet were unknown in the Old World: maize, potatoes (sweet and white), and many kinds of beans (snap, kidney, lima beans, and others). The white potato, lthough commonly called "Irish," actually migrated from South America to Europe and only reached North America with the Scotch-Irish immigrants of the 1700s. Other New World food plants were manioc (soon a staple in tropical Africa, consumed in the United States chiefly as tapioca), peanuts, squash, peppers, tomatoes, pumpkins, pineapples, sassafras, papayas, guavas, avocadoes, cacao (the source of chocolate), and chicle (for chewing gum). Europeans soon introduced rice, wheat, barley, oats, wine grapes, melons, coffee, olives, bananas, "Kentucky" bluegrass, daisies, and dandelions.

The beauty of the exchange was that the food plants were more complementary than competitive. They grew in different soils and climates, or on different schedules. Indian corn, it turned out, could flourish almost anywhere—high or low, hot or cold, wet or dry. It spread quickly throughout the world. Before the end of the 1500s American maize and sweet potatoes were staple crops in China. The green revolution exported from the Americas thus helped nourish a worldwide population explosion probably greater than any since the invention of agriculture, something like a fivefold increase between 1630 and 1950, from some 500 million to almost 2.5 billion. Plants domesticated by American Indians now make up about a third of the world's food plants.

Europeans, moreover, adopted many Indian devices: canoes, snowshoes, moccasins, hammocks, kayaks, ponchos, dogsleds, toboggans, and parkas. The rubber ball and the game of lacrosse had Indian origins. New words entered the languages of Europeans in profusion: wigwam, teepee, papoose, succotash, hominy, tobacco, moose, skunk, opossum, woodchuck, chipmunk, tomahawk, mackinaw, hickory, pecan, raccoon, and hundreds of others—and new terms in translation: warpath, warpaint, paleface, medicine man, firewater. And the aborigines left the map

*John White's watercolor of an Indian village depicts agriculture, prayer, burial practices, and other aspects of daily life.*

dotted with place names of Indian origin long after they were gone, from Miami to Yakima, from Penobscot to Yuma.

There were still other New World contributions: tobacco and a number of drugs, including coca (for cocaine and novocaine), curare (a muscle relaxant), and cinchona bark (for quinine), and one common medical device, the enema tube. Indian healers, unlike the snake-oil merchants who traded on their reputation, were seldom quacks. But Europeans presented them with exotic maladies they could not handle, for the Indians had lived in blissful ignorance of many infections that plagued the Old World. Even minor European diseases like measles turned killer in the bodies of Indians who had never encountered them and thus had built no immunity. Major diseases like smallpox and typhus killed all the more speedily. According to an account from the first English colony, sent by Sir Walter Raleigh to Roanoke Island, within a few days after Englishmen visited the Indian villages of the neighborhood, "people began to die very fast, and many in short space. . . . The disease also was so strange that they neither knew what it was, nor how to cure it; the like by report of the oldest man in the country never happened before, time out of mind." Now it happened time and time again. The first contacts with some of Columbus's sailors devastated whole communities, and the epidemics spread rapidly into the interior. But the Indians made some restitution. They got the worst of the bargain, but they infected Europeans with syphilis in return.


## PROFESSIONAL EXPLORERS

Undeterred by new diseases, professional explorers, mostly Italians, hired themselves out to the highest bidder to look for that open sesame to riches, a western passage to the Orient. One after another these men probed the shorelines of America during the early sixteenth century in the vain search for an opening, and thus increased by leaps and bounds European knowledge of the vast expanse of the new discoveries. The first to sight the North American continent was John Cabot, or Giovanni Caboto, a Venetian whom Henry VII of England sponsored after having missed a chance to sponsor Columbus. Acting on the theory that Cathay was opposite England, Cabot sailed from Bristol across the North Atlantic in 1497 and fetched up at Cape Breton or southern Newfoundland. Cabot never returned from a second voyage in 1498, but his landfall at what the king called "the newe founde lande" gave England the basis for a later claim to all of North America. For many years little was done to follow up the discovery except by fishermen who after 1500 more and more exploited the teeming waters of the Grand Banks. In 1513 the Spaniard Vasco Nuñez de Balboa became the first European to sight the Pacific Ocean, but only after he had crossed the Isthmus of Panama on foot.

The Portuguese, who from their base in the Azores explored the coasts of Newfoundland and Labrador, and named the latter, meanwhile stole the march by going the other way. In 1498, while Columbus prowled the Caribbean, Vasco da Gama reached the East by sailing around Africa and soon afterward set up the trading posts of a commercial empire stretching from India to the Moluccas (or Spice Islands) of Indonesia. The Spaniards, however, reasoned that the line of demarcation established by the Treaty of Tordesillas ran around the other side of the earth as well. Hoping to show that the Moluccas lay near South America within the Spanish sphere, Ferdinand Magellan, a Portuguese seaman in the employ of Spain, set out to find a passage through or around South America. Departing Spain in 1519, he found his way through the dangerous strait which now

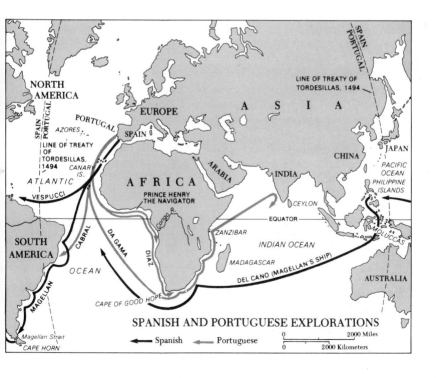

SPANISH AND PORTUGUESE EXPLORATIONS

bears his name, then moved far to the north before he found winds to bear him westward. On a journey far longer than he had bargained for, he touched upon Guam and eventually made a landfall in the Philippines, where he lost his life in a fight with the natives.

Led by Magellan's navigator, Sebastian del Cano, however, the remaining two ships made their way to the Moluccas, picked up a cargo of spices, and one of them, the *Victoria*, returned to Spain in 1522. This first voyage around the globe quickened Spanish ambitions for empire in the East, but after some abortive attempts at establishing themselves there, the Spaniards, beset by war with France, sold Portugal their claims to the Moluccas. From 1565, however, Spaniards would begin to penetrate the Philippines, discovered by Magellan and named for the Spanish prince who became Philip II. In the seventeenth century the English and the Dutch would oust Portugal from most of its empire, but for a century the East Indies were Portuguese.

### THE SPANISH EMPIRE

And the New World was Spanish, except for Brazil. The Caribbean Sea was the funnel through which Spanish power entered the New World. Columbus himself founded the first colony on Hispaniola in 1493; a few years later his brother Bartholomew started to build a castle (ruins of which still exist) at Santo Domingo, which became the capital of the West Indies. From there colonization proceeded eastward to Puerto Rico (1508) and westward to Cuba (1511–1514).

CORTÉS'S CONQUEST   In the islands, Spaniards found only primitive cultures of hunters and gatherers. On the mainland, however, it was different, for there they found civilizations in some ways equal to their own, but almost as vulnerable to their power. The great adventure of mainland conquest began in 1519, when Hernando Cortés and 600 men landed on the site of Vera Cruz, which he founded, and then, far exceeding his orders, set about a daring conquest of the Aztec Empire. The 200-mile march from Vera Cruz through difficult mountain passes to the Aztec capital of Tenochtitlán (Mexico City), and the subjugation of the Aztecs, was one of the most remarkable feats in human history.

But Cortés had some assets and made the most of them. An acute judge of character and a gifted diplomat as well as military leader, he landed in a region where the people were still fighting

*In this 1599 woodcut, Cortés holds out his hand in friendship to the Aztec ruler Montezuma; Cortés would soon destroy Montezuma and enslave the Aztec nation.*

off the spread of Aztec power and were ready to embrace new allies. To the Aztecs and their enemies alike, Cortés seemed to fulfill legends of the Toltec god Quetzalcoatl, who was due to return in the form of a white man and conquer the Aztecs. By a combination of threats and wiles, after several battles Cortés was able to enter Tenochtitlán peacefully and to make the emperor, Montezuma, his puppet. This state of affairs lasted until the spring of 1520, when the Aztecs rebelled and stoned Montezuma to death. The Spaniards lost about a third of their men as they fought their way out of the city. Their allies remained loyal, however, and Cortés gradually regrouped. In 1521 he took the city again. After that the resistance collapsed, and Cortés and his officers simply replaced the former Aztec overlords as rulers over the Indian empire.

In doing so they set the style for other conquistadores to follow, who within twenty years had established a Spanish empire far larger than Rome's had ever been. Between 1522 and 1528 various lieutenants of Cortés, the most notable being Pedro de

Alvarado, conquered the remnants of Mayan-Toltec culture in Yucatán and Guatemala. In 1531 Francisco Pizarro took a band of soldiers down the Pacific coast from Panama toward Cuzco, the seat of the Inca. Along the way he was able to play off against each other the supporters of rival claimants to the throne of the Inca, and to capture the leading claimant, seize his treasure, and execute him in 1533. From Peru, conquistadores extended Spanish authority through Chile by about 1553, and to the north, in present-day Colombia, conquered the Chibcha Empire in 1536–1538.

The Spanish were great believers in form. Before entering upon each new conquest, Spanish generals read a *Requerimiento* (Requirement) to the native people. This curious document recited Christian history from the creation to the time of the current pope and called upon the Indians to accept the authority of the Castilian crown, as granted by the pope. Failure to do so would result in subjugation and loss of property, and even more dire consequences. "The resultant deaths and damages shall be your fault," the paper added, not that of the Spaniards. The *Requerimiento* was repeatedly pronounced before battle, and while it may have helped to salve consciences, it required a strange naïveté. "It is not Christianity that leads them on," the great Spanish dramatist Lope de Vega had the devil say in his play *The New World*, "but rather gold and greed."

SPANISH AMERICA    The course of empire was nevertheless marked by Spain's centuries-long crusade to expel the Islamic Moors from their foothold in the Iberian peninsula. By coincidence it was in 1492, the very year of discovery, that the Catholic monarchs captured the last Moorish stronghold, Granada, and there ordered the expulsion of all Jews (previously tolerated by the Moors) unless they converted to Christianity.

The conquest of America seemed almost like an extension of this crusade into a new world—first conquest, then conversion, by force if need be. The conquistadores transferred to America and there elaborated a system known as the *encomienda*, whereby Christian knights had acquired rights over land and people captured from the Moors. In America favored officers took over Indian villages or groups of villages. As *encomenderos* they were called upon to protect and care for the villages and support missionary priests. In turn they could levy tribute in goods and labor. Spanish America therefore developed from the start a society of extremes: conquistadores and encomenderos who sometimes found wealth beyond the dreams of avarice, if more often just a crude affluence, and subject peoples who were held in poverty.

What were left of them, that is. By the mid-1500s Indians were nearly extinct in the West Indies, reduced more by European diseases than by Spanish exploitation. To take their place the colonizers as early as 1503 began to bring in black slaves from Africa, the first in a melancholy traffic that eventually would bring over 9 million people across the Atlantic in bondage. In all of Spain's New World empire, by one informed estimate, the Indian population dropped from about 50 million at the outset to 4 million in the seventeenth century, and slowly rose again to 7.5 million. Whites, who totaled no more than 100,000 in the mid-sixteenth century, numbered over 3 million by the end of the colonial period.

The Indians did not always want for advocates, however. Catholic missionaries in many cases offered a sharp contrast to the conquistadores. Setting examples of self-denial, they went out into remote areas, often without weapons or protection, to spread the gospel—and often suffered martyrdom for their efforts. Among them rose defenders of the Indians, the most noted of whom was Bartolomeo de las Casas, a priest in Hispaniola and later bishop of Chiapas, Guatemala, author of *A Brief Relation of the Destruction of the Indies* (1552). Las Casas won some limited reforms from the Spanish government, but ironically had a more lasting influence in giving rise to the so-called Black Legend of Spanish cruelty which the enemies of Spain gleefully spread abroad, often as a cover for their own abuses.

From such violently contrasting forces Spanish America gradually developed into a settled society. The independent conquistadores were replaced quickly by a second generation of bureaucrats and the *encomienda* was replaced by the *hacienda* (a great farm or ranch) as the claim to land became a more important source of wealth than the claim to labor. The empire was organized first into two great regions, the Viceroyalties of New Spain and Perú; eventually the Viceroyalties of New Granada and La Plata were split off from the latter. From the outset these were separate realms of the Castilian crown, united with Spain and with each other only in the person of the monarch. And from the outset, in sharp contrast to the later English experience, the crown took an interest in regulating every detail of colonial administration. After 1524 the Council of the Indies, directly under the crown, issued laws for America, served as the appellate court for civil cases arising in the colonies, and had general oversight of the bureaucracy. Trade, finances, and taxation were closely watched by the *Casa de Contratación,* or House of Trade, set up at Seville in 1503.

The culture of Spanish America would be fundamentally unlike the English-speaking world that would arise to the north. In fact a difference already existed in pre-Columbian America, with largely nomadic tribes to the north and the more complex civilizations in Mesoamerica. On the latter world the Spaniards imposed an overlay of their own peculiar ways, but without uprooting the deeply planted cultures they found. Just as Spain itself harbored reminders of the one-time Arab rule, so its colonies preserved reminders of the Aztec and Incan cultures. Catholicism, which for long centuries had absorbed pagan gods and transformed pagan feasts into such holy days as Christmas and Easter, in turn adapted Indian beliefs and rituals to its own purposes. The Mexican Virgin of Guadalupe, for instance, evoked memories of feminine divinities in native cults. Thus Spanish America, in the words of Mexican writer Octavio Paz, became a land of superimposed pasts. "Mexico City was built on the ruins of Tenochtitlán, the Aztec city that was built in the likeness of Tula, the Toltec city that was built in the likeness of Teotihuacán, the first great city on the American continent. Every Mexican bears within him this continuity, which goes back two thousand years."

SPANISH EXPLORATIONS   For more than a century after Columbus no European power other than Spain had more than a brief foothold in the New World. Spain had not only the advantage of having sponsored the discovery, but of having stumbled onto those parts of America that would bring the quickest returns. While France and England struggled with domestic quarrels and religious conflict, Spain had forged an intense national unity. Under Charles V, heir to the throne of Austria and the Netherlands, and Holy Roman Emperor to boot, Spain dominated Europe as well as America. The treasures of the Aztecs and the Incas added to Spain's power, but they would prove to be a mixed blessing. The easy reliance on American gold and silver undermined the basic economy of Spain and tempted the government to live beyond its means, while American bullion contributed to price inflation throughout Europe.

To the north of Mexico the Spaniards never got a secure footing, but the "Spanish borderlands" of the southern United States from Florida to California preserve many reminders of the Spanish presence. Spanish mariners probably saw the Gulf coast of North America before 1500, but the earliest known exploration

SPANISH EXPLORATIONS
OF THE MAINLAND

•••• Balboa 1513
▬▬▬ Ponce de León 1513
▬ ▬ Cortés 1519
▬▬▬ Narvaez 1528
▬▬▬ Pizarro 1531-1533
▬ ▬ Cabeza de Vaca 1535-1536
•••••• De Soto 1539-1542
▬ ▬ ▬ Coronado 1540-1542

| 0 | | 1000 Miles |
|---|---|---|
| 0 | | 1000 Kilometers |

(of Florida) was made in 1513 by Juan Ponce de León, then governor of Puerto Rico, who later tried but failed to plant a colony on the Gulf coast in 1521. Meanwhile Spanish explorers skirted the Gulf coast from Florida to Vera Cruz, scouted the Atlantic coast from Cuba to Newfoundland, and established a short-lived colony on the Carolina coast.

Sixteenth-century knowledge of the interior came mostly from would-be conquistadores who sought but found little to plunder in the hinterlands. The first, Pánfilo de Narváez, landed in 1528 at Tampa Bay, marched northward to Appalachee, an Indian village in present-day Alabama, then back to the coast near St. Marks, where his party contrived crude vessels in hope of reaching Mexico. Wrecked on the coast of Texas, a few survivors

under Nuñez Cabeza de Vaca worked their way painfully overland and after eight years stumbled into a Spanish outpost in
western Mexico. Hernando de Soto followed their example in
1540–1543. With 600 men he landed on the Florida west coast,
hiked up as far as western North Carolina, then westward
beyond the Mississippi, and up the Arkansas River. In the spring
of 1542 de Soto died near the site of Memphis; the next year the
survivors floated down the Mississippi and 311 of the original
band found their way to Mexico. In 1540 Francisco Vasquez de
Coronado, inspired by rumors of gold, traveled northward into
New Mexico and eastward across Texas and Oklahoma as far as
Kansas. He came back in 1542 without gold but with a more real-
istic view of what lay in those arid lands.

The first Spanish base in the present United States came in response to French encroachments on Spanish claims. In the 1560s
French Huguenots (Protestants) established short-lived colonies
in South Carolina and Florida. In 1565 a Spanish outpost, St. Augustine, became the first European town in the present-day
United States, and is now its oldest urban center except for the
pueblos of New Mexico. While other outposts failed, St. Augustine survived as a defensive outpost perched on the edge of a
continent.

In New Mexico the Spanish launched missionary efforts in
1581. Santa Fe, the capital and second-oldest European city in
the United States, was founded in 1609 or 1610. An Indian uprising in 1680, the great Pueblo Revolt, chased the Spaniards out,
but they returned in the 1690s. Spanish outposts on the Florida
and Texas Gulf coasts and in California did not come until the
eighteenth century.

## The Protestant Reformation

While Spain built her empire, a new movement was growing elsewhere in Europe, the Protestant Reformation, which
would embitter national rivalries, and by encouraging serious
challenges to Catholic Spain's power, profoundly affect the
course of early American history. When Columbus sailed in
1492 all of western Europe acknowledged the Catholic church
and its pope in Rome. The unity of Christendom began to crack
in 1517, however, when Martin Luther, a German monk and
theologian, posted his "Ninety-five Theses" in protest against
abuses in the church and especially against the sale of indul-
gences for the remission of sins. Sinful men, Luther argued,

*Martin Luther.*

could win salvation neither by good works nor through the mediation of the church, but only by faith in the redemptive power of Christ and through a direct relationship to God—the "priesthood of all believers." And the only true guide to the will of God was the Bible.

Fired with these beliefs, Luther set out to reform the church and ended by splitting it. Lutheranism spread rapidly among the people and their rulers—some of them with an eye to seizing church properties—and when the pope expelled Luther from the church in 1520, reconciliation became impossible. The German states fell into conflict over religious differences until 1555, when they finally patched up a peace whereby each prince determined the religion of his subjects. Generally, northern Germany, along with Scandinavia, became Lutheran. The principle of close association between church and state thus carried over into Protestant lands, but Luther had unleashed ideas that ran beyond his personal control.

Other Protestants pursued Luther's doctrine to its logical end and preached religious liberty for all. Further divisions on doctrinal matters led to the appearance of various sects such as Anabaptists, who rejected infant baptism and favored the separation of church and state. Other offshoots including the Mennonites, Amish, Dunkers, Familists, and Schwenkfelders appeared later in America, but the more numerous like-minded groups would be Baptists and Quakers, who derived from English origins.

CALVINISM    Soon after Luther began his revolt a number of Swiss cantons, influenced by the teachings of Huldreich Zwingli in Zurich, began to throw off the authority of Rome. In Geneva the reform movement looked to John Calvin, a Frenchman who had fled to Switzerland and who brought his adopted city under the

*John Calvin.*

sway of his beliefs. In his great theological work, *The Institutes of the Christian Religion* (1536), Calvin set forth a stern doctrine. All men, he taught, were damned by the original sin of Adam, but the sacrifice of Christ made possible their redemption by faith. The experience of faith, however, was open only to those who had been elected by God and thus predestined to salvation from the beginning of time. It was a hard doctrine, but the infinite wisdom of God was beyond human understanding.

Calvinism required a stern moral code, for the outward sign of true faith was correct behavior. If this did not of itself prove that one was of the elect, an immoral life clearly proved the opposite. Calvin therefore insisted upon strict morality and hard work, a teaching which especially suited the rising middle class. Moreover, he taught that men serve God through any legitimate calling, and permitted laymen a share in the governance of the church through a body of elders and ministers called the consistory or presbytery. The doctrines of Calvin became the basis for the beliefs of the German Reformed and Dutch Reformed churches, the Presbyterians in Scotland, some of the Puritans in England, and the Huguenots in France. Through these and other groups Calvin later exerted more effect upon religious belief and practice in the English colonies than any other single leader of the Reformation.

THE REFORMATION IN ENGLAND    In England the Reformation, like so many other things, followed a unique course. The Church of England, or Anglican church, took form through a gradual process of Calvinizing English Catholicism. Rejection of papal authority came about at first, however, for purely political reasons. Henry VIII (1509–1547), the second of the Tudor dynasty, had in fact won from the pope the title of Defender of the Faith, for his *Defense of the Seven Sacraments* (1521), a refutation of Luther's ideas. But Henry's marriage to Catherine of Aragon had produced no male heir, and for that reason he required an annulment. In the past popes had found ways to accommodate such requests, but Catherine was the aunt of Charles V, king of Spain and emperor of the Holy Roman Empire, whose support was vital to the church's cause on the continent, so the pope refused. Unwilling to accept the rebuff, Henry severed the connection with Rome, named a new archbishop of Canterbury who granted the annulment, and married the lively Anne Boleyn. And she, in one of history's great ironies, presented him not with the male heir he sought, but a daughter, who as Elizabeth I would reign from 1558 to 1603 over one of England's greatest eras.

Elizabeth could not be a Catholic, for in the Catholic view she was illegitimate. During her reign, therefore, the Church of England became Protestant, but in its own way. The structure of organization, the bishops and archbishops, remained much the same, but the doctrine and practice changed: the Latin liturgy became, with some changes, the English *Book of Common Prayer*, the cult of saints was dropped, and the clergy were permitted to marry. The thirty-nine Articles of Faith, prepared by a

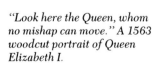

*"Look here the Queen, whom no mishap can move." A 1563 woodcut portrait of Queen Elizabeth I.*

committee of bishops and announced in 1571, defined the Anglican creed in Protestant terms, though sometimes evasively. For the sake of unity the "Elizabethan Settlement" allowed some latitude in theology and other matters, but this did not satisfy all. Some tried to enforce the letter of the law, stressing traditional practice. Many others, however, especially those under Calvinist influence from the continent, wished to "purify" the church so that it more nearly fit their views of biblical authority. Some of these Puritans would later despair of the effort to reform the Anglican church and would leave England to build their own churches in America.

## CHALLENGES TO SPANISH EMPIRE

The Spanish monopoly of New World colonies remained intact throughout the sixteenth century, but not without challenge from national rivals spurred now by the emotion unleashed by the Protestant Reformation. The French were the first to pose a serious challenge as Huguenot seamen promised to build France into a major seapower. Spanish treasure ships from the New World held out a tempting lure to French corsairs, and at least as early as 1524 one of them was plundered off the Azores by a French privateer. That same year the French king sent an Italian named Giovanni da Verrazzano in search of a passage to Asia. Sighting land (probably at Cape Fear, North Carolina), Verrazzano ranged along the coast as far north as Maine. On the way he viewed Pamlico Sound across the North Carolina Outer Banks, and beguiled by hope, mistook it for the Pacific Ocean. On a second voyage in 1538, his career came to an abrupt end in the West Indies at the hands of the fierce Caribs.

Unlike the Verrazzano voyages, those of Jacques Cartier about a decade later led to the first French effort at colonization. On three voyages Cartier explored the Gulf of St. Lawrence and up the St. Lawrence River looking for another fantasy kingdom compounded of European greed and Indian tall tales. Twice he got as far as present Montréal, and twice wintered at or near the site of Québec, near which a short-lived French colony appeared in 1542–1543. From that time forward, however, French kings lost interest in Canada. France after mid-century plunged into religious civil wars, and the colonization of Canada had to await the coming of Samuel de Champlain, the "Father of New France," after 1600.

From the mid-1500s forward, greater threats to Spanish power arose from the growing strength of the Dutch and English.

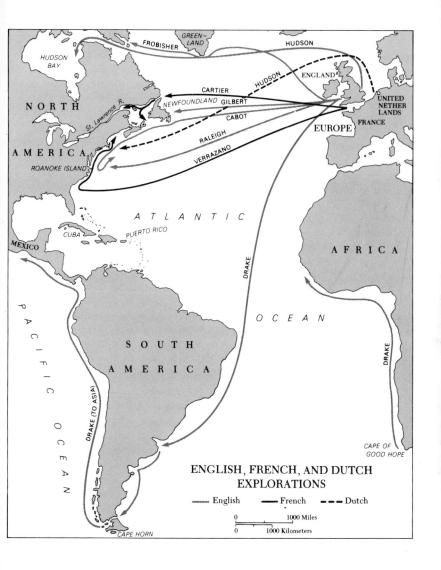

ENGLISH, FRENCH, AND DUTCH
EXPLORATIONS

——— English    ——— French    = = = Dutch

0           1000 Miles

0          1000 Kilometers

The provinces of the Netherlands, which had passed by inheritance to the Spanish king, and which had become largely Protestant, rebelled against Spanish rule in 1567. A protracted and bloody struggle for independence was interrupted by a twelve-year truce, but Spain did not accept the independence of the Dutch Republic until 1648.

Almost from the beginning of the revolt the Dutch "Sea Beggars," privateers working out of both English and Dutch ports, plundered Spanish ships in the Atlantic and carried on illegal trade with the Spanish colonies. The Dutch "Sea Beggars" soon had their counterpart in the Elizabethan "Sea Dogges": John Hawkins, Francis Drake, and others. While Elizabeth steered a tortuous course to avoid open war with Catholic Spain, she encouraged both Dutch and English captains in smuggling and piracy. Sir John Hawkins, first of the great Sea Dogs, got his start as a smuggler in 1562 when he picked up some 300 black slaves in Sierra Leone and traded them at a profit in Hispaniola. Two years later he took a cargo to the Spanish Main (in Venezuela and Panamá). A third voyage, in 1567–1568, however, ended in disaster when a Spanish fleet surprised him at Vera Cruz. Only two of his five ships escaped, commanded respectively by Hawkins and his cousin, Francis Drake, whose exploits soon overshadowed his own.

Drake now abandoned the pretense of legal trade and set out to loot Spanish treasure. In 1577 he embarked in the *Golden Hind* on his famous adventure around South America to raid Spanish towns along the Pacific and surprise a treasure ship from Perú. Continuing in a vain search for a passage back to the Atlantic, he was driven out to sea. He closed with the American coast at about 43° North and spent seven weeks at Drake's Bay in "New Albion," as he called California. Eventually he found his way westward around the world and back home in 1580. Elizabeth, who had secretly backed the voyage, shared a profit of 4,600 percent, and knighted Sir Francis upon his return.

THE ARMADA'S DEFEAT   Such depredations continued for some twenty years before circumstances provoked open war. In 1568 Elizabeth's cousin Mary, "Queen of Scots," ousted by Scottish Presbyterians in favor of her infant son, fled to refuge in England. Mary, who was Catholic, had a claim to the English throne by descent from Henry VII, and soon became the focus for Spanish-Catholic intrigues to overthrow Elizabeth. Finally, after an abortive plot to kill Elizabeth and elevate Mary to the throne, the queen yielded to the demands of her ministers and had Mary beheaded in 1587.

In revenge Philip II decided to crush once and for all the Protestant power of the north and began to gather his ill-fated Armada, whereupon Francis Drake swept down upon Cadiz and destroyed part of the fleet before it was ready. His "singeing of the King of Spain's beard" postponed for a year the departure of the "Invincible Armada," which set out in 1588. From the beginning it was a case of incompetence and mismanagement compounded by bad luck. The Spanish idea of naval warfare was to

*The defeat of the Spanish Armada, depicted in a contemporary English oil painting.*

bring rival ships together for what in effect was an infantry battle at sea. The heavy Spanish galleons, however, could not cope with the smaller and faster English vessels commanded by Drake and others. The English harried the Spanish ships through the English Channel on their way to the Netherlands, where the Armada was to pick up an army of invasion. But caught up in a powerful "Protestant Wind" from the south, the storm-tossed fleet never got there. It was swept into the North Sea instead, and what was left of it finally found its way home around the British Isles, leaving wreckage scattered on the shores of Scotland and Ireland.

Defeat of the Armada marked the beginning of English supremacy on the sea and cleared the way for English colonization. It was the climactic event of Elizabeth's reign, and it brought to a crescendo the surging patriotism that had been born of the epic conflict with Spain. The great literature of the Elizabethan age reflected a spirit of confidence and pride. The historical plays of William Shakespeare, especially, celebrated the glories of the House of Tudor and linked them to the spirit of the nation: "This blessed plot, this earth, this realm, this England." England was in the springtime of her power, filled with a youthful zest for new worlds and new wonders that were opening up before the nation.

ENGLISH EXPLORATIONS   A significant figure in channeling this energy was Richard Hakluyt, an Oxford clergyman, who as a youth was inspired by the example of his cousin, the elder Richard Hakluyt, to collect and publish accounts of the great voyages of exploration. He set out systematically to read whatever accounts he could find in Latin, Greek, Italian, Spanish, Portuguese, French, and English. In the process he rescued some accounts from destruction. In 1582 Hakluyt brought out his first book, *Divers Voyages touching the discoverie of America*, and in the summer of the Armada he finished *The Principall Navigations, voiages and discoveries of the English Nation*.

Hakluyt, moreover, became an active promoter of colonization. In 1584, at the request of Sir Walter Raleigh, he prepared for the queen *A Discourse of Western Planting* (first published three centuries later) in which he pleaded for colonies to accomplish diverse objects: to extend the reformed religion, to expand trade, to employ the idle, to supply England's needs from her own dominions, to provide bases in case of war with Spain, to enlarge the queen's revenues and navy, and to discover a Northwest Passage to the Orient.

While Hawkins and Drake ransacked the Spanish Main, other seamen renewed the search for the Northwest Passage, inspired by Sir Humphrey Gilbert's *A discourse of a Discoverie for a New Passage to Cataia*. Three voyages by Martin Frobisher (1576–1578) and three by John Davis (1585–1587) discovered new lands (and Eskimos) to the west of Greenland, but no passage. The history of English colonization must begin with Gilbert and his half-brother, Sir Walter Raleigh. In 1578 Gilbert, who had long been a confidant of the queen, secured a royal patent to possess and hold "heathen and barbarous landes countries and territories not actually possessed of any Christian prince or people." Significantly the patent guaranteed to Englishmen and their descendants in such a colony the rights and privileges of Englishmen "in suche like ample manner and fourme as if they were borne and personally residaunte within our sed Realme of England." And laws had to be "agreable to the forme of the lawes and pollicies of England." Gilbert, after two false starts, finally set out with a colonial expedition in 1583, intending to settle near Narragansett Bay (in present-day Rhode Island). He landed in Newfoundland, took possession of the land for Elizabeth by right of John Cabot's discovery, and read his commission to some mystified fishermen on the shore. With the season far advanced and his largest vessels lost, Gilbert resolved to return home. On the last day of his life he was seen with a book in his hand—probably Sir Thomas More's *Utopia*, which inspired his last recorded words. From the deck of his pinnace *The Squirrel*, Gilbert shouted across to his other ship the haunting words: "We are as near to heaven by sea as by land." The following night his ship vanished and was never seen again.

RALEIGH'S LOST COLONY   The next year, 1584, Raleigh persuaded the queen to renew Gilbert's patent in his own name, and sent out a ship to reconnoiter a site. Sailing by way of the West Indies, they came to the Outer Banks of North Carolina, which Verrazzano had visited sixty years before, found an inlet to Pamlico Sound, and discovered Roanoke Island, where the soil seemed fruitful and the natives friendly. The Outer Banks afforded some protection, and rivers to the interior fostered dreams of a route to the Pacific. In 1585 Raleigh's first colony went out under the command of Sir Richard Grenville with Ralph Lane as governor. Grenville went via the West Indies, plundering Spanish vessels to help defray the cost, and left the colonists on Roanoke Island before returning to England. They survived a mild winter, but the following June friction with the natives led to a fight, and when Francis Drake arrived to warn them of a threatened Spanish attack, the colonists decided to go

*The English arrival at the Outer Banks, with Roanoke Island at left.*

home. Soon afterward Grenville returned, but not finding the colonists, left fifteen men behind to hold the fort and departed.

Raleigh then set about trying again, and in 1587 sponsored a colony of 117, including women and children, under Gov. John White. The plan was to pick up Grenville's men at Roanoke and proceed to Chesapeake Bay, since Roanoke was inaccessible to large vessels. But the ship's pilot, claiming the season was too far advanced—and probably eager to get on with plundering Spanish vessels—insisted that the colony remain at Roanoke. After a month in Roanoke, Governor White returned to England to get supplies, leaving behind his daughter Elinor and his granddaughter Virginia Dare, the first English child born in the New World. White, however, could not get back because of the war with Spain. He finally returned in 1590 to find the city of "Ralegh" abandoned and despoiled.

No trace of the colonists was ever found, nor any of the men Grenville left behind. Hostile Indians may have destroyed the colony, or hostile Spaniards—who certainly planned to attack—may have done the job. The only clue was one word carved on a doorpost, "Croatoan," the name of a friendly tribe of Indians and also of their island, the present Ocracoke. A romantic legend later developed that the colonists joined the Croatan Indians and finally were absorbed by them. There is no solid evidence for this, and while some may have gone south, the main body of colonists appears to have gone north to the southern shores of the Chesapeake Bay, as they had talked of doing, and lived there for some years until killed by local Indians. Such stories were picked up from the Indians by English settlers at Jamestown some two decades later. Unless some remnant of the Lost Colony did survive in the woods, there was still not a single Englishman in North America when Queen Elizabeth died in 1603.

FURTHER READING

Many scholars have at one time or another looked at pre-Columbian American Indian life. Probably the most readable and comprehensive of the anthropological accounts is Harold E. Driver's *Indians of North America* (2nd ed., 1969). Recent historical treatments include Alvin M. Josephy's *The Indian Heritage of America* (1968) and Wilcomb E. Washburn's *The Indian in America* (1975).°

° These books are available in paperback editions.

Several works explore the theme of cultural conflict. Henry Warner Bowden's *American Indians and Christian Missions: Studies in Cultural Conflict* (1981) and James Axtell's *The Invasion Within* (1986) are interpretive. More theoretical is Richard Drinnon's *Facing West: The Metaphysics of Indian Hating and Empire Building* (1980). Karen O. Kupperman's *Settling with the Indians: The Meeting of English and Indian Cultures in America, 1580–1640* (1980) stresses the racist nature of the conflict. R. C. Padden's *The Hummingbird and the Hawk* (1967) describes Cortés's conquest of the Aztecs; also useful is Charles Gibson's *The Aztecs under Spanish Rule* (1964).

Alfred W. Crosby, Jr.'s *The Columbian Exchange* (1972) discusses the biological aspects of the cultural collision. Crosby's *Ecological Imperialism: The Biological Expansion of Europe, 900–1900* (1986) is a full exploration of the ecological side of European expansion.

For evidence that Viking explorers came to North America before Columbus, see Paul H. Chapman's *The Norse Discovery of America* (1981).°

A number of fine overviews of European exploration are available. The most comprehensive are two volumes by Samuel E. Morison, *The European Discovery of America: The Northern Voyages*, A.D. *500–1600* (1971), and *The Southern Voyages*, A.D. *1492–1616* (1974). David B. Quinn's *North America from Earliest Discovery to First Settlements* (1977) is also useful. Scholarship on Columbus is best handled by Samuel E. Morison's *Admiral of the Ocean Sea* (2 vols., 1942), which was condensed into *Christopher Columbus, Mariner* (1955).° A good outline of the forces of exploration is John H. Parry's *The Age of Reconnaisance* (1963). On the recent controversy regarding the site of the first landfall, see the articles on Columbus and the New World in *National Geographic*, November 1986, pp. 566–605.

Clarence H. Haring's *The Spanish Empire in America* (1947) stresses the institutional framework of Spanish imperial government. James Lang's *Conquest and Commerce: Spain and England in the Americas* (1975) compares the Spanish and English processes of colonization. See also Charles Gibson's *Spain in America* (1966), and for the French experience, William J. Eccles's *France in America* (1972). The most comprehensive view of how European mercantile practices led to the "modernization" of the rest of the world is presented in Louis Hartz's *The Founding of New Societies: Studies in the History of the United States, Latin America, South Africa, Canada, and Australia* (1964).

The English efforts that led to the Roanoke Island colony are documented in David B. Quinn's *England and the Discovery of America, 1481–1620* (1974). The most readable account of the colony itself is Karen O. Kupperman's *Roanoke* (1984); Quinn's *Set Fair for Roanoke* (1985) is more comprehensive. For background on the motives for English exploration and settlement, see Alfred L. Rouse's *The Expansion of Elizabethan England* (1955) and Carl Bridenbaugh's *Vexed and Troubled Englishmen, 1590–1642* (1968). The link between English settlements and the Irish experience is explored in David B. Quinn's *The Elizabethans and the Irish* (1966). The first volumes of Bernard Bailyn's comprehensive narrative of the transatlantic migration of peoples from the Old World to the New are *The Peopling of British North America: An Introduction* (1986) and *Voyagers to the West: A Passage in the Peopling of America on the Eve of the Revolution* (1986).

# 2

## ENGLAND AND HER COLONIES

The England which Elizabeth bequeathed to James I, like the colonies it would plant, was a unique blend of elements. The language and the people themselves mixed Germanic and Latin ingredients. The Anglican church mixed Protestant theology and Catholic forms in a way unknown on the continent. And the growth of royal power paradoxically had been linked with the rise of English liberties, in which even Tudor monarchs took pride. In the course of their history the English people have displayed a genius for "muddling through," a gift for the pragmatic compromise that defied logic but in the light of experience somehow worked.

### THE ENGLISH BACKGROUND

Set off from continental Europe by the English Channel, that "moat defensive to the house" in Shakespeare's words, England had safe frontiers after the union of the English and Scottish crowns in 1603. In her comparative isolation, England developed institutions to which the continent had few parallels. By 1600 the decline of feudal practices was far advanced. The great nobles, decimated by the Wars of the Roses, had been brought to heel by Tudor monarchs and their ranks filled with men loyal to the crown. In fact the only nobles left, strictly speaking, were those few peers of the realm who sat in the House of Lords. All others were commoners, and among their ranks the aristocratic pecking order ran through a great class of landholding squires, distinguished mainly by their wealth and bearing the simple titles of "esquires" and "gentlemen," as did many well-to-do townsmen. They in turn mingled freely and often intermarried with the classes of yeomen (small freehold farmers) and merchants.

ENGLISH LIBERTIES   It was to these middle classes that the Tudors looked for support and, for want of bureaucrats or a standing army, for local government. Chief reliance in the English counties was on the country gentlemen, who usually served as officials without pay. Government therefore allowed a large measure of local initiative. Self-rule in the counties and towns became a habit—one that, along with the offices of justice of the peace and sheriff, English colonists took along as part of their cultural baggage.

Even the Tudors, who acted as autocrats, preserved the forms of constitutional procedure. In the making of laws the king's subjects consented through representatives in the House of Commons. By custom and practice the principle was established that the king taxed his subjects only with the consent of Parliament. And by its control of the purse strings Parliament would draw other strands of power into its hands. This structure of habit broadened down from precedent to precedent to form a constitution that was not written in one place, or for that matter, not fully written down at all. The *Magna Carta* (Great Charter) of 1215, for instance, had been a statement of privileges wrested by certain nobles from the king, but it became part of a broader tradition that the people as a whole had rights which even the king could not violate.

A further buttress to English liberty was the great body of common law, which had developed since the twelfth century in royal courts established to check the arbitrary power of local

*The House of Commons in 1640.*

nobles. Without laws to cover every detail, judges had to exercise their own ideas of fairness in settling disputes. Decisions once made became precedents for later decisions, and over the years a body of judge-made law developed, the outgrowth more of experience than of abstract logic. Through the courts the principle evolved that a subject could be arrested or his goods seized only upon a warrant issued by a court, and that he was entitled to a trial by a jury of his peers (his equals) in accordance with established rules of evidence.

ENGLISH ENTERPRISE   The liberties of Englishmen inspired a certain initiative and vigor of which prosperity and empire were born. The ranks of entrepreneurs and adventurers were constantly replenished by the young sons of the squirearchy, cut off from the estate which the oldest son inherited by the law of primogeniture (or first born). The growth of commerce was spurred at first by the growth of the trade in woolen cloth built up after 1400 by the Company of Merchant Adventurers, which greatly expanded markets on the continent. The company was the prototype of the regulated company, actually a trade association of merchants who sold on their own accounts under the supervision of the company, which secured markets and privileges.

With time, however, investors formed joint-stock companies, ancestors of the modern corporation, in which stockholders shared the risks and profits, sometimes in a single venture but more and more on a permanent basis. When the cloth market became saturated in the mid-1500s, English merchants began to scan broader horizons for new outlets, new goods, new patterns of trade, and found themselves incurring greater risks. In the late 1500s some of the larger companies managed to get royal charters which entitled them to monopolies in certain areas and even governmental powers in their outposts: the Muscovy Company, the Levant Company, the Barbary Company, the Guinea Company, and the East India Company. Companies like these would become the first instruments of colonization.

For all the vaunted glories of English liberty and enterprise, it was not the best of times for the common people of the realm. For more than two centuries serfdom had been on the way to extinction, as the feudal duties of serfs were commuted into rents. But while tenancy gave a degree of independence, it also gave landlords the ability to increase demands and, as the trade in woolen products grew, to enclose farmlands and evict the tenants in favor of sheep. The enclosure movement of the sixteenth century thus gave rise to the great numbers of sturdy beggars and rogues who people the literature of Elizabethan times and gained immortality in Mother Goose: "Hark, hark, the dogs do bark. The beggars have come to town." The problem was met only in part by Elizabethan poor laws which obligated each parish to care for its own (a practice passed on to the colonies), and the needs of this displaced population became another argument for colonial expansion—the more because the cloth market weakened and the nation's economy sought other outlets.

PARLIAMENT AND THE STUARTS    With the death of Elizabeth the Tudor line ran out and the throne fell to the first of the Stuarts, whose dynasty spanned most of the seventeenth century, a turbulent time during which, despite many distractions at home, the English planted an overseas empire. In 1603 James VI of Scotland, son of the ill-fated Mary, Queen of Scots, and great-great-grandson of Henry VII, became James I of England—as Elizabeth had planned. A man of ponderous erudition, James fully earned his reputation as the "wisest fool in all Christendom." He lectured Englishmen on every topic but remained blind to English traditions and sensibilities. Where the Tudors had wielded absolute power through constitutional forms, the learned James demanded a more consistent logic and advanced at every chance the theory of divine right, beginning with a lecture to his first Parliament. Where the Puritans hoped to find a

*James I, the successor to Queen Elizabeth and the first of England's Stuart kings.*

*Charles I, in a portrait by Van Dyck that vividly captures the ill-fated monarch's arrogance.*

Presbyterian ally in their opposition to Anglican trappings, they found instead a testy autocrat. "No bishop, no king," he told them, and promised to "harry them out of the land." He even offended Anglicans by sensibly deciding to end Elizabeth's war with Catholic Spain—and old privateers by suppressing what had now become piracy.

Charles I, who succeeded his father in 1625, proved even more stubborn about royal prerogative, ruled without Parliament from 1628 to 1640, and levied taxes by royal decree. The archbishop of Canterbury, William Laud, directed a systematic persecution of Puritans but finally overreached himself when he tried to impose Anglican worship on Presbyterian Scots. In 1638 Scotland rose in revolt and in 1640 Charles called Parliament to rally support and raise money. The "Long Parliament" (new elections had been delayed now for twenty years) impeached Laud instead, condemned to death the king's chief minister, and abolished the "prerogative courts" established by the crown. In 1642, when the king tried to arrest five members of Parliament, civil war broke out between the "Roundheads" who backed Parliament and the "Cavaliers" who supported the king.

In 1646 royalist resistance collapsed and parliamentary forces captured the king. Parliament, however, could not agree on a permanent settlement. A dispute arose between Presbyterians and Independents (who preferred a congregational church government), and in 1648 the New Model Army of the Independents purged the Presbyterians, leaving a "Rump Parliament" which then instigated the trial and execution of Charles I on charges of treason.

Oliver Cromwell, commander of the army, became in effect a military dictator, ruling first through a council chosen by Parliament (the Commonwealth), and after forcible dissolution of Parliament as Lord Protector (the Protectorate). Cromwell extended religious toleration to all except Catholics and Anglicans, but his arbitrary governance and his moralistic codes made the regime more and more unpopular. When, after his death in 1658, his son proved too weak to carry on, the army once again took control, permitted new elections for Parliament, and supported the restoration of the monarchy under Charles II, son of the martyred king, in 1660.

Charles accepted as terms of the Restoration settlement the principle that he must rule jointly with Parliament, and managed by tact or shrewd maneuvering to hold his throne. His younger brother, the duke of York, was less flexible. Succeeding as James II in 1685, he openly avowed Catholicism and assumed the same unyielding stance as the first two Stuarts. Englishmen could bear it so long as they expected one of his Protestant daughters, Mary or Anne, to succeed him, but in 1688 the birth of a son who would be reared a Catholic finally brought matters to a crisis. Leaders of Parliament invited Mary and her husband, William of Orange, a Dutch prince, to assume the throne jointly, and James fled the country.

By this "Glorious Revolution" Parliament finally established its freedom from royal control. Under the Bill of Rights, in 1689, William and Mary gave up the prerogatives of suspending laws, erecting special courts, keeping a standing army, or levying taxes except by Parliament's consent. They further agreed to frequent sessions and freedom of speech in Parliament, freedom of petition to the crown, and restrictions against excessive bail and cruel and unusual punishments. Under the Toleration Act of 1689 a degree of freedom of worship was extended to all Christians except Catholics and Unitarians, although dissenters from the established church still had few political rights. In 1701 the Act of Settlement ensured a Protestant succession through Queen Anne (1702–1714). And by the Act of Union in 1707 England and Scotland became the United Kingdom of Great Britain.

### SETTLING THE CHESAPEAKE

During these eventful years all but one of the thirteen North American colonies and several more in the islands of the Caribbean had their start. After the ill-fated efforts of Gilbert and Raleigh, the joint-stock company of merchants and gentlemen became the chief vehicle of colonization. In 1606 James I chartered a Virginia Company with two divisions, the First Colony of London and the Second Colony of Plymouth. The London group could plant a settlement between the Thirty-fourth and Thirty-eighth Parallels, the Plymouth group between the Forty-first and Forty-fifth Parallels, and either between the Thirty-eighth and Forty-first Parallels, provided they kept a hundred miles apart. The stockholders expected a potential return from

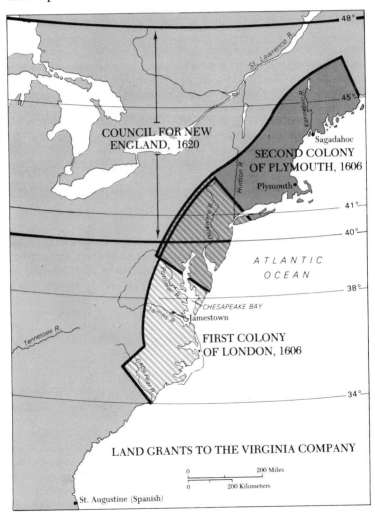

LAND GRANTS TO THE VIRGINIA COMPANY

gold and other minerals; products, such as wine, citrus fruits, and olive oil, to free England from dependence on Spain; trade with the Indians; pitch, tar, potash, and other forest products needed for naval stores; and perhaps a passage to East Asia. Some investors dreamed of finding another Aztec or Inca Empire, but there were in fact relatively few Indians in eastern North America; others thought of a pirate base for plundering Spanish treasure ships. Few if any foresaw what the first English colony would actually become: a place to grow tobacco.

From the outset the pattern of English colonization would diverge from the Spanish. For one thing the English had a different model in their experience. The Spanish had retaken their homeland from the Moors and in the process worked out patterns of colonization later used in America. The English, after four centuries of sporadic intervention in Ireland, proceeded under Elizabeth to conquer the Irish by military force. While the interest in America was growing, the English were already involved in planting settlements, or "plantations" in Ireland. Within their own pale (or limit) of settlement the English set about reconstructing their familiar way of life insofar as possible. The term "wild Irish," which today seems more comic than serious, was then taken in dead earnest. The English went to Ireland, one historian said, with "a preconceived idea of a barbaric society and they merely tailored the Irishman to fit this ideological straitjacket." In English eyes, Irish Catholicism was mere paganism. What the English saw as a "savage nation" that lived "like beastes" could therefore be subjected without compunction. The same pattern would apply to the Indians of North America. In America, moreover, the English settled along the Atlantic seaboard, where the native populations were relatively sparse. There was no Aztec or Inca Empire to conquer and rule. Even without the example of Ireland, the colonists would have no alternative to setting up their own "pales" of settlement.

VIRGINIA  In August 1607 the Plymouth Company landed about 100 men at Sagadahoc on the Kennebec River in Maine, but abandoned the site after a hard winter of Indian hostility, bungling, and short supplies. Meanwhile the London Company, under the vigorous lead of Sir Thomas Smith, a prominent merchant, had already planted the first permanent colony in Virginia. On December 20, 1606, three ships borrowed from the Muscovy Company—the *Susan Constant,* the *Godspeed,* and the *Discovery*—sailed out from the Thames River with 104 men. On May 6, 1607, having traveled south via the West Indies to catch the trade winds, they sighted the capes of Chesapeake Bay. Following instructions, they chose a river with a northwest bend—in hope of a passage to Cathay—and settled about 40 miles from the sea to hide from marauding Spaniards. The river they called the James, and the settlement, Jamestown. Contrary to instructions to choose an island, they settled on a peninsula where the 105 survivors could see any approach from downstream and defend a narrow neck of land against the Indians. They were defenseless, however, from the mosquitoes of the neighboring swamps.

The colonists began building a fort, thatched huts, a storehouse, and a church. They explored the James up to the falls near present Richmond, where they reached the limits of tribes dominated by the chief Powhatan. The colonists set to planting, but they were either townsmen unfamiliar with farming or, fully two-thirds of them, "gentleman" adventurers who scorned manual labor. Ignorant of woodlore, they could not exploit the abundant game and fish. Supplies from England were undependable, and only John Smith's leadership and their trade with the Indians, who taught them to grow maize, enabled them to survive.

The Indians of the region were loosely organized in what Thomas Jefferson later called the "Powhatan Confederacy." Neither that nor the title "emperor" which the English gave to the Indian *weroance* accurately conveys the structure of their society. Powhatan, chief of the Pamunkey tribe, had merely extended an insecure hegemony over some thirty tribes in the coastal area. Despite occasional clashes with the colonists, the Indians adopted a stance of watchful waiting. The reason probably was that Powhatan at first hoped for trade and alliance with newcomers who might serve his purposes, and realized too late their growing design to possess the country.

The colonists, as it happened, had more than a match for Powhatan in Capt. John Smith, a man of humble origins but rare powers, a soldier of fortune whose tales of exploits in eastern Europe are so extravagant as to strain belief, except that they stand up wherever they can be checked against other evidence. When the colonists opened their sealed instructions, they found that Smith, who had quarreled with the expedition's leaders and had been clapped into chains on board ship, was to be a member of the governing council. The council was at first beset by disagreement and vacillation, but by force of will and ability Smith was soon in charge. With the colonists on the verge of starvation, he imposed discipline, forced all to work on pain of expulsion, bargained with the Indians, and explored and mapped the Chesa-

100 Miles

100 Kilometers

MARYLAND

VIRGINIA

St. Mary's
(1634)

Henrico (1610)

Jamestown (1607)

Susquehanna R.

Delaware R.

Potomac R.

DELAWARE BAY

CHESAPEAKE BAY

James R.

York R.

ATLANTIC OCEAN

**EARLY VIRGINIA
AND MARYLAND**

Original grant to
Lord Baltimore

---- Present-day boundary
of Maryland

ROANOKE ISLAND
(1580s)

peake region. Despite his efforts, however, only 53 of the 120 colonists were alive at the end of 1608.

In 1609 the Virginia Company moved to reinforce the Jamestown colony. A new charter redefined the colony's boundaries and replaced the largely ineffective council with an all-powerful governor whose council was only advisory. In a dramatic promotion the company lured new subscribers from all ranks of society and attracted new settlers with the promise of free land after seven years of labor. The company in effect had given up hope of prospering except through the sale of lands which would rise in value as the colony grew. The governor, the noble Lord De La Warr (Delaware), sent as interim governor Sir Thomas Gates. In May 1609 Gates set out with a fleet of nine vessels and about 500 passengers and crew. On the way Gates was shipwrecked on Bermuda, where he and the other survivors wintered in comparative ease, subsisting on fish, fowl, and wild pigs. (Their story was transformed by William Shakespeare into his play *The Tempest*.)

Part of the fleet did reach Jamestown, however, and deposited some 400 settlers, who overwhelmed the remnant of about 80. These leaderless settlers, said one observer, included "many unruly gallants packed thether by their friends to escape il destinies." But their destinies were "il" indeed. All chance that John Smith might control things was lost when he suffered a gunpowder burn and sailed back to England in October 1609.

The consequence was anarchy and the "starving time" of the winter of 1609–1610, during which most of the colonists, weakened by hunger, fell prey to pestilence. By May, when Gates and his companions made their way to Jamestown on two small ships painfully built in Bermuda, only about 60 remained alive. All poultry and livestock (including horses) had been eaten, and one man was even said to have dined on his wife. Jamestown was falling into ruins, the Indians had turned hostile, and the decision was made to give it up.

In June 1610, as the colonists made their way down the river, Lord Delaware providentially arrived with three ships and 150 men, whereupon instead of leaving Virginia, the colonists returned to Jamestown and hived off the first new settlements upstream at Henrico (Richmond) and two more downstream near the mouth of the river. It was a critical turning point for the colony, whose survival required a combination of stern measures and not a little luck. Effective leadership came with Delaware, and after his departure, under his deputies. In 1611 Thomas Gates took charge and established a strict system of *Lawes Divine, Moral, and Martiall,* inaccurately called "Dale's Code," after Thomas Dale who enforced them as marshal. Severe even

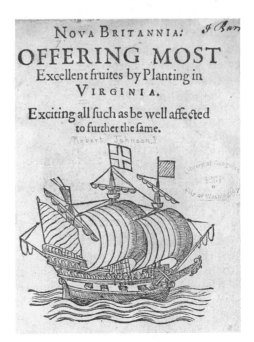

*A 1609 handbill of the Virginia Company attempts to lure settlers to Jamestown.*

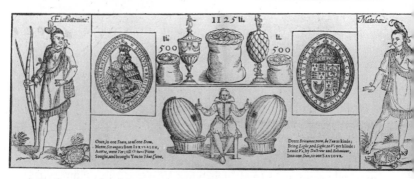

A Declaration for the certaine time of drawing the great standing
Lottery. *While the Jamestown colony limped along in its early years, the
Virginia Company resorted to raising funds through lotteries, such as
this one held in 1615.*

by the standards of a ruthless age, the code enforced a militaristic
discipline needed for survival.

Over the seven years that followed the colony limped along
until it gradually found a reason for being: tobacco. In 1612 John
Rolfe had begun to experiment with the harsh and biting Virginia
tobacco. Eventually he got hold of some seed for the more savory
Spanish varieties, and by 1616 the weed had become an export
staple. Meanwhile Rolfe had made another contribution to stability by marrying Pocahontas, the daughter of Powhatan. Pocahontas had been a familiar figure in Jamestown almost from the
beginning. In 1607, then only twelve, she figured in perhaps the
best-known story of the settlement, her plea for the life of John
Smith, who credited to his own charm what was perhaps the climax to a ritual threat of execution, a bit of play-acting to impress
Smith with Powhatan's authority. In 1613, however, on a foray
to extort corn from the Indians, Dale's men had captured Pocahontas and held her for ransom. To fend off the crisis, Rolfe proposed marriage to Pocahontas, Powhatan agreed, and a wary
peace ensued. Distinguished Virginians still boast of their descent from the Indian "princess."

In 1618 Sir Edwin Sandys, a prominent member of Parliament,
became head of the company and set about a series of reforms.
First of all he inaugurated a new head-right policy. Anybody who
bought a share in the company who could transport himself to
Virginia, could have fifty acres, and fifty more for any servants he
might send or bring. The following year, 1619, was memorable
in several ways. The company now relaxed the tight regimen of

the *Lawes* and promised that the settlers should have the "rights of Englishmen," including a representative assembly. A new governor arrived with instructions to put the new order into effect, and on July 30, 1619, the first General Assembly of Virginia, including the governor, six councilors, and twenty-two burgesses, met in the church at Jamestown and deliberated for five days, "sweating & stewing, and battling flies and mosquitoes." It was an eventful year in two other respects. The promoters also saw a need to send out wives for the men who, Sir Edwin Sandys noted, "By defect thereof (as is credibly reported) stay there but to get something and then return for England." During 1619 a ship arrived with ninety young women, to be sold to likely husbands of their own choice for the cost of transportation (about 125 pounds of tobacco). And a Dutch man-of-war, according to an ominous note in John Rolfe's diary, stopped by and dropped off "20 Negars," the first blacks known to have reached English America. It would be another year before the fabled *Mayflower* came.

Despite its successes the company again fell upon evil days. Sandys quarreled with other leaders in the company, and in 1622 Powhatan's brother and successor, Opechancanough, led a concerted uprising which killed 347, including John Rolfe. Some 14,000 people had migrated to the colony since 1607, but the population in 1624 stood at a precarious 1,132. Despite the broad initial achievements of the company, after about 1617 a handful of insiders had engrossed large estates and began to monopolize the indentured workers. In a tobacco boom of those years some made fortunes, but most of the thousands sent out died before they could prove themselves. At the behest of Sandys's opponents, the king appointed a commission to investigate, and on its recommendation a court dissolved the company. In 1624 Virginia became a royal colony.

The king did not renew instructions for an assembly, but his governors found it impossible to rule the troublesome Virginians without one, and annual assemblies met after 1629, although not recognized by the crown for another ten years. After 1622, relations with the Powhatan Confederates continued in a state of what the governor's council called "perpetual enmity" until the aging Opechancanough staged another concerted attack in 1644. The English suffered as many casualties as they had twenty-two years before, but put down the uprising with such ferocity that nothing quite like it happened again.

Sir William Berkeley, who arrived as governor in 1642, presided over the colony's growth for most of the next thirty-four

### Apparrell.

|  | li. | s. | d. |
|---|---|---|---|
| One Monmouth Cap | 00 | 01 | 10 |
| Three falling bands | — | 01 | 03 |
| Three fhirts | — | 07 | 06 |
| One wafte-coate | — | 02 | 02 |
| One fuite of Canuafe | — | 07 | 06 |
| One fuite of Frize | — | 10 | 00 |
| One fuite of Cloth | — | 15 | 00 |
| Three paire of Irifh ftockins | — | 04 | — |
| Foure paire of fhooes | — | 08 | 08 |
| One paire of garters | — | 00 | 10 |
| One doozen of points | — | 00 | 03 |
| One paire of Canuafe fheets | — | 08 | 00 |
| Seuen ells of Canuafe, to make a bed and boulfter, to be filled in *Virginia* 8.s. | — | — | — |
| One Rug for a bed 8. s. which with the bed feruing for two men, halfe is | — | 08 | 00 |
| Fiue ells coorfe Canuafe, to make a bed at Sea for two men, to be filled with ftraw, iiij. s. | — | — | — |
| One coorfe Rug at Sea for two men, will coft vj. s. is for one | — | 05 | 00 |
|  | 04 | 00 | 00 |

*Apparell for one man, and fo after the rate for more.*

### Victuall.

|  | li. | s. | d. |
|---|---|---|---|
| Eight bufhels of Meale | 02 | 00 | 00 |
| Two bufhels of peafe at 3.s. | — | 06 | 00 |
| Two bufhels of Oatemeale 4.s. 6.d. | — | 09 | 00 |
| One gallon of *Aquauitae* | — | 02 | 06 |
| One gallon of Oyle | — | 03 | 06 |
| Two gallons of Vineger 1. s. | — | 02 | 00 |
|  | 03 | 03 | 00 |

*For a whole yeere for one man, and fo for more after the rate.*

### Armes.

|  | li. | s. | d. |
|---|---|---|---|
| One Armour compleat, light | — | 17 | 00 |
| One long Peece, fiue foot or fiue and a halfe, neere Mufket bore | 01 | 02 | — |
| One fword | — | 05 | — |
| One belt | — | 01 | — |
| One bandaleere | — | 01 | 06 |
| Twenty pound of powder | — | 18 | 00 |
| Sixty pound of fhot or lead, Piftoll and Goofe fhot | — | 05 | 00 |
|  | 03 | 09 | 06 |

*For one man, but if halfe of your men haue armour it is fufficient fo that all haue Peeces and fwords.*

### Tooles.

|  | li. | s. | d. |
|---|---|---|---|
| Fiue broad howes at 2.s. a piece | — | 10 | — |
| Fiue narrow howes at 16.d. a piece | — | 06 | 08 |
| Two broad Axes at 3.s. 8.d. a piece | — | 07 | 04 |
| Fiue felling Axes at 18.d a piece | — | 07 | 06 |
| Two fteele hand fawes at 16.d. a piece | — | 02 | 08 |
| Two two-hand fawes at 5. s. a piece | — | 10 | — |
| One whip-faw, fet and filed with box, file, and wreft | — | 10 | — |
| Two hammers 12.d. a piece | — | 02 | 00 |
| Three fhouels 18.d. a piece | — | 04 | 06 |
| Two fpades at 18.d. a piece | — | 03 | — |
| Two augers 6.d. a piece | — | 01 | 00 |
| Sixe chiffels 6.d. a piece | — | 03 | 00 |
| Two percers ftocked 4.d. a piece | — | 00 | 08 |
| Three gimlets 2.d. a piece | — | 00 | 06 |
| Two hatchets 21.d. a piece | — | 03 | 06 |
| Two frowes to cleaue pale 18.d. | — | 03 | 00 |
| Two hand-bills 20. a piece | — | 03 | 04 |
| One grindleftone 4.s. | — | 04 | 00 |
| Nailes of all forts to the value of | 02 | 00 | — |
| Two Pickaxes | — | 03 | — |
|  | 06 | 02 | 08 |

*For a family of 6. perfons and fo after the rate for more.*

### Houfhold Implements.

|  | li. | s. | d. |
|---|---|---|---|
| One Iron Pot | — | 00 | 07 |
| One kettle | — | 06 | — |
| One large frying pan | — | 02 | 06 |
| One gridiron | — | 01 | 06 |
| Two fkillets | — | 05 | — |
| One fpit | — | 02 | — |
| Platters, difhes, fpoones of wood | — | 04 | — |
|  | 01 | 08 | 00 |

*For a family of 6. perfons, and fo for more or leffe after the rate.*

For Suger, Spice, and fruit, and at Sea for 6. men — 00 | 12 | 06

So the full charge of Apparrell, Victuall, Armes, Tooles, and houfhold ftuffe, and after this rate for each perfon, will amount vnto about the fumme of — 12 | 10 | —

The paffage of each man is — 06 | 00 | —

The fraight of thefe prouifions for a man, will bee about halfe a Tun, which is — 01 | 10 | —

So the whole charge will amount to about — 20 | 00 | 00

*Nets, hookes, lines, and a tent muft be added, if the number of people be greater, as alfo fome kine.*

*And this is the vfuall proportion that the Virginia Company doe beftow vpon their Tenants which they fend.*

Whofoeuer tranfports himfelfe or any other at his owne charge vnto *Virginia*, fhall for each perfon fo tranfported before Midfummer 1625. haue to him and his heires for euer fifty Acres of Land vpon a firft, and fifty Acres vpon a fecond diuifion.

Imprinted at London by Felix Kyngston. 1622.

## The Inconveniencies That Have Happened to Some Persons Which Have Transported Themselves from England to Virginia. *The Virginia Company recommended that prospective settlers bring to America these "provisions necessary to sustain themselves."*

years. The brawling populace of men on the make over which he held sway was a far cry from the cultivated gentry of the next century. But among them were the Byrds, Carters, Masons, and Randolphs who made the fortunes that nurtured the celebrated aristocrats of later generations.

MARYLAND  In 1634, ten years after Virginia became a royal colony, a neighboring settlement appeared on the northern shores of Chesapeake Bay, the first proprietary colony, granted to Lord Baltimore by Charles I and named Maryland in honor of Queen

Henrietta Maria. Sir George Calvert, the first Lord Baltimore, had announced in 1625 his conversion to Catholicism and sought the colony as a refuge for English Catholics who were subjected to discriminations at home. He had in fact undertaken to colonize Newfoundland in 1623 under a previous grant, but that colony was abandoned five years later after a successful clash with the French was followed by a severe winter. Calvert had tried Virginia too. In October 1629 he had landed with his family and some followers at Jamestown, but was ordered to leave because he refused to take the Oaths of Allegiance and Supremacy to the monarch.

Nevertheless Calvert kept the favor of King Charles and sought a charter in the region, which was issued in 1632 after his death. His son, Cecilius Calvert, the second Lord Baltimore, actually founded the colony. The charter, which set a precedent for later proprietary grants, gave the proprietor powers similar to those of an independent monarch, though the charter specified that the laws must be in accordance with those of England. References to religion were vague except for a mention that chapels should be established according to the ecclesiastical law of England.

In 1634 Calvert planted the first settlement in Maryland at St. Mary's on a small stream near the mouth of the Potomac. St. Mary's in fact was already there, a native settlement purchased from friendly Indians along with the cleared fields around it. Calvert brought Catholic gentlemen as landholders, but a majority of the servants from the beginning were Protestants. The charter gave Calvert power to make laws with the consent of the freemen (all property holders). The first legislative assembly met in 1635, and divided into two houses in 1650, with governor and council sitting separately. This was instigated by the predominantly Protestant freemen—largely servants who had become landholders, or immigrants from Virginia. The charter also empowered the proprietor to grant manorial estates, and Maryland had some sixty before 1676, but the Lords Baltimore soon found that to draw settlers they had to offer farms. Because of their flexibility, the Calverts bent rather than broke in the prevailing winds. Ousted from the proprietorship only for brief periods under Cromwell and William III, they continued even then to hold their property rights and coined a fortune in America before the end of the colonial period. The colony was meant to rely on mixed farming, but its fortunes, like those of Virginia, soon came to depend on tobacco.

## SETTLING NEW ENGLAND

The Virginia Company of Plymouth never got back to colonization after the Sagadahoc failure in 1607, although it did bestir itself to hire John Smith as an explorer. After his return from a visit in 1614 Smith published *A Description of New England* (1616) and thus named the region. Having watched the London Company's transition from commerce to real estate, the leader of the Plymouth Company, Sir Ferdinando Gorges, reorganized his moribund enterprise into the Council for New England (1620), which had the right to issue land grants between the Fortieth and Forty-eighth Parallels.

PLYMOUTH    The first permanent settlers landed in New England by no design of the council, which had some notion of creating vast feudal domains for its members. In fact they landed there by no design of their own—at least none that they acknowledged.

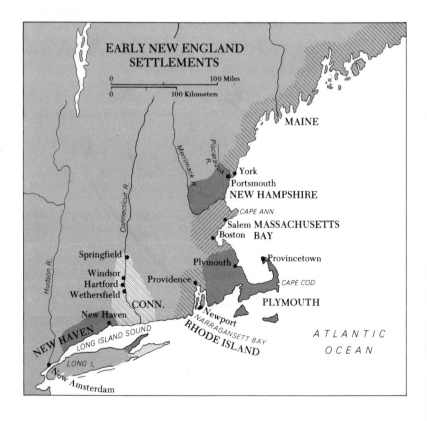

EARLY NEW ENGLAND
SETTLEMENTS

0            100 Miles
0            100 Kilometers

MAINE

*Merrimack R.*

*Piscataqua R.*

York
Portsmouth
NEW HAMPSHIRE

*CAPE ANN*

Salem MASSACHUSETTS
Boston  BAY

*Connecticut R.*

Springfield

Plymouth

Provincetown

Windsor

Providence

*CAPE COD*

*Hudson R.*

Hartford
Wethersfield

CONN.

PLYMOUTH

New Haven

Newport

NEW HAVEN

NARRAGANSETT BAY

ATLANTIC

LONG ISLAND SOUND

RHODE ISLAND

OCEAN

LONG I.

New Amsterdam

They meant to go to Virginia, they said. The Pilgrims who established Plymouth colony belonged to the most extreme and uncompromising sect of Puritans, the Separatists, who had severed all ties with the Church of England. They stemmed from a congregation established at Scrooby in eastern England, members of which had slipped away to Holland in 1607 to escape persecution. The Calvinistic Dutch granted them asylum and toleration, but restricted them mainly to unskilled labor. After ten years in the Dutch city of Leyden, they had wearied of the struggle. Watching their children turn into Dutchmen, drifting away to become sailors, soldiers, or worse, so that "their posterity would be in danger to degenerate and be corrupted," they longed for English ways and the English flag. If they could not have them at home, perhaps they might transplant them to the New World. King James would not promise outright toleration if they set up a colony, but did agree to leave them alone, or as he put it, to "connive at them."

The Leyden group got the support of London merchants, led by Thomas Weston, who secured a land patent from the Virginia Company and set up a joint-stock company. In July 1620 a group of thirty-five Pilgrims led by William Bradford left Leyden on the *Speedwell.* At Southampton, England, a larger ship, the *Mayflower,* and a larger group of colonists joined them. At Plymouth, however, they had to abandon the leaky *Speedwell* and in September they crammed the *Mayflower* with their party of 101, both "saints" and "strangers," the latter including John Alden, a cooper, and Miles Standish, a soldier hired to organize their defenses. A stormy voyage led them in November to Cape Cod, far north of Virginia. Heading south, they encountered rough waters and turned back to seek safety at Provincetown. "Being thus arrived at safe harbor, and brought safe to land," William Bradford wrote in his history, *Of Plymouth Plantation,* "they fell upon their knees and blessed the God of Heaven who had brought them over the vast and furious ocean, and delivered them from all the perils thereof, again to set their feet on the firm and stable earth, their proper element." Exploring parties then scouted Cape Cod Bay and hit upon a place John Smith had called Plymouth for their settlement. Since they were outside the jurisdiction of any organized government, forty-one of the Pilgrim Fathers entered into a formal agreement to abide by laws made by leaders of their own choosing—the Mayflower Compact of November 21, 1620.

On December 26 the *Mayflower* reached Plymouth harbor and stayed there until April to give shelter and support while the Pilgrims raised and occupied their dwellings amid the winter snows. Nearly half the colonists died of exposure and disease, but friendly relations with the neighboring Wampanoag Indians proved their salvation. In the spring of 1621 the colonists were introduced to Squanto, an Indian who spoke English and showed the colonists how to grow maize. A few years earlier Squanto had been kidnapped aboard a passing English ship and sold into slavery in Spain, whence he had somehow found his way back to England and, aboard a trading ship, back home, where he found himself to be the sole survivor of the Pawtuxet tribe, which had been wiped out by a pestilence. By autumn the Pilgrims had a bumper crop of corn, a flourishing fur trade, and a supply of lumber for shipment. To celebrate they held a harvest feast in company with Chief Massasoit and the Wampanoags. But after the ship *Fortune* arrived with thirty-five new colonists, the enlarged group again faced hunger before a food supply arrived in the spring. To make matters worse, on the way home the *Fortune* lost its cargo of furs and lumber to a French privateer.

But the colony soon stabilized. In 1621 it got a land patent from the Council for New England. Two years later it gave up its original communal economy to the extent that each settler was to provide for his family from his own land. A group of settlers bought out the sponsoring merchants in 1626 and promised to pay the purchase price in nine annual installments, although final settlement was delayed until 1648. In 1630 Governor Bradford secured a new title, the "Bradford Patent," from the Council for New England, which confirmed possession and defined the boundaries more clearly.

Throughout its separate existence, until absorbed into Massachusetts in 1691, the Plymouth colony remained in the anomalous position of holding a land grant but no charter of government from any English authority. The government grew instead out of the Mayflower Compact, which was neither exactly a constitution nor a precedent for later constitutions, but rather the obvious recourse of a group who had made a covenant (or agreement) to form a church and who believed that God had made a covenant with men to provide a way to salvation. Thus the civil government grew naturally out of the church government, and the members of each were identical at the start. The signers of the compact at first met as the General Court, which chose the governor and his assistants (or council). Later others were admitted as members, or "freemen," but only church members were eligible. Eventually, as the colony grew, the General Court became in 1639 a body of representatives from the various towns.

*The Plymouth Meetinghouse, built in 1683 with funds from the sale of confiscated Indian lands.*

Plymouth Colony's population never rose above 7,000, and after ten years it was overshadowed by its larger neighbor, Massachusetts Bay Colony. Plymouth's area, Cape Cod and the neighboring mainland, had relatively poor land, lacked ready access to furs from the interior, and was not in the best location for fisheries. But its imprint on the national mind would be greater than its size would warrant—William Bradford's unpretentious history, *Of Plymouth Plantation* (completed in 1651) brought the colony vividly to life. And Plymouth invented Thanksgiving—at least later generations persuaded themselves that its 1621 harvest festival was the first Thanksgiving.

During the decade of the 1620s a scattering of settlements appeared along the neighboring coasts, mainly fishing posts occupied only in season, plus a few rugged hermits like Samuel Maverick, who engaged in fishing, fur trading, and sometimes a little farming on his island in Massachusetts Bay. The Pilgrims got their first neighbors when Thomas Weston, who had helped them get a start, sent about fifty "rude and lusty fellows" via Plymouth to Wessagussett (now Weymouth), but that lasted only one winter. Another try by one Captain Wollaston at Mount Wollaston (now part of Quincy) likewise failed, and Wollaston moved to Virginia. He left behind Thomas Morton, who persuaded some thirty men to stay in what he renamed Merry Mount. There, only twenty-five miles from Plymouth, Morton's company of Indian traders brought Renaissance England to the

New World, "drinking and dancing about" a maypole, in Governor Bradford's words, "inviting the Indean women for their consorts, dancing and frisking together . . . and worse practices." But his chief sin was selling the Indians firewater and firearms. It was all too much for the Pilgrims, who sent Miles Standish ("Captaine Shrimpe," in Morton's satiric account) to seize the reprobate and ship him back to England in 1628.

MASSACHUSETTS BAY  Massachusetts Bay Colony, the Puritan Utopia, had its genesis in one of the fishing posts near Plymouth. In 1623 a group of Dorchester merchants with a patent from the Council for New England set up a permanent fishing village on Cape Ann. For three years they occupied the site of the present Gloucester, but the venture proved unprofitable and the promoters withdrew. Back in Dorchester the Rev. John White, a moderate Puritan and a leading force in the Gloucester settlement, held to his hope for a Christian mission to the English fishermen and Indians along the coast. In answer to White's appeal, a group of Puritans and merchants formed the New England Company in 1628, and got a land patent from the Council for New England. Then to confirm its legality the company turned to Charles I, who issued a charter in 1629 under the new name of Massachusetts Bay Company.

Leaders of the company at first looked upon it mainly as a business venture, but a majority faction led by John Winthrop, a well-to-do lawyer from East Anglia recently discharged from a government job, resolved to use the colony as a refuge for persecuted Puritans and as an instrument for building a "wilderness Zion" in America. The charter had one fateful omission: the usual proviso that the company maintain its home office in England. Winthrop's group therefore decided to take the charter with them, thereby transferring the entire government of the

*Gov. John Winthrop, in whose vision the Massachusetts Bay colony would be as "a city upon a hill."*

colony to Massachusetts Bay, where they hoped to ensure Puritan control. By the Cambridge Agreement of 1629 twelve leaders resolved to migrate on these conditions, and the company's governing body agreed.

In March 1630 the *Arbella*, with Gov. John Winthrop and the charter aboard, embarked with six other ships for Massachusetts. In a sermon, "A Model of Christian Charity," delivered on board the *Arbella*, Winthrop told his fellow Puritans "we must consider that we shall be a city upon a hill"—an example to all people. By the end of 1630 seventeen ships bearing 1,000 more arrived. As new settlers poured in, a small group at Salem was joined by a new settlement, Charlestown, and soon Mystic, Newton, Watertown, and Dorchester. Boston, on the Shawmut Peninsula, became the chief city and capital. The *Arbella* migrants thus proved but the vanguard of a massive movement, the Great Migration, that carried some 40,000–50,000 Englishmen to the New World over the next decade, fleeing persecution and economic depression at home. They went not only to New England and the Chesapeake, but now also to new English settlements in the Lesser Antilles: St. Christopher (first settled in 1624), Barbados (1625),

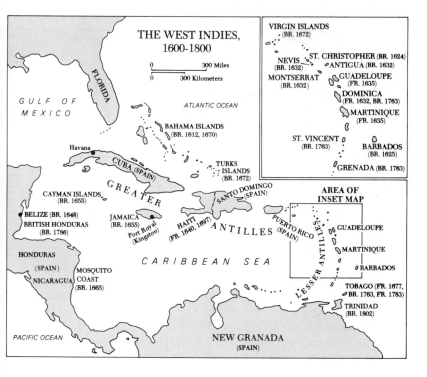

*THE*

# OATH
## OF A
# FREE-MAN

I A . B . being by Gods Providence an Inhabitant and FREEMAN within the Iurifdiction of this Commonwealth; doe freely acknowledge myfelfe to be fubject to the Government thereof.
AND therefore doe here fweare by the Great and Dreadful NAME of the Everliving GOD, that I will be true and faithfull to the fame, and will accordingly yield affiftance & fupport thereunto with my perfon and eftate as in equity I am bound; and will alfo truly endeavour to maintaine & preferve all the liberties & priviledges thereof, fubmitting myfelfe to the wholefome Lawes & Orders made and eftablifhed by the fame. +++ AND further that I will not Plot or practife any evill againft it, or confent to any that fhall fo doe: but will timely difcover and reveal the fame to lawfull authority now here eftablifhed, for the fpeedy preventing thereof.

MOREOVER I doe folemnly bind myfelfe in the fight of GOD, that when I fhall be called to give my voyce touching any fuch matter of this State in which FREEMEN are to deale +++ I will give my vote and fuffrage as I fhall judge in mine own confcience may beft conduce and tend to the publicke weale of the body without refpect of perfon or favour of any man.
So help me GOD in the LORD IESVS CHRIST.

Printed at Cambridge in New England:
by Order of the Generall Courte:
Moneth the Firft - 1639

*The Oath of a Free-Man: "I will give my vote and suffrage as I shall judge in mine own conscience . . ." (1639).*

Nevis (1632), Montserrat (1632), and Antigua (1632). The West Indian islands started out to grow tobacco but ended up in the more profitable business of producing cane sugar.

The transfer of the Massachusetts charter, whereby an English trading company evolved into a provincial government, was a unique venture in colonization. Under this royal charter power in the company rested with the General Court, which elected the governor and assistants. The General Court consisted of shareholders, called freemen (those who had the "freedom of the company"), but of those who came, few besides Winthrop and his assistants had such status. This suited Winthrop and his friends, but then 108 more settlers asked to be admitted as freemen. Rather than risk trouble, the inner group invited applications and finally admitted 118 in 1631. A further provision was made at that time that only church members, a limited category, could become freemen.

At first the freemen had no power except to choose assistants, who in turn chose the governor and deputy governor. The procedure violated provisions of the charter, but Winthrop kept the document hidden and few knew of the exact provisions. In the Watertown Protest of 1632, the people of one town objected to paying taxes levied by the governor and assistants "for fear of bringing themselves and posterity into bondage." Winthrop rebuked them, but that year restored to the body of freemen election of the governor and his deputy. Controversy simmered for two more years until 1634, when each town sent two delegates to Boston to confer on matters coming before the General Court. There they demanded to see the charter, which Winthrop reluctantly produced, and they read that the power to pass laws and levy taxes rested in the General Court. Winthrop argued that the body of freemen had grown too large, but when it met, the General Court responded by turning itself into a representative body with two or three deputies to represent each town. They also chose a new governor, and Winthrop did not resume the office until three years later.

A final stage in the evolution of the government, a two-house legislature, came in 1644 when, according to Winthrop, "there fell out a great business upon a very small occasion." The "small occasion" involved a classic melodrama which pitted a poor widow against a well-to-do merchant over ownership of a stray sow. The General Court, being the supreme judicial as well as legislative body, was the final authority in the case. Popular sympathy and the deputies favored the widow, a Mrs. Sherman, but the assistants disagreed. The case was finally settled out of court, but the assistants feared being outvoted on some greater occasion. They therefore secured a separation into two houses and Massachusetts thenceforth had a bicameral assembly, the deputies and assistants sitting apart, with all decisions requiring a majority in each house.

Thus over a period of fourteen years the Massachusetts Bay Company, a trading corporation, was transformed into the governing body of a commonwealth. Membership in a Puritan church replaced the purchase of stock as the means of becoming a freeman, which was to say, a voter. The General Court, like Parliament, became a representative body of two houses, the

House of Assistants corresponding roughly to the House of Lords, the House of Deputies to the House of Commons. The charter remained unchanged, but practice under the charter was quite different from the original expectation.

RHODE ISLAND   More by accident than design Massachusetts became the staging area for the rest of New England as new colonies grew out of religious quarrels within the fold. Puritanism created a volatile mixture: on the one hand the search for God's will could lead to a rigid orthodoxy; on the other hand it could lead troubled consciences to diverse, radical, even bizarre convictions. Young Roger Williams, who arrived in 1631, was among the first to cause problems, precisely because he was the purest of Puritans, troubled by the failure of Massachusetts Nonconformists to repudiate the Church of England. He held a brief pastorate in Salem, then tried Separatist Plymouth, where according to Governor Bradford he "began to fall into strange opinions," specifically questioning the king's right to grant Indian lands "under a sin of usurpation of others' possession," and returned to Salem. Williams's belief that a true church must have no truck with the unregenerate led him eventually to the absurdity that no true church was possible, unless perhaps consisting of his wife and himself—and he may have had doubts about her.

But bizarre as Williams's beliefs may have been, they led him to principles that later generations would honor for other reasons. The purity of the church required complete separation of church and state and freedom from coercion in matters of faith. Williams therefore questioned the authority of government to

*Religious quarrels within the Puritan fold led to the founding of new colonies. Here a seventeenth-century cartoon shows wrangling sects tossing a Bible in a blanket.*

impose an oath of allegiance and rejected laws imposing religious conformity. Such views were too advanced even for the radical church of Salem, which finally removed him, whereupon Williams retorted so hotly against churches that were "ulcered and gangrened" that the General Court in 1635 banished him to England. Governor Winthrop, however, out of personal sympathy, permitted him to slip away with a few followers among the Narragansett Indians, whom he had befriended. In the spring of 1636 Williams established the town of Providence at the head of Narragansett Bay, the first permanent settlement in Rhode Island.

Anne Hutchinson fell into dispute with the Puritan leaders for different reasons. The articulate wife of a well-to-do settler, she called groups together in her home to discuss the sermons of the Rev. John Cotton. In the course of the talks it began to appear that she held to a belief in an inner light from the Holy Spirit. Only Cotton, it seemed, along with her brother-in-law, the Rev. John Wheelwright, preached the appropriate "covenant of grace"; the others had a "covenant of works." Her adversaries likened her beliefs to the Antinomian heresy, technically a belief that one is freed from the moral law by one's faith and by God's grace. The important point here was that Mrs. Hutchinson offended authority. Upon being hauled before the General Court, she was lured into convicting herself by claiming direct divine inspiration—blasphemy to the orthodox. Banished in 1638, she too took refuge in Narragansett country with a group of followers under William Coddington, who founded Pocasset (Portsmouth) on Aquidneck Island. Eventually she went to Long Island, under Dutch jurisdiction, and died there in an Indian attack in 1643. Her fate, Winthrop wrote, was "a special manifestation of divine justice."

When dissentions split Portsmouth, Coddington founded Shawomet (Warwick) on the mainland below Providence, and another Massachusetts outcast, Samuel Gorton, established Newport at the southern end of Aquidneck. Thus the colony of Rhode Island and Providence Plantations grew up in Narragansett Bay. It was a disputatious lot of dissenters who agreed mainly on one thing: that the state had no right to coerce belief. In 1640 they formed a confederation and in 1644 secured their first charter—from the Puritan Parliament. Williams lived until 1683, an active and beloved citizen of the commonwealth he founded in a society which, during his lifetime at least, lived up to his principles of religious freedom and a government based on the consent of the people.

CONNECTICUT    Connecticut had a more orthodox start in groups of Puritans seeking better lands and access to the fur trade farther west. In 1633, ignoring Fort Good Hope which the Dutch had established near the present-day site of Hartford, a group from Plymouth settled Windsor, ten miles farther up the Connecticut River. In 1636, activated by the leadership of Thomas Hooker, three entire church congregations from Watertown, Dorchester, and Newton (now Cambridge) trekked westward by the "Great Road," driving their hogs and cattle like the westering pioneers of a later day, and moved respectively to the Connecticut River towns of Wethersfield, Windsor, and Hartford, which earlier arrivals had laid out the previous year. A fourth group, from Roxbury, founded Springfield. Meanwhile in 1635 John Winthrop, Jr., had planted another town at the mouth of the river—Saybrook, named after its two proprietors, Lord Saye and Sele and Lord Brooke, who had acquired a grant from the Council for New England.

For a year the settlers in the river towns were governed under a commission from the Massachusetts General Court, but finding that only Springfield lay within Massachusetts, the inhabitants of Wethersfield, Windsor, and Hartford organized the self-governing colony of Connecticut in 1637. The impulse to organize came when representatives of the towns met to consider ways of meeting the danger of attack from the Pequot Indians, who lived east of the river. Before the end of the year the Pequots had attacked Wethersfield, and the settlers, with help from Massachusetts, responded with ferocity, surprising and burning the chief Pequot town on the Mystic River and slaughtering some 400 men, women, and children; stragglers were sold into slavery. All but a remnant of the Pequots perished in the holocaust.

In 1639 the Connecticut General Court adopted the "Fundamental Orders of Connecticut," a series of laws which provided for a government like that of Massachusetts, except that voting was not limited to church members. New Haven had by then appeared within the later limits of Connecticut. A group of English Puritans, led by their minister and a wealthy merchant, had migrated first to Massachusetts and then, seeking a place to establish themselves in commerce, to New Haven on Long Island Sound in 1638. Mostly city dwellers, they found themselves reduced to hardscrabble farming, despite their intentions. The New Haven colony became the most rigorously Puritan of all. Like all the other offshoots of Massachusetts, it too lacked a charter and maintained a self-governing independence until 1662, when it was absorbed into Connecticut under the terms of that colony's first royal charter.

NEW HAMPSHIRE AND MAINE   To the north of Massachusetts, most of what are now New Hampshire and Maine was granted in 1622 by the Council for New England to Sir Ferdinando Gorges and Capt. John Mason and their associates. In 1629 Mason and Gorges divided their territory at the Piscataqua River, Mason taking the southern part which he named New Hampshire. The first settlement had already appeared at Rye in 1623, the same year as the Gloucester fishing settlement. In the 1630s Puritan immigrants began filtering in, and in 1638 the Rev. John Wheelwright, one of Anne Hutchinson's group, founded Exeter. Maine consisted of a few scattered and small settlements, mostly fishing stations, the chief of them being York.

An ambiguity in the Massachusetts charter brought the proprietorships into doubt, however. The charter set the boundary three miles north of the Merrimack River and the Bay colony took that to mean north of the river's northernmost reach, which gave it a claim on nearly the entire Gorges-Mason grant. During the English time of troubles in the early 1640s Massachusetts took over New Hampshire, and in the 1650s extended its authority to the scattered settlements in Maine. This led to lawsuits with the heirs of the proprietors and in 1677 English judges and the Privy Council decided against Massachusetts in both cases. Two years later New Hampshire became a royal colony, but Massachusetts bought out the Gorges heirs and continued to control Maine as its proprietor. A new Massachusetts charter in 1691 finally incorporated Maine into Massachusetts.

## THE ENGLISH CIVIL WAR IN AMERICA

Before 1640 English settlers in New England and around Chesapeake Bay had established two great beachheads on the Atlantic coast, separated by the Dutch colony of New Netherland in between. After 1640, however, the struggle between king and Parliament distracted attention from colonization and migration dwindled to a trickle of emigrants for more than twenty years. During the time of civil war and Cromwell's Puritan dictatorship the struggling colonies were left pretty much to their own devices, especially in New England where English Puritans saw little need to intervene. In 1643 four of the New England colonies—Massachusetts, Plymouth, Connecticut, and New Haven—looked to their own safety by forming the New England Confederation. The purpose was mainly joint defense against the Dutch, French, and Indians, but the colonies agreed also to support the Christian faith, to render up fugitives, and to

*Oliver Cromwell, England's
Lord Protector from 1653 until
his death in 1658.*

settle disputes through the machinery of the Confederation. Two commissioners from each colony met annually to transact business. In some ways the Confederation behaved like a sovereign power. It made treaties with New Netherland and French Acadia, and in 1653 voted a war against the Dutch who were supposedly stirring the Indians against Connecticut. Massachusetts, far from the scene of trouble, failed to cooperate, however, and the Confederation was greatly weakened by the inaction of its largest member. The commissioners nevertheless continued to meet annually until 1684, when Massachusetts lost its charter.

Virginia and Maryland remained almost as independent as New England. At the behest of Gov. William Berkeley, the Virginia Burgesses in 1649 denounced the execution of Charles and recognized his son, Charles II, as the lawful king. In 1652, however, the Assembly yielded to parliamentary commissioners backed by a parliamentary fleet and overruled the belligerent governor. In return for the surrender the commissioners let the Assembly choose its own council and governor, and the colony grew rapidly in population during its years of independent government—some of the growth came from the arrival of royalists who found a friendly haven in the Old Dominion, despite its capitulation to the Puritans.

The parliamentary commissioners who won the submission of Virginia proceeded to Maryland, where the proprietary governor faced particular difficulties with his Protestant majority, largely Puritan but including some earlier refugees from Anglican Virginia. At Governor Stone's suggestion the Assembly had passed, and the proprietor had accepted, the Maryland Toleration Act of 1649, an assurance that Puritans would not be molested in their religion. In 1652 Stone yielded to the commissioners, who nevertheless removed him temporarily, revoked the Toleration Act, and deprived Lord Baltimore of his governmental rights, though not of his lands and revenues. Still, the more extreme Puritan elements were dissatisfied and a brief clash in 1654 brought civil war to Maryland, deposing the governor. But the Calverts had a remarkable skill at retaining favor. Oliver Cromwell took the side of Lord Baltimore and restored him to full rights in 1657, whereupon the Toleration Act was reinstated. The act deservedly stands as a landmark to human liberty, albeit enacted more out of expediency than conviction, and although it limited toleration to those who professed belief in the Holy Trinity.

Although Cromwell let the colonies go their own way, he was not indifferent to the nascent empire. He fought trade wars with the Dutch and harassed England's traditional enemy, Catholic Spain, in the Caribbean. In 1655 he sent out an expedition which conquered Jamaica from the Spaniards, thereby improving the odds for English privateers and pirates who pillaged Spanish ships—and often any others that chanced by.

The Restoration of King Charles II in England was followed by an equally painless restoration of previous governments in the colonies. The process involved scarcely any change, since little had occurred under Cromwell. The Virginia Assembly gladly restored Governor Berkeley to his office, an act soon confirmed by the crown. The king promptly confirmed Lord Baltimore in his rights, which Cromwell had already restored. Emigration rapidly expanded population in both colonies. Fears of reprisals against Puritan New England proved unfounded, at least for the time being. Agents hastily dispatched by the colonies won reconfirmation of the Massachusetts charter in 1662 and the very first royal charters for Connecticut and Rhode Island in 1662 and 1663. All three retained their status as self-governing corporations. Plymouth still had no charter, but went unmolested. New Haven, however, disappeared as a separate entity, absorbed into the colony of Connecticut.

SETTLING THE CAROLINAS

The Restoration of Charles II, the Merry Monarch, opened a new season of enthusiasm for colonial expansion, directed mainly by royal favorites. Within twelve years the English had

EARLY SETTLEMENTS
IN THE SOUTH

conquered New Netherland, had settled Carolina, and very
nearly filled out the shape of the colonies. In the middle region
formerly claimed by the Dutch, four new colonies sprang into
being: New York, New Jersey, Pennsylvania, and Delaware.
Without exception the new colonies were proprietary, awarded
by the king to men who had remained loyal, or had brought
about his restoration, or in one case to whom he was indebted. In
1663 he granted Carolina to eight True and Absolute Lords Proprietors: Sir John Colleton, a Barbadian planter and prime mover
of the enterprise; George Monk, the duke of Albemarle, Cromwell's army commander who engineered the Restoration; Edward Hyde, earl of Clarendon; Sir Anthony Ashley-Cooper, later.
earl of Shaftesbury; Lord John Berkeley and his brother, Gov.
William Berkeley of Virginia; William Craven, earl of Craven;
and Sir George Carteret. The list is nearly a complete rollcall of
the movers and shakers in Restoration expansion. Six of the eight
were connected with the Royal African and Hudson's Bay Companies. Two—Carteret and Lord Berkeley—became the proprietors of New Jersey, and six, including Berkeley and Carteret,
became proprietors of the Bahamas. Five served on the Council
of Trade, six on the Council for Foreign Plantations, both important committees of the Privy Council.

NORTH CAROLINA    Carolina was from the start made up of two widely separated areas of settlement, which finally became separate colonies. The northernmost part, long called Albemarle, had been entered as early as the 1650s by stragglers who drifted southward from Virginia. For half a century Albemarle remained a remote scattering of settlers along the shores of Albemarle Sound, isolated from Virginia by the Dismal Swamp and lacking easy access for ocean-going vessels. For many years its reputation suffered from the belief that it served as a rogue's harbor for the offscourings of Virginia. Later the aristocratic William Byrd, who helped survey the dividing line between Virginia and North Carolina, dubbed the neighboring colony Lubberland: "Surely there is no place in the world where the inhabitants lived with less labor than in North Carolina. . . . When the weather is mild, they stand leaning with both their arms upon the cornfield fence and gravely consider whether they had best go and take a small beat at the hoe but generally find reasons to put it off. . . ." Albemarle had no governor until 1664 when Sir William Berkeley

*Advertisement for settlers showing the proprietors' interest in South Carolina.*

A Brief DESCRIPTION
OF
The Province
OF
CAROLINA
On the COASTS of FLOREDA.
AND

More perticularly of a *New-Plantation*
begun by the *ENGLISH* at *Cape-Feare*,
on that River now by them called *Charles-River*,
the 29th of *May*. 1664.

*Wherein is set forth*
The *Healthfulness* of the *Air* ; the *Fertility* of
the *Earth*, and *Waters* ; and the great *Pleasure* and
*Profit* will accrue to those that shall go thither to enjoy
the same.

*Also*,
Directions and advice to such as shall go thither whether
on their own accompts, or to serve under another.

*Together with*
A most accurate MAP of the whole *PROVINCE*.

*London*, Printed for *Robert Horne* in the first Court of *Gresham-
Colledge* neer *Bishopsgate street*. 1666.

exercised proprietary authority to appoint William Drummond, no assembly until 1665, and not even a town until a group of French Huguenots founded the village of Bath in 1704.

SOUTH CAROLINA   The proprietors neglected Albemarle from the outset, and focused on more promising sites to the south. They proposed to find settlers who had already been seasoned in the colonies, and from the outset Barbadians showed a lively interest. Colleton had connections in Barbados, where the rise of large-scale sugar production had persuaded small planters to try their luck elsewhere. Sir Anthony Ashley-Cooper finally spurred the enterprise by persuading his colleagues to take on more of the financial burden of settlement. In 1669 three ships left London with about 100 settlers recruited in England. The expedition sailed first to Barbados, to pick up more settlers, then north to Bermuda. The goal was Port Royal, at what is now the southern tip of South Carolina, but the settlers decided to go farther north to put more distance between themselves and Spanish St. Augustine. The choice fell on a place several miles up the Ashley River, where Charles Town (later known as Charleston) remained from 1670 to 1680, when it was moved across and downstream to Oyster Point, overlooking Charleston Harbor where, as proud Charlestonians later claimed, the Ashley and Cooper Rivers "join to form the Atlantic Ocean."

The government of this colony rested on one of the most curious documents of colonial history, the "Fundamental Constitutions of Carolina," drawn up by Lord Ashley with the help of his

*A view of Charles Town (Charleston), South Carolina, early in the eighteenth century.*

secretary, the philosopher John Locke. Its cumbersome frame of government and its provisions for an elaborate nobility had little effect in the colony except to encourage a practice of large land grants, but from the beginning smaller "headrights" were given to every immigrant who paid his own way. The provision that had greatest effect was a grant of religious toleration, designed to encourage immigration, which gave South Carolina a greater degree of indulgence (extending even to Jews and heathens) than either England or any other colony except Rhode Island, and once it was established, Pennsylvania.

For two decades the South Carolina proprietors struggled to find a staple crop. Indeed the colonists at first had trouble providing their own subsistence. The first profitable enterprise was the Indian trade developed by Dr. Henry Woodward, who had left an expedition to live among the Indians and learn their languages four years before the founding of Charles Town. Through his contacts with the coastal tribes, and later with the Indians along the Savannah River, enterprising colonists built up a flourishing trade in deerskins and redskins. Ambitious Barbadians, case-hardened by African slavery in the tropics, dominated the colony and did not scruple at organizing a major trade in Indian slaves, whom the Westo Indians obligingly drove to the coast for shipment to the Caribbean. The first major export other than furs and slaves was cattle, and a staple crop was not developed until the introduction of rice in the 1690s. Meanwhile the continuing Indian trade led to repeated troubles with the proprietors, who tried in vain to regulate Indian affairs and stabilize the colony. Ultimately the struggle would lead to a rebellion against proprietary rule and an appeal to the crown to take charge. South Carolina became a separate royal colony in 1719. North Carolina remained under the proprietors' rule for ten more years, when the proprietors surrendered their governing rights to the crown.

## SETTLING THE MIDDLE COLONIES AND GEORGIA

NEW NETHERLAND BECOMES NEW YORK  Charles II resolved early to pluck out that old thorn in the side of the English colonies—New Netherland. The Dutch colony was older than New England, and had been planted when the two Protestant powers enjoyed friendly relations in opposition to Catholic Spain. The Dutch East India Company (organized in 1620) had hired an English captain, Henry Hudson, to seek the elusive passage to

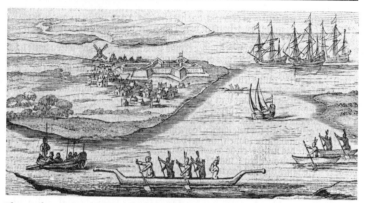

*The earliest view of Fort New Amsterdam, at the southern tip of Manhattan, around 1636–1639.*

Cathay. Coasting North America in 1609, Hudson had discovered Delaware Bay and explored the river named for him, to a point probably beyond Albany where he and a group of Mohawks made merry with brandy. From the contact stemmed a lasting trade relation between the Dutch and the Iroquois nations, a group of whom had met a hostile reception from the French explorer Champlain the year before. In 1614 the Dutch established fur-trading posts on Manhattan Island and upriver at Fort Orange (later Albany). Ten years later a newly organized West India Company began permanent settlement, the first on Governor's Island. In 1626 Gov. Peter Minuit purchased Manhattan from the resident Indians and a Dutch fort appeared at the lower end of the island. The village of New Amsterdam, which grew up around the fort, became the capital of New Netherland.

Dutch settlements gradually dispersed in every direction where furs might be found. They moved not only into surrounding locales like Staten Island and Long Island, but north around Fort Orange, south around Fort Nassau on the Delaware, and eastward to Fort Good Hope on the Connecticut River, which was soon surrounded by New England settlers and eventually surrendered to them in 1653. In 1638 a Swedish trading company established Fort Christina at the site of the present Wilmington and scattered a few hundred settlers up and down the Delaware River. The Dutch, at the time allied to the Swedes in the Thirty Years' War, made no move to challenge the claim until 1655, when a force outnumbering the entire Swedish colony subjected them without bloodshed to the rule of New Netherland. The chief contribution of the short-lived New Sweden to American culture was the idea of the log cabin, which the Swedes and a few Finnish settlers with them had brought over from the woods of Scandinavia.

The Dutch West India Company was interested mainly in the fur trade and less in agricultural settlements. In 1629, however, the company provided that any stockholder might obtain a large estate (a patroonship) if he peopled it with fifty adults within four years. The patroon was obligated to supply cattle, tools, and buildings. His tenants, in turn, paid him rent, used his grist mill, gave him first option on surplus crops, and submitted to a court he established. It amounted to transplanting the feudal manor into the New World, and met with as little luck as similar efforts in Maryland and South Carolina. Volunteers for serfdom were hard to find when there was land to be had elsewhere, and the only successful patroonship was that of Kiliaen van Rensselaer, a pearl merchant of Amsterdam, who secured lands covering what are now two counties around Albany. Most settlers took advantage of the company's provision that one could have as farms (*bouweries*) all the lands one could improve.

The government of the colony was under the almost absolute control of a governor sent out by the company, subject to little check from his council or from the directors back in Holland. The three successors to Minuit proved stubborn autocrats, either corrupt or inept, especially at Indian relations. They depended on a small professional garrison for defense, and the inhabitants (including a number of English on Long Island) betrayed almost total indifference in 1664 when Gov. Peter Stuyvesant called them to arms against a threatening British fleet. Almost defenseless, old soldier Stuyvesant blustered and stomped about on his wooden leg, but finally surrendered without a shot and stayed on quietly at his farm in what had become the colony of New York.

The plan of conquest had been hatched by the king's brother, the duke of York and Albany, later King James II. As lord high admiral and an investor in the African trade, York had already engaged in harassing Dutch shipping and forts in Africa. When he and his advisors counseled that New Netherland could easily be reduced, Charles II simply granted the region to his brother as proprietor, permitted the hasty gathering of a force, and the English transformed New Amsterdam into New York and Fort Orange into Albany, replaced Stuyvesant with Col. Richard Nicolls, and held the country thereafter, except for a brief Dutch reoccupation in 1673–1674. The Dutch, however, left a permanent imprint on the land and the language: the Dutch vernacular faded away but place names like Block Island, Wall Street (the original wall was for protection against Indians), Broadway (Breede Wegh) remained, along with family names like Rensselaer, Roosevelt, and Van Buren. The Dutch presence lingered in the Dutch Reformed church; in words like boss, cooky, crib, snoop, stoop, spook, and kill (for creek); in the legendary Santa Claus, Rip Van Winkle, and the picturesque Dutch governors, preserved in the satirical caricatures of Washington Irving's *Knickerbocker History*.

NEW JERSEY    Shortly after the conquest, still in 1664, the duke of York granted his lands between the Hudson and the Delaware Rivers to Sir George Carteret and Lord John Berkeley (brother of Virginia's governor), and named the territory for Carteret's native island of Jersey. The New Jersey proprietorship then passed through a sequence of incredible complications. In 1674 Berkeley sold his share to a Quaker leader, whose affairs were so encumbered that their management fell to three trustees, one of whom was William Penn, another prominent Quaker. In 1676 by mutual agreement the colony was divided by a diagonal line into East and West New Jersey, with Carteret taking the east—a division that corresponded to New Jersey's status later as hinterland and commuter bedroom for New York and Philadelphia. Finally in 1682 Carteret sold out to a group of twelve, including Penn, who in turn brought into partnership twelve more proprietors, for a total of twenty-four! In East New Jersey, peopled at first by perhaps 200 Dutch who had crossed the Hudson, new settlements gradually arose: some disaffected Puritans from New Haven founded Newark, Carteret's brother brought a group to found Elizabethtown (Elizabeth), and a group of Scots founded Perth Amboy. In the west, which faces the Delaware, a scattering of Swedes, Finns, and Dutch remained, soon to be overwhelmed by swarms of English Quakers. In 1702 East and West New Jersey were united as a royal colony.

PENNSYLVANIA AND DELAWARE    The Quaker sect, as the Society of Friends was called in ridicule, was the most influential of many radical groups that sprang from the turbulence of the English Civil War. Founded by George Fox about 1647, the Quakers carried further than any other group the doctrine of individual inspiration and interpretation—the "inner light," they called it. Discarding all formal sacraments and formal ministry—all spoke only as the spirit moved them—they refused deference to persons of rank, used the familiar "thee" and "thou" in addressing

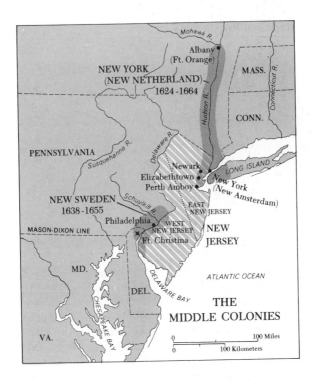

THE
MIDDLE COLONIES

0          100 Miles
0          100 Kilometers

everyone, refused to take oaths because that was contrary to Scripture, and embraced pacifism. Quakers were subjected to persecution—often in their zeal they seemed to invite it—but never inflicted it on others. Their toleration extended to complete religious freedom for all, of whatever belief or disbelief, and to the equality of sexes and the full participation of women in religious affairs.

In 1673 George Fox had returned from an American visit with the vision of a Quaker commonwealth in the New World and had enticed others with his idea. The entrance of Quakers into the New Jersey proprietorships had encouraged Quakers to migrate, especially to the Delaware River side. And soon, across the river, arose Fox's "Holy Experiment," William Penn's Quaker Commonwealth, the colony of Pennsylvania. William Penn was the son of Admiral Sir William Penn, who had supported Parliament in the Civil War and had led Cromwell's conquest of Jamaica but later helped in the Restoration. Young William was reared as a proper gentleman, but as a student at Oxford had turned to Quakerism. His father disowned him, but after a reconciliation, sent him off to France to get his mind on other things. It worked for a while, but Penn later came back to the faith.

*William Penn, the Quaker who founded the Pennsylvania colony in 1681.*

Upon his father's death he inherited the friendship of the Stuarts and a substantial estate, including a claim of £16,000 his father had lent the crown. Whether in settlement of the claim or out of simple friendship he got from Charles II in 1681 proprietary rights to a tract extending westward from the Delaware for five degrees of longitude and from the "beginning" of the forty-third degree on the north to the "beginning" of the fortieth degree on the south. The land was named, at the king's insistence, for Penn's father: Pennsylvania (literally Penn Woods). The boundary overlapped lands granted to both New York and Maryland. The New York boundary was settled on the basis of the duke of York's charter at 42° North, but the Maryland boundary remained in question until 1767 when a compromise line (nineteen miles south of the Fortieth Parallel) was surveyed by Charles Mason and Jeremiah Dixon—the celebrated Mason-Dixon Line.

When Penn assumed control there was already a scattering of Dutch, Swedish, and English settlers on the west bank of the Delaware, but Penn was soon making vigorous efforts to bring in more settlers. He published glowing descriptions of the colony, which were translated into German, Dutch, and French. They were favorably received, especially by members of Pietist sects whose beliefs paralleled those of the Quakers. By the end of 1681 Penn had about 1,000 settlers in his province, and in October of the next year arrived himself with 100 more. By that time a town was growing up at the junction of the Schuylkill and Delaware Rivers, which Penn called Philadelphia (the City of Brotherly Love). Because of the generous terms on which Penn offered land, because indeed he offered aid to emigrants, the colony grew rapidly.

Indian relations were good from the beginning, because of the

Quakers' friendliness and because of Penn's careful policy of purchasing land titles from the Indians. Penn even took the trouble to learn the language of the Delawares, something few white men even tried. For some fifty years the settlers and the natives lived side by side in peace, in relationships of such trust that Quaker farmers sometimes left their children in the care of Indians when they were away from home.

The government, which rested on three Frames of Government promulgated by Penn, resembled that of other proprietary colonies, except that the councilors as well as the assembly were elected by the freemen (taxpayers and property owners) and the governor had no veto—although Penn, as proprietor, did. "Any government is free . . . where the laws rule and the people are a party to the laws," Penn wrote in the 1682 Frame of Government. He hoped to show that a government could run in accordance with Quaker principles, that it could maintain peace and order without oaths or wars, that religion could flourish without an established church and with absolute freedom of conscience. Because of its tolerance, Pennsylvania became a refuge not only for Quakers but for a variety of dissenters—as well as Anglicans —and early reflected the ethnic mixture of Scotch-Irish and Germans that became common to the middle colonies and the

*A Quaker meeting. The presence of women is evidence of Quaker views on the equality of the sexes.*

southern backcountry. Penn himself stayed only two years in the colony, and although he returned in 1699 for two more years, he continued at home the life of an English gentleman—and Quaker.

In 1682 the Duke of York also granted Penn the area of Delaware, another part of the Dutch territory. At first Delaware became part of Pennsylvania, but after 1701 was granted the right to choose its own assembly. From then until the American Revolution it had a separate assembly, but had the same governor as Pennsylvania.

GEORGIA   Georgia was the last of the British continental colonies to be established, half a century after Pennsylvania. In 1663, despite Spanish claims in the area, Charles II had granted the area from the Thirty-first to Thirty-sixth Parallels to the Carolina proprietors, but in 1732 George II gave the land between the Savannah and Altamaha Rivers to the twenty-one trustees of Georgia. In two respects Georgia was unique among the colonies: it was set up as both a philanthropic experiment and a military buffer against Spanish Florida. Gen. James E. Oglethorpe, who accompanied the first colonists as resident trustee, represented both concerns: as a soldier who organized the defenses, and as a philanthropist who championed prison reform and sought a colonial refuge for the poor and persecuted.

In 1733 a band of 120 colonists founded Savannah near the mouth of the Savannah River. Carefully laid out by Oglethorpe, the old town with its geometrical pattern and its numerous little parks remains a monument to the city planning of a bygone day. A group of Protestant refugees from Salzburg began to arrive in 1734, followed by a number of Germans and German-speaking Moravians and Swiss, who made the colony for a time more German than English. The addition of Scottish Highlanders, Portuguese Jews, Welsh, Piedmontese, and others gave the early colony a cosmopolitan character much like that of its neighbor across the river.

As a buffer against Florida the colony succeeded, but as a philanthropic experiment it failed. Efforts to develop silk and wine production had little success. Land holdings were limited to 500 acres, rum was prohibited, and the importation of slaves forbidden, partly to leave room for servants brought on charity, partly to ensure security. But the utopian rules soon collapsed. The regulations against rum and slavery were widely disregarded, and finally abandoned. By 1759 all restrictions on landholding were removed.

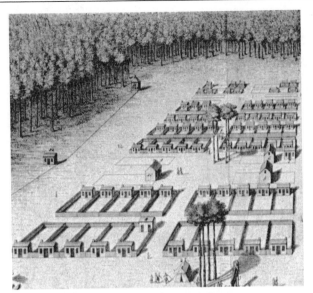

*A view of Savannah in 1734. The town's layout was carefully planned.*

In 1753 the trustees' charter expired and the province reverted to the crown. As a royal colony Georgia acquired for the first time an effective government. The province developed slowly over the next decade, but grew rapidly in population and wealth after 1763. Instead of wine and silk, Georgians exported rice, indigo, lumber, naval stores, beef, and pork, and carried on a lively trade with the West Indies. Georgia's products fitted well into the British economic system and Georgians prospered. The colony, which got off to such a late start, had become a roaring success.

## THRIVING COLONIES

A British historian once wrote that England acquired an empire "in a fit of absence of mind." In the abstract it seems an unlikely way to build an empire, but after a late start the English outstripped both the French and the Spanish in the New World. The lack of plan was the genius of English colonization, for it gave free rein to a variety of human impulses. The centralized control imposed by the monarchs of Spain and France got them off the mark more quickly but eventually brought their downfall

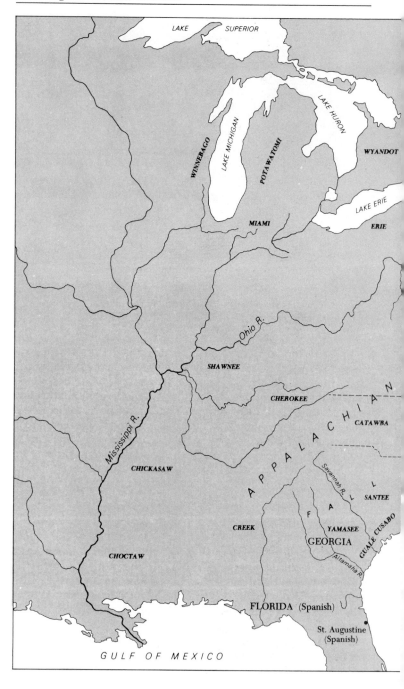

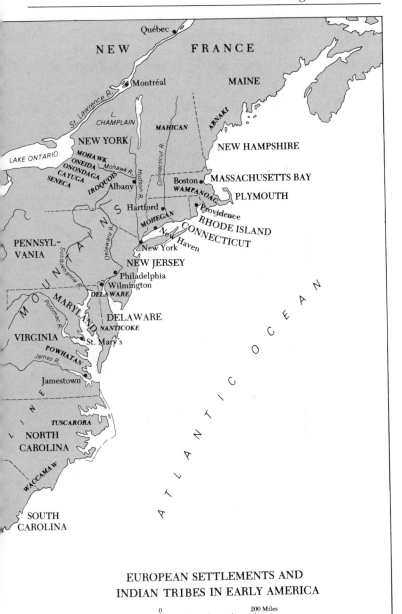

EUROPEAN SETTLEMENTS AND
INDIAN TRIBES IN EARLY AMERICA

0                200 Miles

0             200 Kilometers

because it hobbled innovation and responsiveness to new circumstances. The British acted by private investment and with a minimum of royal control. Not a single colony was begun at the direct initiative of the crown. In the English colonies poor immigrants had a much greater chance of getting at least a small parcel of land. The English, unlike their rivals, welcomed people from a variety of nationalities and dissenting sects who came in search of a new life or a safe harbor. And a degree of self-government made the English colonies more responsive to new circumstances—if sometimes stalled by controversy.

The compact pattern of English settlement contrasted sharply with the pattern of Spain's far-flung conquests or France's far-reaching trade routes to the interior by way of the St. Lawrence and Mississippi Rivers (discussed in Chapter 4). Geography reinforced England's bent for concentrated occupation and settlement of its colonies. The rivers and bays which indented the coasts served as veins of communication along which colonies first sprang up, but no great river offered a highway to the far interior. About a hundred miles back in Georgia and the Carolinas, and nearer the coast to the north, the "fall line" of the rivers presented rocky rapids which marked the head of navigation and the end of the coastal plain. About a hundred miles beyond that, and farther back in Pennsylvania, stretched the rolling expanse of the Piedmont, literally the foothills. And the final backdrop of English America was the Appalachian Mountain range, some 200 miles from the coast in the south, reaching down to the coast at points in New England, with only one significant break—up the Hudson-Mohawk Valley of New York. For 150 years the farthest outreach of settlement stopped at the slopes of the mountains. To the east lay the wide expanse of ocean, which served as a highway for the transit of civilization from Europe to America, but also as a barrier beyond which civilization took to new paths in a new environment.

## FURTHER READING

Several general interpretations handle the sweep of English settlement during the early colonial period. The first volume of Charles M. Andrews's *The Colonial Period of American History* (4 vols., 1934–1938) is detailed and comprehensive. Bernard Bailyn's multivolume work *The Peopling of British North America,* the first two volumes of which have appeared *(The Peopling of British North America: An Introduction* (1986) and *Voyagers to the West: A Passage in the Peopling of America on the Eve of the Revolution* (1986), will provide a comprehensive view of European migration. Shorter and more interpretive are Daniel J. Boorstein's *The Americans: The Colonial Experience* (1958)° and John E. Pomfret and Floyd M. Shumway's *Founding the American Colonies, 1583–1600* (1970). A valuable summary of recent scholarship is *Colonial British America* (1984),° edited by Jack P. Greene and J. R. Pole.

Carl Bridenbaugh's *Vexed and Troubled Englishmen, 1590–1642* (1968) helps explain why so many sought a new home in a strange land. A path-breaking book on the social conditions of pre-industrial England is Peter Laslett's *The World We Have Lost* (3rd ed., 1984). A study of the political institutions of the time is Wallace Notestein's *The English People on the Eve of Colonization, 1603–1630* (1954). English constitutional traditions and their effect on the colonists are examined in Julian H. Franklin's *John Locke and the Theory of Sovereignty* (1978) and David S. Lovejoy's *The Glorious Revolution in America* (1972).° John Phillips Kenyon documents the internal dynamics of English politics in *Stuart England* (2nd ed., 1985).°

Carl Bridenbaugh's *Jamestown, 1544–1699* (1980) traces the English experience on the Chesapeake. See also *The Chesapeake in the 17th Century: Essays on Anglo-American Society and Politics* (1980),° edited by Thad Tate and David Ammerman. On the role of Capt. John Smith, see Alden T. Vaughan's *American Genesis: Captain John Smith and the Founding of Virginia* (1975).°

Still a good starting point for the northern colonies is James T. Adam's *The Founding of New England* (1921). A useful and enlightening primary source is William Bradford's narrative of the Pilgrim experience, *Of Plymouth Plantation, 1620–1647* (1952),° edited by Samuel E. Morison.

Scholarship abounds on Puritanism. To learn about the English roots of the movement, see Charles H. George and Katherine George's *The Protestant Mind of the English Reformation, 1570–1640* (1961). More analytical and psychological is Michael Walzer's *The Revolution of the Saints: A Study in the Origins of Radical Politics* (1965).° David G. Allen's *In English Ways* (1981)° traces the migration of English societies to Massachusetts. The classic works of Perry Miller demonstrate how Puritan ideology evolved once transplanted to the New World; see especially *The New England Mind* (2 vols., 1939–1953)° and *Errand into the Wilderness* (1956).° The problem of translating idea into governance is treated elegantly in Edmund S. Morgan's *The Puritan Dilemma: The Story of John Winthrop* (1958).°

Useful works on the problem of dissent in a theocracy include Edmund S. Morgan's *Roger Williams, the Church, and the State* (1967)° and Emery Battis's *Saints and Sectaries: Anne Hutchinson and the Antinomian Controversy in Massachusetts Bay Colony* (1962). The religious theme in the settlement of Connecticut is handled in Mary J. A. Jones's *Congregational Commonwealth: Connecticut, 1636–1662* (1968). See also Sydney V. James's *Colonial Rhode Island* (1975).

No comprehensive work explores the overall pattern of settlement in the Middle Colonies, yet good scholarship exists for each colony.

° These books are available in paperback editions.

Thomas J. Condon's *New York Beginnings: The Commercial Origins of New Netherlands* (1968) examines the Dutch connection. The influence of Quakers can be studied through Gary B. Nash's *Quakers and Politics: Pennsylvania, 1681–1726* (1968). Other useful studies on the colony level include Michael G. Kammen's *Colonial New York* (1975), Joseph E. Illick's *Colonial Pennsylvania* (1976), John E. Pomfret's *Colonial New Jersey* (1973), and John A. Munroe's *History of Delaware* (1979).

Settlement of the areas along the south Atlantic is traced in Wesley F. Craven's *The Southern Colonies in the Seventeenth Century, 1607–1689* (1949) and Clarence L. Ver Steeg's *Origins of a Southern Mosaic* (1975). The early chapters of Hugh T. Lefler and Albert R. Newsome's *North Carolina* (3rd ed., 1973) and Robert M. Weir's *Colonial South Carolina* (1983) cover the activities of the Lords Proprietors. For an imaginative study of race and the settlement of South Carolina, see Peter Wood's *Black Majority: Negroes in Colonial South Carolina from 1670 through the Stono Rebellion* (1975).° To study Oglethorpe's aspirations, consult Paul S. Taylor's *Georgia Plan: 1732–1752* (1971).

# 3

# COLONIAL WAYS OF LIFE

## The Shape of Early America

THE ECOLOGY   One of the cherished legends of American history has it that the English settlers entered a pristine environment, an unspoiled wilderness little touched by human intervention. It is true that on the Atlantic seaboard the settlers encountered a sparser native population than they might have elsewhere, and one already devastated by European germs which traders and fishermen had brought.

For thousands of years, however, the pre-Columbian inhabitants had modified the environment of the eastern seaboard. The hunting practices of Stone Age Indians, one student of the subject has said, led to the "greatest known loss of wild species" in American history, about 10,000 years ago. Over the millennia that followed the plant and animal life of North America were profoundly transformed. A common practice had been slash-and-burn agriculture, which halted the normal forest succession and, especially in the Southeast, created large stands of longleaf pines, still the most common source of timber in the region. In New England, as farther south, the Indians had burned woods to create croplands. They also burned the undergrowth in hardwood forests to open them for easier travel and to make way for grasses, berries, and other forage for the animals they hunted.

In many places—Plymouth, for instance, or St. Mary's, Maryland—settlers occupied the sites of former Indian towns. And maize, corn, beans, and squash quickly became colonial staples, along with new crops brought from Europe. The colonists too transformed the landscape of course. Their very ideas of property in land, so foreign to most Indians, changed things. In time a denser population of both humans and their domestic animals created a new environment of fields, meadows, fences, barns, and houses.

POPULATION GROWTH    England's first footholds in America were bought at a fearful price. The beachhead in Virginia, one historian pointed out, "cost far more casualties, in proportion to numbers engaged, than did the conquest of any of the Japanese-held islands in World War II." But once the seasoning time was past and the colony was on its feet, Virginia and all its successors grew at a prodigious rate. After Virginia put down the last major Indian uprising in 1644, its population quadrupled from about 8,000 to 32,000 over the next thirty years, then more than doubled, to 75,000, by 1704. Throughout the mainland colonies the yearly growth rate during the eighteenth century ran about 3

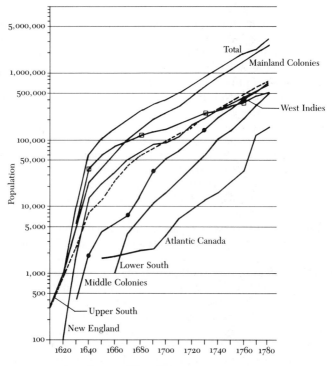

*Population of British America, 1610–1780.*

percent. In 1625 the English colonists numbered little more than 2,000 in Virginia and Plymouth together; by 1700 the population in the colonies was perhaps 250,000, and during the eighteenth century it doubled at least every twenty-five years. By 1750 the number of colonists had passed 1 million; by 1775 it stood at about 2.5 million. In 1700 the English at home outnumbered the colonists by about 20 to 1; by 1775, on the eve of the American Revolution, the ratio was about 3 to 1.

The prodigious increase of colonial population did not go unnoticed of course. In 1770 Ezra Stiles, the future president of Yale College, predicted in his diary that English would "become the vernacular Tongue of more people than any one Tongue on Earth, except the Chinese." Benjamin Franklin of Pennsylvania, a keen observer of many things, published in 1751 his *Observations Concerning the Increase of Mankind* in which he pointed out two facts of life which distinguished the colonies from Europe: land was plentiful and cheap; labor was scarce and dear. Just the opposite conditions prevailed in the Old World. From this reversal of conditions flowed many if not most of the changes which European culture underwent in the New World—not the least being that good fortune beckoned the immigrant and induced the settlers to replenish the earth with large families. Where labor was scarce, children could lend a hand, and once they were grown could find new land for themselves if need be. Colonists tended, as a result, to marry and start new families at an earlier age.

THE BIRTH RATE    At the time many English women never married at all, and those who did often waited until their mid or later twenties, and men until even later. But in England women outnumbered men, while in the first waves of colonial settlement the sex ratio was reversed. The result was that the average age at marriage for colonial women dropped to twenty or twenty-one, for men to twenty-five or twenty-six, and the birth rate rose accordingly, since those who married earlier had time for about two additional pregnancies during the childbearing years. Later a gradual reversion to a more even sex ratio brought the average age at marriage back toward the European norm. Even so, given the better economic prospects in the colonies, a greater number of American women married and the birth rate remained higher than in Europe, probably about 45–50 births per 1,000 women per year in the colonies in contrast to about 28 per 1,000 in Europe.

THE DEATH RATE   What was equally important, however, was a startlingly lower death rate in the New World. Infants generally had a better chance to reach maturity, and adults had a better chance to reach old age. In seventeenth-century New England, apart from childhood mortality, men would expect to reach seventy and women nearly that age. This longevity was less the result of what Massachusetts Gov. William Shirley called the "Healthfulness of the Climates on this Continent" than of the character of the settlements. Since the land was more bountiful, famine seldom occurred after the first year, and while the winters were more severe than in England, firewood was plentiful. Being younger on the whole—the average age in the colonies in 1790 was sixteen!—Americans were less susceptible to disease than were Europeans. More widely scattered, they were also less exposed to disease. This began to change, of course, as population centers grew and trade and travel increased. By the mid–eighteenth century the colonies were beginning to have levels of contagion much like those in Europe. In 1735–1737, for instance, a diphtheria epidemic swept the northern colonies, taking the lives of thousands. In this case the lack of previous exposure now left the young especially vulnerable for want of a chance to develop immunity.

The greatest variations on these patterns occurred in the earliest testing times of the southern colonies. During the first cen-

*Mr. John Freake, and Mrs. Elizabeth Freake and Baby Mary. Elizabeth married John at age nineteen; Mary, born when Elizabeth was thirty-two, was the Freakes' eighth and last child.*

*"Youth is a Fading Flower." The death rate in colonial America was relatively low, but Peter Bancroft's gravestone bears testimony to the ever-present specter of childhood mortality.*

tury after the Jamestown settlement, down to about 1700, a high rate of mortality and a chronic shortage of women meant that the population increase there could be sustained only by immigration. In the southern climate English settlers proved vulnerable to malaria, dysentery, and a host of other diseases. The mosquito-infested rice paddies of the Carolina tidewater were notoriously unhealthy. And ships that docked at the Chesapeake tobacco plantations brought in with their payloads unseen cargoes of smallpox, diphtheria, and other infections. Given the higher mortality, families were often broken by the early death of parents. One consequence was to throw children on their own at an earlier age. Another was probably to make the extended family support network, if not the extended household, more important in the South.

SEX RATIOS AND THE FAMILY  Whole communities of religious or ethnic groups migrated more often to the northern colonies than to the southern, bringing more women in their company. There was no mention of any women at all among the first arrivals at

Jamestown. Virginia's seventeenth-century sex ratio of two or three white males to each female meant that many men never married, although nearly every adult woman did. Counting only the unmarried, the ratio went to about eight men for every woman. In South Carolina around 1680 the sex ratio stood at about three to one, but since about three-quarters of the women were married, it was something like seven to one for singles.

A population made up largely of bachelors without strong ties to family and to the larger community made for instability of a high order in the first years. And the high mortality rates of the early years further loosened family ties. While the first generations in New England proved to be long-lived, and many more children there knew their grandparents than in the motherland, young people in the seventeenth-century South were apt never to see their grandparents, and in fact to lose one or both of their parents before reaching maturity. But after a time of seasoning, immunities built up. Eventually the southern colonies reverted to a more even sex ratio and family sizes approached those of New England. In eighteenth-century Virginia, Col. William Byrd of Westover asserted, matrimony thrived "so excellently" that an "Old Maid or an Old Bachelor are as scarce among us and reckoned as ominous as a Blazing Star." And early marriage re-

"A little commonwealth." *This eighteenth-century American family shows the "stairstep" pattern of childbearing, in which children were born at approximately two-year intervals.*

mained common. The most "antique Virgin" Byrd knew was his own daughter, of about twenty.

Survival was the first necessity and for the 90–95 percent of colonists who farmed, a subsistence or semi-subsistence economy remained the foundation of being. Life moved more by the rhythms of the seasons, the rising and setting of the sun, than by the dictates of the clock. Not only food, but shelter, implements, utensils, furnishings, and clothing had to be made at home from the materials at hand. As the primary social and economic unit, the family became a "little commonwealth" which took on functions performed by the community in other times and places. Production, religion, learning, health care, and other activities centered around the home. Fathers taught their sons by example how to farm, hunt, and fish. Mothers taught their daughters how to tend to the chickens, the gardens, and the countless household chores that fell to the women of that time. Extended kinship ties added meaning to life and stability to communities.

Though colonists began in the early years to manifest such traditional American traits as practicality, acquisitiveness, restlessness, and a propensity for violence, it would be far too easy to read back into colonial times exaggerated notions of American individualism. Whatever the changes to be wrought by environment, the earliest settlers were transplanted Europeans whose ideas and practices adjusted to new circumstances only by degrees. Clusters of ethnic and religious groups that sprang up, such as the "tribal cult" of Puritans in New England, or the settlements of Germans in Pennsylvania, suggest that European values persisted in the New World for some time. Conditions in America did cause changes in family life, the implications of which social historians have only begun to work out, but this much seems clear. The conjugal unit, or nuclear family of parents and children, was not a new development in the colonies but the familiar arrangement in both England and America. The household that included an extended family of three or more generations was rare, although given the greater life span, large networks of kinship ties did develop. These networks included servants attached to households, who were often young kinspeople apprenticed to learn a trade.

THE SOCIAL HIERARCHY   The earliest settlers also brought in their cultural baggage certain fixed ideas of hierarchy and rank. People of the lower orders deferred to their "betters" almost without question. Devereux Jarratt, son of a carpenter and later an Episcopal evangelist, recalled that in the Virginia of his youth:

"We were accustomed to look upon, what were called *gentle folks,* as beings of a superior order. . . . Such ideas of the differences between *gentle* and *simple,* were, I believe, universal among all of my rank and age. . . ." John Winthrop, looking out from a higher station in life, asserted it to be God's will that "in all times some must be rich, some poore, some high and eminent in power and dignitie, others meane and in subjection."

But from Jamestown onward persons of "meane" birth like John Smith revealed rare qualities when confronted with the wilderness. The breadth of opportunity to be plucked from danger impelled settlers to shake off the sense of limitations that haunted the more crowded lands of Europe. J. Hector St. John de Crevecoeur, a French immigrant, wrote from his New York farm in the 1780s: "A European, when he first arrives, seems limited in his intentions, as well as in his views; but he very suddenly alters his scale; . . . he no sooner breathes our air than he forms schemes, and embarks in designs he never would have thought of in his own country."

Still, the new experience of social mobility took some getting used to. The fear lingered that it threatened the equilibrium of society, and efforts persisted to keep the "meaner sort" in their place. But attempts to regulate dress as the outward sign of social class ran up against a human weakness for finery. Even in Puritan New England, which got an undeserved reputation for austerity, the scorn of fancy dress was reserved mainly for those who affected to rise above their station. In 1651 the Massachusetts General Court declared its "utter detestation and dislike" that persons of mean condition "should take upon them the garb of gentlemen" and prescribed fines for those with estates of less than £200 who wore gold or silver lace and other such finery.

WOMEN IN THE COLONIES    The status of women too altered in the new conditions of life. The acute shortage of women in the early years made them the more highly valued, and by many accounts brought subtle improvements in their status—a condition which tended to move with successive frontiers westward. The general labor shortage meant that both women and children were treated more indulgently than in the Europe of their times, not that their standing in the law or in their assigned roles in society was drastically altered. "Here, as in England," the historian Julia Cherry Spruill wrote, "women were without political rights, and generally wives were legal nonentities" whose property the husband controlled—although single women and widows had practically the same legal rights as men.

*Prudence Punderson's needlework, "The First, Second, and Last Scene of Mortality" (c. 1776), shows the domestic path, from cradle to coffin, followed by most colonial women.*

Despite the conventional mission of women to serve in the domestic sphere, the scarcity of labor opened new lines of action. Quite a few women by necessity or choice went into gainful occupations. In the towns they commonly served as tavern hostesses and shopkeepers, but occasional notices in colonial papers listed women also in such employments as doctors, printers, upholsterers, glaziers, painters, silversmiths, tanners, and shipwrights—often, but not always, widows carrying on their husbands' trades. Some managed plantations, again usually carrying on in the absence of husbands. One exceptional early case was "Mistress Margarett Brent, Spinster," of Maryland, who arrived in 1638 with two brothers and a sister. All four came on their own ventures, with servants and patents for large tracts of land. Margaret Brent ran her plantation so well that her brothers entrusted their affairs to her in their absence. As executrix of Gov. Leonard Calvert's estate she settled his complex affairs and arranged to pay the local militia and avert a mutiny. As "his Lordship's Attorney" she boldly demanded a vote in the Assembly the better to see after his affairs. The governor, in response, acknowledged her gifts, but denied her request. When she became perhaps the first American suffragette, she had overstepped the bounds of acceptance.

The colonists everywhere had much in common. But as the land filled with population behind the frontier, the differences of geography and climate, and the diverse human elements entering the New World, produced ways of life that differed from north to south, from east to west. New England evolved into a center of fishing and commerce, the Puritan and the Yankee; the southern colonies into the land of tobacco and rice, the country gentleman, the yeoman farmer, and the black slave; the Middle Colonies into the colonial "breadbasket" of wheat and barley, the home of the Quaker, the Dutchman, and the Scotch-Irish.

## SOCIETY AND ECONOMY IN THE SOUTHERN COLONIES

STAPLES   The southern colonies had one unique advantage—the climate. They could grow exotic staples (market crops) that withered in northern latitudes and were prized by the mother country. Virginia, as Charles I put it, was "founded upon smoke." Within four years of John Rolfe's first experiments the passion for the "joviall weed" reached such heights that Gov. Thomas Dale required two acres of corn as a prerequisite for growing it. By 1619 production had reached 20,000 pounds, and in the year of the Glorious Revolution, 1688, it was up to 18 million pounds.

After 1690 rice was as much the staple in South Carolina as tobacco in Virginia or sugar in Barbados. The process by which it got established is obscure. One cherished story is that the colony conjured the industry out of a single bag of seed from Madagascar, but there are other stories of seed from India and Africa

*A Virginia tobacco plantation. England's King James I described the habit of "drinking smoke" as "a custom lothsome to the eye, hatefull to the Nose, harmefull to the braine, and dangerous to the Lungs."*

(black slaves, already familiar with rice growing in Africa, may have taught whites how to go about it) and there is solid evidence that the Lords Proprietors planned experiments with rice from the beginning. From whatever source the rice came, the rise and fall of tidewater rivers made the region ideally suited to a crop that required alternate flooding and draining of the fields. In 1699 the young colony exported at least 366 tons of rice.

Much later, in the 1740s, another exotic staple appeared—indigo, the blue dyestuff which found an eager market in the British woolens industry. An enterprising young lady named Eliza Lucas, daughter of the governor of Antigua, produced the first crop on her father's Carolina plantation, left in her care when she was only seventeen. She thereby founded a major industry, and as the wife of Charles Pinckney, later brought forth a major dynasty which flourished in the golden age of Charleston.

From the southern woods came harvests of lumber and naval stores (tar, pitch, and turpentine) as well. From their early leadership in the latter trade North Carolinians would later derive the nickname of Tar Heels. In the interior a fur trade flourished, and in the Carolinas, a cattle industry that pretokened the later industry on the Great Plains—with cowboys, roundups, brandings, and long drives to market.

English customs records showed that for the years 1698–1717 South Carolina and the Chesapeake colonies bought English goods averaging £154,000 in value annually, and sent back American goods averaging £246,000 leaving a balance of £92,000 in favor of the colonies. But the balance was more than offset by "invisible" charges: freight payments to shipper, profits, commissions, storage charges, and interest payments to English merchants, insurance premiums, inspection and customs duties, and outlays to purchase indentured servants and slaves. Thus began a pattern that would plague the southern staple-crop system into the twentieth century. Planter investments went into land and slaves while the profitable enterprises of shipping, trade, investment, and manufacture fell under the sway of outsiders.

LAND    Land could be had almost for the asking throughout the colonial period, although many a frontier squatter who succumbed to the lure ignored the formalities of getting a deed. In colonial law land titles rested ultimately upon grants from the crown, and in colonial practice the evolution of land policy in the first colony set patterns that were followed everywhere save in New England. In 1614 when Governor Dale gave each of the

Virginia Company's colonists three acres for his own use, it was the beginning of a policy that every colonist could claim a plot of his own. In 1618 the company, lacking any assets other than land, promised each investor a fifty-acre "share-right" for £12.10s, and each settler a "headright" for paying his own way or for bringing in others. When Virginia became a royal colony in 1624, the headright system continued to apply, administered by the governor and his council. Lord Baltimore adopted the same practice in Maryland, and successive proprietors in the other southern and middle colonies adopted variations on the plan.

As time passed certain tracts were put up for sale and throughout the colonies special grants (often sizable) went to persons of rank or persons who had performed some meritorious service, such as fighting the Indians. Since land was plentiful and population desired, the rules tended to be generously interpreted and carelessly applied. With the right connections, persons or companies might engross handsome estates and vast speculative tracts in the interior, looking toward future growth and rising land values. From the beginning of colonization—and even before that—the real-estate boomer was a stock figure in American history, and access to power was often access to wealth. But by the early 1700s acquisition of land was commonly by purchase under more or less regular conditions of survey and sale by the provincial government. The later national land surveys followed the southern practice.

The first grants were made without any conditions attached, but at an early date the crown and proprietors decided to recover something from the giveaways by the levy of annual quit-rents on the land. In the Middle Ages such payments would quit (release) the tenant from military and other duties to his lord. In the New World, however, such levies had no roots in a feudal tradition and came to be a point of chronic protest, resistance, and evasion. But they remained on the books.

Some promoters of colonization, including Ferdinando Gorges, Lord Baltimore, and the Lords Proprietors of Carolina, had dreams of reviving the feudal manor in the New World. Their plans went awry, it is commonly said, because of the New World environment. With land aplenty, there was little call to volunteer for serfdom. Yet in unexpected ways the southern colonies gave rise to something analogous, a new institution with a new name: the plantation. The word originally carried the meaning of colony. The plantations in the New World were the colonies and planters were the settlers who had "planted" them. Gradually the name attached itself to individual holdings of large size.

*An idyllic view of a tidewater plantation. Note the easy access to ocean-going vessels.*

If one distinctive feature of the South's staple economy was a good market in England, another was a trend toward large-scale production. Those who planted tobacco soon discovered that it quickly exhausted the soil, thereby giving an advantage to the planter who had extra fields to rotate in beans and corn or to leave fallow. With the increase of the tobacco crop, moreover, a fall in prices meant that economies of scale might come into play —the large planter with lower cost per unit might still make a profit. Gradually he would extend his holdings along the river-fronts, and thereby secure the advantage of direct access to the ocean-going vessels that moved freely up and down the water-ways of the Chesapeake, discharging goods from London and taking on hogsheads of tobacco. So easy was the access in fact that the Chesapeake colonies never required a city of any size as a center of commerce, and the larger planters functioned as merchants and harbormasters for their neighbors.

LABOR  If the planter found no volunteers for serfdom, and if wage labor was scarce and expensive, one could still purchase an indentured servant for £6 to £30 (a substantial sum, which in much of the seventeenth and eighteenth centuries would equal perhaps 900 to 5,000 pounds of tobacco) and get his labor for a term of years. Voluntary indentured servitude accounted for probably half the arrivals of white settlers in all the colonies out-side New England. The name derived from the indenture, or contract, by which a person could bind himself to labor in return for transportation to the New World. Usually one made the contract with a shipmaster who would then sell it to a new master upon arrival. Not all went voluntarily. The London underworld developed a flourishing trade in "kids" and "spirits," who were kidnapped or spirited into servitude. On occasion orphans were bound off to the New World; from time to time the mother country sent convicts into colonial servitude, the first as early as 1617. After 1717, by act of Parliament, convicts guilty of certain crimes could escape the hangman by "transportation." Most of these, like Moll Flanders, the lusty heroine of Daniel Defoe's novel, seem to have gone to the Chesapeake. And after 1648 political and military offenders met a like fate, beginning with some captives of the Parliamentary armies.

In due course, however, the servant reached the end of his term, usually after four to seven years, claimed the freedom dues set by custom and law—some money, tools, clothing, food—and took up land of his own. And with the increase of the colonies, servants had a wider choice of destination. Pennsylvania became more often the chosen land, "one of the best poor man's countries in the world," in the verdict of a judge at the time.

SLAVERY  But captive Africans, although they might cost a bit more, had no choice and served for life. Slavery, long a dying institution in Europe, had undergone a revival in Spanish America a full century before the Jamestown colony. It gradually evolved in the Chesapeake after 1619, when a Dutch vessel dropped off twenty Negroes in Jamestown. Some of the first were treated as indentured servants, with a limited term, and achieved freedom and landownership. They themselves sometimes acquired slaves and white indentured servants. But gradually, with rationalizations based on color difference or heathenism, the practice of perpetual slavery became the custom of the land. Evidence that in 1640 some blacks were being held in hereditary life service appears in Virginia court records. In 1660 and 1661, and 1663 in Maryland, the colonial Assembly recognized slavery by laws that later expanded into elaborate and restrictive slave codes. In South Carolina, by contrast, Barbadians after 1670 simply transplanted the institution of slavery full-blown from the Caribbean before they discovered its value in the rice paddies, where indentured servants could hardly be enticed to work in the mud and heat.

The sugar islands of the French and British Antilles and the cane fields of Portuguese Brazil had the most voracious appetite

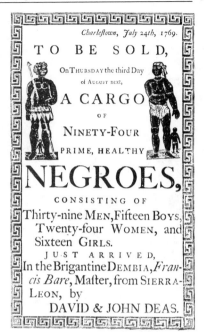

*Advertisement for the sale of slaves—men, boys, women, and girls.*

for human cargoes, using them up in the tropical heat and miasmas on the average within seven years. By 1675 the English West Indies had over 100,000 slaves while the colonies in North America had only about 5,000. But as the staple crops became established on the American continent, the demand for slaves grew. And as readily available lands diminished, Virginians were less eager to bring in indentured servants who would lay claim to them at the end of their service. Though British North America took less than 5 percent of the total slave imports to the Western Hemisphere during the more than three centuries of that squalid traffic—400,000 out of some 9,500,000—it offered better chances for survival if few for human fulfillment. The natural increase of black immigrants in America approximated that of whites by the end of the colonial period.

Negro slavery was recognized in the laws of all the colonies, but flourished in the Tidewater South—one colony, South Carolina, had a black majority through most of the eighteenth century. By one estimate, about 40 percent of the slaves imported into North America came in through Sullivan's Island in Charleston Harbor, which was to black Americans what New York's Castle Garden and Ellis Island were later to millions of European

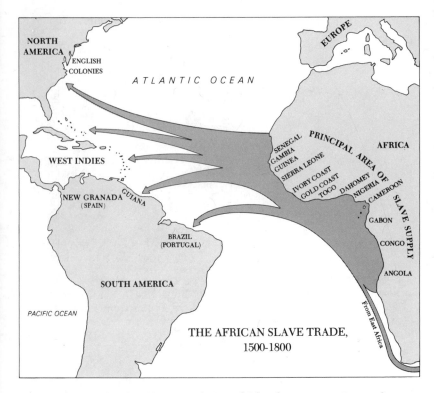

THE AFRICAN SLAVE TRADE,
1500-1800

From East Africa

immigrants or San Francisco's Angel Island to Asians. To say that black Africans made up the largest single group of non-English immigrants to the colonies, however, would be to ignore the great ethnic diversity of unwilling arrivals from lands as remote from each other as Angola and Senegambia, the west coast of Africa, and the area around the hump in between. About half the total came from Congo-Angola and the Bight of Biafra, and nearly all the rest from the Atlantic coast up to Senegambia. Thrown indiscriminately together, people who spoke Mandingo, Wolof, Ibo, Hausa, Kongo, and countless other tongues added to those who spoke various European and Indian languages to make the Deep South the most relentless melting pot in British America.

As a result, blacks with diverse homelands developed a new identity as Afro-Americans, though not without leaving obscurely entwined in the fabric of American culture more strands of African heritage than historians and anthropologists can ever disentangle. Among them were new words that entered the language, such as tabby, tote, cooter, goober, yam, banana, and the names of the Coosaw, Peedee, and Wando Rivers. More important were African influences in music, folklore, and religious practices. (For a discussion of these, see pp. 583–586.)

Most of the slaves were fated to become fieldhands, but not all did. Blacks from the lowlands of Africa used their skills as boatmen in the coastal waterways. Some had linguistic skills that made them useful interpreters. Others tended cattle and swine in the wilderness, or hacked away at the forests and operated sawmills. In a society which had to construct itself they became skilled artisans: blacksmiths, carpenters, coopers, bricklayers, and the like. Some of the more fortunate entered domestic service.

Slavery and the growth of a biracial South had economic, political, and cultural effects far into the future, and set America on the way to tragic conflicts. Questions about the beginnings of slavery still have a bearing on the present. Did a deep-rooted color prejudice lead to slavery, for instance, or did the existence of slavery produce the prejudice? Clearly slavery evolved because of the desire for a supply of controlled labor, and Englishmen fell in with a trade established by the Portuguese and Spanish more than a century before—the very word "Negro" is Spanish for "black." But while Englishmen often enslaved Indian captives, they did not bring their white captives into slav-

*The survival of African culture among American slaves is evident in this late-eighteenth-century painting of a South Carolina plantation. The musical instruments, pottery, and clothing are of African origin, probably Yoruba.*

ery. Color was the crucial difference, or at least the crucial rationalization.

One historian has marshalled evidence that the seeds of slavery were already planted in Elizabethan attitudes. Englishmen associated the color black with darkness and evil; they stamped the different appearance, behavior, and customs of Africans as "savagery." At the very least such perceptions could soothe the consciences of people who traded in human flesh. On the other hand most of the qualities which colonial Virginians imputed to blacks to justify slavery were the same qualities that Englishmen assigned to their own poor to explain *their* status: their alleged bent for laziness, improvidence, treachery, and stupidity, among other shortcomings. Similar traits, moreover, were imputed by ancient Jews to the Canaanites and by the Mediterranean peoples of a later date to the Slavic captives sold among them. The names Canaanite and Slav both became synonymous with slavery—the latter lingers in our very word for it. Such expressions would seem to be the product of power relationships and not the other way around. Dominant peoples repeatedly assign ugly traits to those they bring into subjection.

THE GENTRY    By the early eighteenth century Virginia and South Carolina were moving into the golden age of the Tidewater gentry, leaving the more isolated and rustic colony of North Carolina as "a valley of humiliation between two mountains of conceit." The first rude huts of Jamestown had given way to frame and brick houses. Some of the seventeenth-century homes, like Governor Berkeley's Green Springs or Nathaniel Bacon's "Castle," were spacious, but even the most prosperous generally lived in houses of four to seven small rooms. It was only as the seventeenth century yielded to the eighteenth that the stately country seats in the Georgian, or "colonial," style began to emerge along the banks of the great rivers: Tuckahoe, Stratford, Westover, Berkeley, Carter's Grove, Nomini Hall, and others which still stand as monuments to a graceful age. The great mansions, flanked by storehouses and servants' quarters, characteristically faced both ways, looking down to the waterfront dock and the expanse of river, and to a landward front where a drive from the road led up to the imposing steps and doorways. In South Carolina the mansions along the Ashley, Cooper, and Wando, or along the tidal creeks that set the Sea Islands imperceptibly off from the mainland, came to be noted for their spacious gardens and avenues of moss-hung live oaks. The Charleston town houses of the gentry varied the Georgian style by turning their sides to

*Two Virginia mansions attest to the growing wealth of the gentry.*
*Nathaniel Bacon's "Castle" (top), built in the seventeenth century,*
*appears humble when compared to the Georgian grandeur of*
*William Byrd's Westover, built in 1730 (bottom).*

the street and adding to their fronts long piazzas in the West Indian style to catch the sea breezes.

The new aristocracy patterned its provincial lifestyle after that of the English country gentlemen. The great houses became centers of sumptuous living and legendary hospitality to neighbors and passing strangers. In their zest for the good life the planters kept in touch with the latest refinements of London style and fashion, living on credit extended for the next year's crop and the years' beyond that, to such a degree that in the late colonial period Thomas Jefferson called the Chesapeake gentry "a species of property annexed to certain English mercantile houses." Dependence on outside capital remained a chronic southern problem far beyond the colonial period.

In season the carriages of the Chesapeake elite rolled to the villages of Annapolis and Williamsburg, and the city of Charleston became the center of political life and high fashion where the new-issue aristocrats could reel and roister for days on end and patronize the taverns, silversmiths, cabinetmakers, milliners, and tailors. Through much of the year the outdoors beckoned planters to the pleasures of hunting and fishing and horsemanship. Gambling on horse races, cards, and dice became consuming passions for men and women alike. But a cultivated few courted high culture with a diligence that violated genteel indulgence. William Byrd II of Westover pursued learning with a passion. He built a library of some 3,600 volumes and often rose early to keep up his Latin, Greek, and Hebrew. Robert "King" Carter of Nomini Hall practiced music several hours a day. The Pinckneys of the Carolina low country, when they were at home, practiced their musical instruments and read from such authors as Vergil, Milton, Locke, Addison, Pope, and Richardson. Such families commonly sent their sons—and often their daughters—abroad for an education, usually to England, sometimes to France.

RELIGION   The first colonists in Virginia brought with them an Anglican minister, but only in Virginia and Maryland was the Church of England established (tax supported) before the end of the seventeenth century. In the early eighteenth century it became the established church in all the South—and some counties of New York and New Jersey, despite the presence of many dissenters. In the new environment, however, the Anglican church evolved into something quite unlike the state church of England. The scattered population and the absence of bishops made centralized control difficult. After 1632 the bishop of London held theoretical jurisdiction over the colonial churches, but regulation was generally entrusted to governors more concerned with political matters.

In practice therefore, if not in theory, the Anglican churches became as independent of any hierarchy as the Puritans of New England. Governance fell to lay boards of vestrymen, who chose the ministers, and usually held them on a tight rein by granting short-term contracts. In Virginia ministerial salaries depended on the taxes paid in the parish, and in 1662 were set uniformly at the value of 13,333 pounds of leaf; the salary therefore fluc-

*The elegant pulpit at Christ's Church, an eighteenth-century Anglican church in Virginia.*

tuated with the price of tobacco. Often the parishes were too large for an effective ministry. Isolated chapels might have lay readers and get only infrequent visits by clergymen. Standards were often lax, and the Anglican clergy around the Chesapeake became notorious for its "sporting parsons," addicted to fox-hunting, gambling, drunkenness, and worse. Some parishes went for long periods without ministers: ordination by a bishop could be had only in England, and the pay was too uncertain.

No bishop ever resided in the colonies, and only a bishop could ordain ministers or confirm members, a fact which of itself caused a falling off. Certain functions of supervision and discipline, however, could be delegated to "commissaries," the first and most noted of whom was James Blair, who brought some order into Virginia's church affairs after 1689. At his death in 1743 only two parishes lacked ministers. Commissary Thomas Bray, appointed to Maryland in 1696, spent less than a year in the colony during which he established a library in nearly every parish, but was more significant for work back in England which led King William to charter the Society for the Propagation of the Gospel in Foreign Parts (the SPG, sometimes called the "Venerable Society"). The first missionary of the SPG arrived in

South Carolina on Christmas Day 1702; for the next eighty years the SPG sponsored hundreds of missionaries, who worked especially in New England and the Middle Colonies where the Anglican church was weakest. The missionaries kept up a sporadic agitation to have a bishop assigned to the colonies, but none ever was. Opposition came from various quarters: most of the colonists were dissenters; some in England feared that the appointment of bishops might make the colonies more independent, while some in the colonies feared that it would make them less so; commercial and landed interests worried that it might make the colonies less attractive to dissenters, and so inhibit growth.

## Society and Economy in New England

**TOWNSHIPS**  By contrast to the seaboard planters who transformed the English manor into the southern plantation, the Puritans transformed the English village into the New England town. Land policy in New England had a stronger social and religious purpose than elsewhere. Towns shaped by English precedent and Puritan policy also fitted the environment of a rockbound land, confined by sea and mountains and unfit for large-scale cultivation.

Neither headrights nor quitrents ever took root in New England. There were cases of large individual grants, but the standard system was one of township grants to organized groups. A group of settlers, often gathered already into a church, would petition the General Court for a town (what elsewhere was commonly called a "township") then divide it according to a rough principle of equity—those who invested more, or had larger families or greater status, might receive more land—retaining some pasture and woodland in common and holding some for later arrivals. In some early cases the towns arranged each settler's land in separate strips after the medieval practice, but with time land was commonly divided into separate farms to which landholders would move out, away from the close-knit village. And still later, by the early eighteenth century, the colonies used their remaining land as a source of revenue by selling townships to proprietors whose purpose, more often than not, was speculation and resale.

**ENTERPRISE**  The life of the New England farmer was typically a hardscrabble subsistence. Simply clearing the glacier-scoured soil of rocks might require sixty days of hard labor per acre. The growing season was short, and no exotic staples grew in that hard climate. If the town resembled the English village, the crops too were those familiar to the English countryside: wheat, barley, oats, some cattle and swine, and where the woodland predators could be killed off—especially on islands like Nantucket or Martha's Vineyard—sheep grazed on the land. By the end of the seventeenth century New England farmers were developing some surpluses for export but never any staples that met the demands of the English market.

With virgin forests ready for conversion into masts, lumber, and ships, and rich fishing grounds that stretched northward to Newfoundland, it is little wonder that New Englanders turned to the sea for livelihood—the fisheries in fact antedated settlement by more than a century. The Chesapeake region afforded a rich harvest of oysters, but New England, by its proximity to waters frequented by cod, mackerel, halibut, and other varieties, became the more important maritime center. Marblehead, Salem, Ipswich, and Charlestown early became important commercial fishing towns. Whales too abounded in New England waters and supplied whale oil for lighting and lubrication, as well as ambergris, a secretion used in perfumes. New England ships eventually were chasing whales from Baffin Bay to Antarctica and out across the Pacific on voyages that lasted years.

The fisheries, unlike the farms, supplied a staple of export to Europe, while lesser grades of fish went to the West Indies as food for slaves. Fisheries encouraged the development of ship-

The trade card of a Boston chandler, advertising candles made from whale oil.

building, and experience at seafaring spurred commerce. This in turn encouraged wider contacts in the Atlantic world and a certain cosmopolitanism which clashed with more provincial aspects of the Puritan utopia.

Abundant forests near the shore yielded lumber, masts, pitch, and tar, and as early as July 4, 1631, John Winthrop launched a ship of sixty tons, the *Blessing of the Bay,* which marked the beginning of an American merchant marine. By the mid–seventeenth century shipyards had developed at Boston, Salem, Dorchester, Gloucester, Portsmouth, and other towns. New England remained the center of shipbuilding throughout the colonial period. Lumber provided not only raw material for ships but a prime cargo. As early as 1635 what may have been the first sawmill appeared at Portsmouth, New Hampshire. Sawmills soon abounded throughout the colonies, often together with gristmills using the same source of waterpower.

TRADE  Commercially the colonies by the end of the seventeenth century had become part of a great North Atlantic connection, trading not only with the British Isles and the British West Indies, but also—and often illegally—with Spain, France, Portugal, Holland, and their colonies from America to the shores of Africa. Out of necessity the colonists had to import manufactured goods from Britain and Europe: hardware, machinery, paint, instruments of navigation, various household items. The function of the colonies as a market for English goods was important to the mother country. The central problem for the colonies was to find the means of paying for the imports—the eternal problem of the balance of trade.

The mechanism of trade in New England and the Middle Colonies differed from that of the South in two respects: their lack of staples to exchange for English goods was a relative disadvantage, but the abundance of their own shipping and mercantile enterprise worked in their favor. After 1660, in order to protect English agriculture and fisheries, the English government raised prohibitive duties against certain major exports of these colonies: fish, flour, wheat, and meat, while leaving the door open to timber, furs, and whale oil. Consequently New York and New England in the years 1698–1717 bought more from England than they sold there, incurring an unfavorable trade balance.

The northern colonies met the problem partly by using their own ships and merchants, thus avoiding the "invisible" charges for trade and transport, and by finding other markets for the staples excluded from England, thus acquiring goods or bullion to

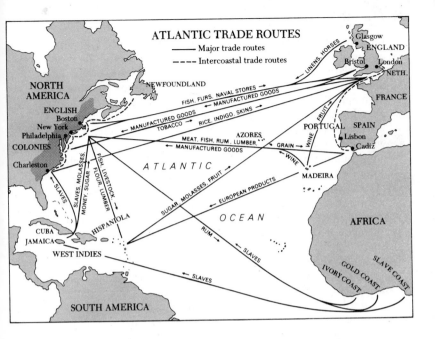

ATLANTIC TRADE ROUTES
—— Major trade routes
- - - - Intercoastal trade routes

pay for imports from the mother country. American lumber and fish therefore went to southern Europe, Madeira, and the Azores for money or in exchange for wine; lumber, rum, and provisions went to Newfoundland; and all of these and more went to the West Indies, which became the most important outlet of all. American merchants could sell fish, bread, flour, corn, pork, bacon, beef, and horses to West Indian planters who specialized in sugarcane. In return they got money, sugar, molasses, rum, indigo, dyewoods, and other products, much of which went eventually to England. This gave rise to the famous "triangular trade" (more a descriptive convenience than a rigid pattern) in which New Englanders shipped rum to the west coast of Africa and bartered for slaves, took the slaves on the "Middle Passage" to the West Indies, and returned home with various commodities including molasses, from which they manufactured rum. In another version they shipped provisions to the West Indies, carried sugar and molasses to England, and returned with manufactured goods from Europe.

The generally unfavorable balance of trade in the colonies left a chronic shortage of hard money, which drifted away to pay for imports and invisible charges. Since England restricted the export of bullion, such coins as found their way to the colonies were mostly foreign: the Portuguese johannes (or "joe") and

moidore, the French pistole, and most important of all, the
Spanish piece of eight (eight reals) or the Spanish milled dollar
which later took its place—the ancestor of the American dollar.
Colonists reckoned in terms of English pounds, shillings, and
pence, but it has been said that they were more a medium of expression than a medium of exchange.

Various expedients met the shortage of currency: the use of
wampum or commodities, the monetary value of which colonial
governments tried vainly to set by law. For a time Massachusetts
coined silver "pine tree" shillings, but lost the right after the loss
of its charter in 1684. Promissory notes of individuals or colonial
treasurers often passed as a crude sort of paper money. Most of
the colonies at one time or another issued bills of credit, on
promise of payment later (hence the dollar "bill"), and after
South Carolina took the lead in 1712, most set up land banks
which issued paper money for loans to farmers on the security of
their lands, which were mortgaged to the banks. Colonial
farmers began to recognize that an inflation of paper money led
to an inflation of crop prices, and therefore asked for more and
more paper. Thus began in colonial politics what was to become
a recurrent issue in later times, the question of currency inflation. Wherever the issue arose, debtors commonly favored
growth in the money supply, which would make it easier for
them to settle accounts, whereas creditors favored a limited
money supply, which would increase the value of their capital. In
1741, therefore, in response to influential creditors of Massachusetts, Parliament extended the Bubble Act of 1720 to the colonies. That act, passed in response to speculative frauds in

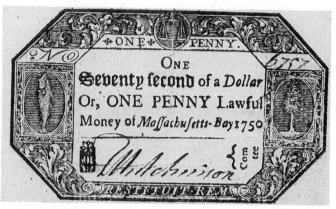

*Massachusetts Bay currency, dated 1750, showing a codfish and
a pine tree.*

*The parlor of the Thomas Hart house, Ipswich, Massachusetts, built around 1640.*

England like the South Sea Bubble, outlawed joint-stock companies not authorized by Parliament. Ten years later, in 1751, Parliament outlawed legal tender paper money in New England, and in 1764 throughout the colonies.

RELIGION  It has been said that in New England one was never far from the smell of fish and brimstone. The Puritans for many years had a bad press. By the standards of later ages they were judged bigots, but they had come to America to escape error, not to tolerate it in their New Zion. And the picture of the dour Puritan, hostile to anything that gave pleasure, is false. Puritans, especially those of the upper class, wore colorful clothing, enjoyed secular music, and imbibed prodigious quantities of rum. "Drink is in itself a good creature of God," said the Rev. Increase Mather, " . . . but the abuse of drink is from Satan." The architecture and household articles of Puritan New England have a continuing aesthetic appeal. The things of the world, in the Puritan view, were made by God and to be enjoyed by man. Sin lay not so much in their use as in their misuse. At the same time man had an obligation to work in this world, and worldly success was important.

The Puritans who settled Massachusetts, unlike the Separatists of Plymouth, proposed only to form a purified version of the Anglican church. They believed that they could remain loyal to the Church of England, the unity of church and state, and the principle of compulsory uniformity. But their remoteness from England led them directly, in fact very quickly, to a congregational form of church government identical with that of the Pilgrim Separatists, and for that matter little different from the practice of southern Anglicans.

Certain things in the Puritan faith were pregnant with meaning for the future. In the Puritan's version of Calvin's theology God had voluntarily entered into a covenant, or contract, with men through which his creatures could secure salvation. By analogy, therefore, an assembly of true Christians could enter into a church covenant, a voluntary union for the common worship of God. From this it was a fairly short step to the idea of a voluntary union for purposes of government. The history of New England affords examples of several such limited steps toward constitutional government: the Mayflower Compact, the Cambridge Agreement of John Winthrop and his followers, the Fundamental Orders of Connecticut, and the informal arrangements whereby the Rhode Island settlers governed themselves until they secured a charter in 1663.

The covenant theory contained certain seeds of democracy in both church and state, but democracy was no part of Puritan political science, which like so much else in Puritan belief began with original sin. Because of man's depravity government became necessary for his restraint. "If people be governors," asked the Rev. John Cotton, "who shall be governed?" The Puritan was dedicated to seeking not the will of the people but the will of God. The ultimate source of authority was the Bible, God's revelation to man. But the Bible had to be known by right reason, which was best applied by those trained to the purpose. Hence most Puritans deferred to an intellectual elite for a true knowledge of God's will. Church and state were but two aspects of the same unity, the purpose of which was to carry out God's will on earth. The New England way might thus be summarized in the historian Perry Miller's phrase as a kind of "dictatorship of the regenerate."

The church exercised a pervasive influence over the life of the town, but unlike the Church of England it had no temporal power. Thus while Puritan New England has often been called a theocracy, the church technically was entirely separated from the state—except that the residents were taxed for its support. And if not all inhabitants were church members, they were impelled, indeed required, to be present for church services. So complete was the consensus of church member and nonmember alike that the closely knit communities of New England have been called peaceable kingdoms. It was a peace, however, under which there bubbled a volcano of soul-searching.

The Puritan lived anything but what Plato had called "the unexamined life." He was assailed by doubts, by a fear of falling away, by the haunting fear that despite his best outward efforts he might not be one of God's elect. Add that to the long winters which kept the family cooped up during the dark, cold months, and one has a formula for seething resentments and recriminations which, for the sake of peace in the family, had to be projected outward toward neighbors. The New Englanders of those peaceable kingdoms therefore built a reputation as the most litigious people on the face of God's earth, continually quarreling over fancied slights, business dealings, and other issues, and building in the process a flourishing legal profession.

SOCIAL STRAINS    All the while, social strains were growing in the community, a consequence of population pressure on the land. In the close-knit towns of New England the fragmentation of family ties seems to have been slowed by the peculiar circumstances of the community. Studies of Andover, Dedham, and Plymouth, Massachusetts, among other towns, suggest that at least in the seventeenth century family ties grew stronger and village life more cohesive than in the homeland. The conjugal unit prevailed, but intermarriage of families blurred the line between family and community. And among the first settlers, fathers exercised strong patriarchal control over their sons through their control of the land. They kept the sons in the town, not letting them set up their own households or get title to their farmland until they reached middle age.

In New England as elsewhere the tendency was to subdivide the land among all the children. But by the eighteenth century, with land scarcer, the younger sons were either getting control of property early or else moving on. Often the younger male children were forced out, with family help and blessings, to seek land elsewhere or new kinds of work in the commercial cities. With the growing pressure on land in the settled regions, poverty was becoming visible in what had once seemed a country of unlimited opportunity.

The emphasis on a direct accountability to God, which lay at the base of all Protestant theology, itself caused a persistent tension and led believers to challenge authority in the name of private conscience. Massachusetts repressed such heresy in the 1630s, but it resurfaced during the 1650s among Quakers and Baptists, and in 1659–1660 the colony hanged four Quakers who persisted in returning after they were expelled. These acts caused such revulsion—and an investigation by the crown—that they were not repeated, although heretics continued to face harassment and persecution.

More damaging to the Puritan Utopia was the increasing worldliness of New England, which placed growing strains on church discipline. More and more children of the "visible saints" found themselves unable to give the required testimony of regeneration. In 1662 an assembly of ministers at Boston accepted the "Half-Way Covenant," whereby baptized children of church members could be admitted to a "halfway" membership and secure baptism for their own children in turn. Such members, however, could neither vote in church nor take communion. A further blow to Puritan hegemony came with the Massachusetts royal charter of 1691, which required toleration of dissenters and based the right to vote in public elections on property rather than on church membership.

The strains that built up in Massachusetts's transition from Pu-

*Four women being hanged as witches in seventeenth-century England. At Salem, nineteen people were hanged for witchcraft.*

ritan utopia to royal colony reached an unhappy climax in the witchcraft hysteria at Salem Village (later Danvers) in 1692. The general upheaval in the colony's political, economic, social, and religious life was compounded in that locale by a conflict of values between a community rooted in the subsistence farm economy and the thriving port of Salem proper.

Seething insecurities and family conflict in the community made it receptive to accusations by adolescent girls that they had been bewitched. Before the hysteria ran its course ten months later, nineteen people (including some men) had been hanged, one man pressed to death by heavy stones, and more than 100 others jailed. The fascination of horror has drawn a disproportionate amount of attention to the witchcraft delusions. It should be noted, however, that most people in the Western world at that time believed in witches who served the devil and his demons. But nearly everybody responsible for the Salem executions later recanted and nothing quite like it happened in the colonies again. In Europe witches were still being executed in the eighteenth century.

## SOCIETY AND ECONOMY IN THE MIDDLE COLONIES

AN ECONOMIC MIX    Both geographically and culturally the Middle Colonies stood between New England and the South, blending their own influences with elements derived from the older regions on either side. In so doing they more completely reflected the diversity of colonial life and more fully foreshadowed the pluralism of the later American nation than the regions on either side. Their crops were those of New England but more bountiful, owing to better land and a longer growing season, and they developed surpluses of foodstuffs for exports to the plantations of the South and the West Indies: wheat, barley, oats, and other cereals, flour, and livestock. Three great rivers—the Hudson, Delaware, and Susquehanna—and their tributaries gave the Middle Colonies a unique access to their backcountry and to the fur trade of the interior, where New York and Pennsylvania long enjoyed friendly relations with the Iroquois, Delaware, and other tribes. As a consequence the region's commerce rivaled that of New England, and indeed Philadelphia in time supplanted Boston as the largest city of the colonies.

Land policies followed the headright system of the South, with all the later embellishments of favoritism to influential speculators. One of the most successful of these was James Logan, a man of staggering erudition. Logan was secretary to William Penn, then Pennsylvania commissioner of property, and holder of numerous other offices from which positions of influence he set himself up as one of the leading merchants and landholders— and owner of the largest private library—in the colonies. In New York the early royal governors, especially Lord Cornbury, went him one better. They carried forward, in practice if not in name, the Dutch device of the patroonship, granting to influential favorites vast estates on Long Island and up the Hudson and Mohawk Valleys. These realms most nearly approached the Old World manor, self-contained domains farmed by tenants who paid dues to use the landlords' mills, warehouses, smokehouses, and wharfs. But with free land elsewhere, New York's population languished and the new waves of immigrants sought the promised land of Pennsylvania.

AN ETHNIC MIX   In the makeup of their population the Middle Colonies stood apart from both the mostly English Puritan settlements and the biracial plantation colonies to the South. In New York and New Jersey, for instance, Dutch culture and language lingered for some time to come, along with the Dutch Reformed church. Up and down the Delaware River the few Swedes and Finns, the first settlers, were overwhelmed by the influx of English and Welsh Quakers, followed in turn by the Germans and Scotch-Irish.

The Germans came mainly from the Rhineland Palatinate, which had been devastated and impoverished first in the Thirty Years' War (1618–1648), then in the repeated wars of the French king Louis XIV (1667–1713). Penn's brochures on the

*The Musical Life of York. Music was an important part of community life in Pennsylvania German towns like York. Benjamin Franklin wrote of a 1756 visit to York, "I was at their Church, where I was entertain'd with good Musick, the Organ being accompanied with Violins, Hautboys [oboes], Flutes, Clarinets, etc."*

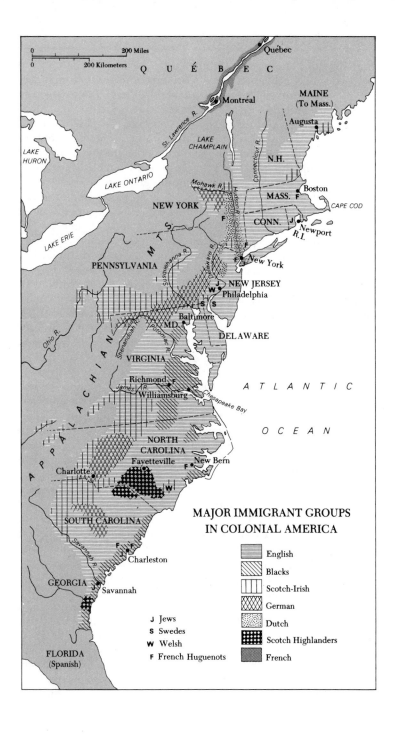

MAJOR IMMIGRANT GROUPS
IN COLONIAL AMERICA

English
Blacks
Scotch-Irish
German
Dutch
Scotch Highlanders
French

J  Jews
S  Swedes
W  Welsh
F  French Huguenots

bounties of Pennsylvania circulated in German translation, and his promise of religious freedom brought a response from persecuted sects, especially the Mennonites, German Baptists whose beliefs resembled those of the Quakers. In 1683 a group of Mennonites founded Germantown near Philadelphia. They were but the vanguard of a swelling migration in the eighteenth century which included Lutherans, Reformed Calvinists, Moravians, Dunkers, and others, a large proportion of whom paid their way as indentured servants, or "redemptioners," as they were commonly called. Back of Philadelphia they created a belt of settlement in which the "Pennsylvania Dutch" (a corruption of *Deutsch*, meaning German) predominated, and a channel for the dispersion of German population through the colonies.

The Scotch-Irish began to arrive later and moved still farther out in the backcountry. "Scotch-Irish" is an enduring misnomer for Ulster Scots, Presbyterians transplanted from Scotland to confiscated lands in Northern Ireland to give that country a more Protestant tone. The Ulster plantation dated from 1607–1609, the years when Jamestown was fighting for survival. A century later the Ulster Scots were on the move again, in flight from economic disaster caused by English tariffs. This time they looked mainly to Pennsylvania.

The Germans and Scotch-Irish became the largest non-English elements in the colonies, but other groups enriched the diversity of population in New York and the Quaker colonies: French Huguenots (Calvinists whose privilege of toleration was revoked in 1685), Irish, Welshmen, Swiss, Jews, and others. New York had inherited from the Dutch a tradition of toleration which had given the colony a motley population before the English conquest: French-speaking Walloons and Frenchmen, Germans, Danes, Portuguese, Spaniards, Italians, Bohemians, Poles, and others, including some New England Puritans. The Protestant Netherlands had given haven to the Sephardic Jews expelled from Spain and Portugal, and enough of them found their way into New Netherland to found a synagogue there.

What could be said of Pennsylvania as a refuge for the persecuted might be said as well of Rhode Island and South Carolina, which practiced a similar religious toleration. Newport and Charleston, like New York and Philadelphia, became centers of minuscule Jewish populations. French Huguenots made their greatest mark on South Carolina, more by their enterprise than by their numbers, and left implanted in the life of the colony such family names as Huger, Porcher, DeSaussure, Legare, Lanneau, and Lesesne. A number of Highland Scots came directly

## PERCENTAGE OF AFRO-AMERICANS
## IN THE TOTAL POPULATION
## OF THE BRITISH COLONIES, 1660–1780

| Year | New England | Middle Colonies | Upper South | Lower South | West Indies |
|------|-------------|-----------------|-------------|-------------|-------------|
| 1660 | 1.7 | 11.5 | 3.6 | 2.0 | 42.0 |
| 1700 | 1.8 | 6.8 | 13.1 | 17.6 | 77.7 |
| 1740 | 2.9 | 7.5 | 28.3 | 46.5 | 88.0 |
| 1780 | 2.0 | 5.9 | 38.6 | 41.2 | 91.1 |

SOURCE: U.S. Bureau of the Census, *Historical Statistics of the United States, Colonial Times to 1970* (Washington, D.C.: U.S. Government Printing Office, 1975), 2 : 1168 (Ser. Z 1–19).

from their homeland rather than by way of Ulster, especially after suppression of a rebellion in 1745 on behalf of the Stuart pretender to the throne, "Bonnie Prince Charlie." A large group of them went to Fayetteville, North Carolina, where Gaelic-speaking Scots settled beside Lumbee Indians who had spoken English for nearly a century.

The eighteenth century was the great period of expansion and population growth in British North America, and during those years a large increase of the non-English stock took place. A rough estimate of the national origins of the white population as of 1790 found it to be 60.9 percent English, 14.3 percent Scots and Scotch-Irish, 8.7 percent German, 5.4 percent Dutch, French, and Swedish, 3.7 percent Irish, and 7 percent miscellaneous or unassigned. If one adds to the 3,172,444 whites in the 1790 census the 756,770 nonwhites, not even considering uncounted Indians, it seems likely that only about half the populace, and perhaps fewer, could trace their origins to England. Of the blacks about 75 percent had been transported from the bend of the African coastline between the Senegal and Niger Rivers; most of the rest came from Congo-Angola.

THE BACKCOUNTRY   Pennsylvania in the eighteenth century became the great distribution point for the diverse ethnic groups of European origin, just as the Chesapeake and Charleston became the distribution points for African peoples. Before the mid–eighteenth century population in the Pennsylvania backcountry was coming up against the Appalachian barrier and, following the line of least resistance, the Scotch-Irish and Germans filtered southward across western Maryland, down the Shenandoah Valley of Virginia, and on into the Carolina and Georgia backcountry. Germans were first in the upper Shenandoah Valley, and to the south of them Scotch-Irish filled the lower valley. Migrants of both stocks continued to move into the Carolina and Georgia backcountry, while others found their way up from Charleston.

Along the fringes of the frontier were commonly found the Scotch-Irish, who had acquired in their homeland and in Ulster a stubborn fighting spirit that brooked no nonsense from the "savages" of the woods. And out on the cutting edge life might be in that "state of nature" described by Thomas Hobbes: "poor, nasty, brutish, and short." It was a lonely life of scattered settlements, isolated log cabins set on plots of land which the pioneer owned or at least occupied, furnished with crude furniture hacked out with axe and adze and pieced together with pegs. The frontier regions bred a rough democracy, because most people were on a nearly equal status, and instilled a stubborn individualism in people who got accustomed to deciding things for themselves. With time, of course, neighborhoods grew up within visiting distance, animal and Indian trails broadened into wagon roads, and crossroads stores grew up into community gathering places where social intercourse could be lubricated with the whiskey that was omnipresent on the Scotch-Irish frontier.

The backcountry of the Piedmont, and something much like it on up to northern New England (Maine, New Hampshire, and what would become Vermont), became a fourth major region that stretched the length of the colonies across the abstract imaginary boundaries which separated the political units. Government was slow to reach these remote settlements, and the system of "every man for himself" sometimes led frontier communities into conditions of extreme disorder.

## COLONIAL CITIES

During the seventeenth century the colonies remained in comparative isolation, evolving subtly distinctive ways and unfolding separate histories. Boston and New York, Philadelphia and Charleston were more likely to keep in closer touch with London than with each other. The Carolina upcountry had more in common with the Pennsylvania backcountry than either had with Charleston or Philadelphia. Colonial cities faced outward to the Atlantic. Since commerce was their chief reason for being, they hugged the coastline or, like Philadelphia, sprang up on streams where ocean-going vessels could reach them. Never holding more than 10 percent of the colonial population, they exerted an influence in commerce, politics, and civilization generally out of proportion to their size.

Five major port cities outdistanced the rest. By the end of the colonial period Philadelphia, with some 30,000 people (counting adjacent suburbs), was the largest city in the colonies and second only to London in the British Empire. New York, with about 25,000, ranked second; Boston numbered 16,000; Charleston, 12,000; and Newport, 11,000. Falling in a range of about 8,000 down to 4,000 were secondary ports and inland towns like New Haven and Norwich, Connecticut; Norfolk; Baltimore; Lancaster, Pennsylvania; Salem; New London; Providence; and Albany.

THE SOCIAL AND POLITICAL ORDER  The upper crust of urban society were the merchants who bartered the products of American farms and forests for the molasses and rum of the West Indies, the wines of Madeira, the manufactured goods of Europe, and the slaves of Africa. Their trade in turn stimulated the activities of rum distilling, ropewalks, sail lofts, instrument makers, and ship chandlers who supplied vessels leaving port. After the mer-

*School Street, Salem, around 1765. The mansion of a wealthy merchant dominates this street scene in Salem, a prosperous port town.*

chants, who constituted the chief urban aristocracy, came a middle class of craftsmen, retailers, innkeepers, and small jobbers who met a variety of needs. And at the bottom of the pecking order were sailors, unskilled workers, and some artisans.

Class stratification in the cities became more pronounced as time went by. One study of Boston found that in 1687 the richest 15 percent of the population owned 52 percent of the taxable wealth; by 1771 the top 15 percent owned about two-thirds and the top 5 percent owned some 44 percent of the wealth. In Philadelphia the concentration of wealth was even more pronounced.

Problems created by urban growth are nothing new. Colonial cities had problems of traffic which required not only paved streets and lighting but regulations to protect children and animals in the streets from reckless riders. Regulations restrained citizens from creating public nuisances by tossing their garbage into the streets. Fires that on occasion swept through closely packed buildings led to preventive standards in building codes, restrictions on burning rubbish, and the organization of volunteer and finally professional fire companies. Crime and violence made necessary more police protection than could be provided by the constable and watch duty that at first was required of ordinary citizens. And in cities the poor became more visible than in

*Fighting a fire in colonial New York, 1762.*

the countryside. Colonists brought with them the English princi-ple of public responsibility. The number of Boston's poor receiv-ing public assistance rose from 500 in 1700 to 4,000 in 1736, New York's from 250 in 1698 to 5,000 in the 1770s. Most of it went to "outdoor" relief in the form of money, food, clothing, and fuel, but almshouses also appeared in colonial cities.

Town governments were not always equal to their multiple tasks. Of the major cities, Boston and Newport had the common New England system of town meetings and selectmen, while New York after 1791 had an elected council responsive to the citizens, although its mayor and other officials were still ap-pointed by the governor. Philadelphia, however, fell under a self-perpetuating closed corporation in which the common run of citizens had no voice, and colonial Charleston never achieved status as a municipal corporation at all, but remained under the thumb of the South Carolina Assembly.

THE URBAN WEB   Little of the colonial population lived far from the navigable streams, except in the interior. The first roads were likely to be Indian trails, which themselves often followed the tracks of bison and perhaps the ancient mastodon through the forests. The trails widened with travel, then were made roads by order of provincial and local authorities. Land travel at first had to go by horse or by foot. The first stagecoach line for the public, opened in 1732, linked Burlington and Perth Amboy, New Jersey, connecting by water to Philadelphia and New York, respectively. That same year a guidebook published in Boston gave roads connecting from Boston through Providence, New York, Philadelphia, and eventually on to Williamsburg and Charleston, with connecting branches. From the main ports good roads might reach thirty or forty miles inland, but all were dirt roads subject to washouts and mudholes. There was not a single hard-surfaced road during the entire colonial period, aside from city streets.

Taverns were an important adjunct of colonial travel, since movement by night was too risky, and they became social and po-litical centers to which the local people repaired to learn news from travelers, to discuss the current issues, to socialize, drink, and gamble. Postal service through the seventeenth century was almost nonexistent—people entrusted letters to travelers or sea captains. Massachusetts set up a provincial postal system in 1677, and Pennsylvania in 1683. In 1691 King William created a monopoly of postal service in Massachusetts, New York, and

Pennsylvania, and Andrew Hamilton of Philadelphia established a weekly service from Portsmouth, New Hampshire, to Philadelphia. The system proved unprofitable though, and was abandoned in 1707. Under a Parliamentary Law of 1710, however, the postmaster of London was authorized to name a deputy in charge of the colonies and a system eventually extended the length of the Atlantic seaboard. Benjamin Franklin, who served as deputy-postmaster from 1753 to 1774, speeded up the service with shorter routes and night-traveling post riders, and increased the volume by inaugurating lower rates.

More reliable deliveries gave rise to newspapers in the eighteenth century. The first printing press in the colonies was set up at Cambridge, Massachusetts, in 1638, in connection with Harvard College; it produced mainly religious tracts and sermons. The first newspaper to endure was the Boston *News-Letter* (1704), which started when the postmaster of Boston began writing letters to friends around Massachusetts to keep them informed of current events. Before 1745 twenty-two newspapers had been started, seven in New England, ten in the Middle Colonies, five in the South, including the *American Weekly Mercury* (1719) of Philadelphia; the *New England Courant* (1721) of Boston, published by James Franklin, older brother of Benjamin; Ben's own *Pennsylvania Gazette* (acquired 1729); the *South Carolina Gazette* (1732); John Peter Zenger's New York *Weekly Journal* (1733); and the *Virginia Gazette* (1736).

An important landmark in the progress of freedom of the press was Zenger's trial for seditious libel for publishing criticisms of New York's governor, William Cosby. Imprisoned for ten months and brought to trial in 1735, he was defended by the aged Andrew Hamilton of Philadelphia, whose cleverness made him perhaps the original "Philadelphia lawyer." The established rule in English common law held that one might be punished for criticism which fostered "an ill opinion of the government." The jury's function was only to determine whether or not the defendant had published the opinion. Hamilton startled the court with his claim that Zenger had published the truth—which the judge ruled an unacceptable defense. Cosby was so unpopular, however, that the jury considered the attacks on him true and held the editor not guilty. The libel law remained standing as before, but editors thereafter were emboldened to criticize officials more freely.

## THE ENLIGHTENMENT

DISCOVERING THE LAWS OF NATURE   It was the cities that, through their commercial contacts, through their newspapers, and through many-fold activities, became the centers for the dissemination of fashion and ideas. In the world of ideas a new fashion was abroad: the Enlightenment. During the first century of English colonization the settlers' contemporaries in Europe went through a scientific revolution in which the old Ptolemaic view of an earth-centered universe was overthrown by the new heliocentric (sun-centered) system of Polish astronomer Nicolaus Copernicus. A climax to the revolution came with Sir Isaac Newton's *Principia* (*Mathematical Principles of Natural Philosophy*, 1687), which set forth his theory of gravitation. Newton had, in short, hit upon the design of a mechanistic universe moving in accordance with natural laws which could be grasped by human reason and explained by mathematics.

By analogy from Newton's world machine one could reason that natural laws governed all things—the orbits of the planets and also the orbits of human relations: politics, economics, and society. Reason could make men aware, for instance, that the natural law of supply and demand governed economics or that natural rights to life, liberty, and property determined the limits and functions of government.

Much of enlightened thought could be reconciled with established beliefs—the idea of natural law existed in Christian theology, and religious people could reason that the worldview of Copernicus and Newton simply showed forth the glory of God. Puritan leaders accepted Newtonian science from the start. Yet carried to its ultimate logic, as the Deists did, the idea of natural law left God eliminated or at best reduced to the position of a remote Creator—as the French *philosophe* Voltaire put it, the master clockmaker who planned the universe and set it in motion. Evil in the world, in this view, resulted not from original sin and innate depravity so much as from an imperfect understanding of the laws of nature. Man, the English philosopher John Locke argued in his *Essay on Human Understanding* (1690), is largely the product of his environment, the human mind a blank tablet on which experience is written. The evils of a corrupt society therefore might corrupt the mind. The way to improve both society and human nature was by the application and improvement of Reason—which was the highest Virtue (enlightened thinkers often capitalized both words).

THE ENLIGHTENMENT IN AMERICA  Whether or not developed to the outermost reaches of its logic, such ideas affected the climate of thought in the eighteenth century. The premises of Newtonian science and the Enlightenment, moreover, fitted the American experience. In the New World people no longer moved in the worn grooves of tradition that defined the roles of priest or peasant or noble. Much of their experience had already been with observation, experiment, and the need to think anew. America was therefore receptive to the new science. Anybody who pretended to a degree of learning revealed a curiosity about natural philosophy, and some carried it to considerable depth.

John Winthrop, Jr. (1606–1676), three times governor of Connecticut, wanted to establish industries and mining in America. These interests led to his work in chemistry and membership in the Royal Society of London. He owned probably the first telescope brought to the colonies. His cousin, John Winthrop IV (1714–1779), was a professional scientist, Hollis Professor of Mathematics and Natural Philosophy at Harvard, who introduced to the colonies the study of calculus and ranged over the fields of astronomy, geology, chemistry, and electricity. Cadwallader Colden, last royal governor of New York, studied and wrote in the fields of botany and physics. David Rittenhouse of Philadelphia, a clockmaker, became a self-taught scientist who built two orreries and probably the first telescope made in America. John Bartram of Philadelphia spent a lifetime traveling and studying American plant life, and gathered in Philadelphia a botanical garden now part of the city's park system.

FRANKLIN'S INFLUENCE  Benjamin Franklin stood apart from all these men as the person who epitomized the Enlightenment, in the eyes of both Americans and Europeans, more than any other single person. It was fitting that Franklin came from Pennsylvania, which in the eyes of Voltaire had fulfilled the Quaker virtues of toleration and simplicity. William Penn, Voltaire wrote, had "brought to the world that golden age of which men talk so much and which probably has never existed anywhere except in Pennsylvania." Franklin came from the ranks of the common man and never lost the common touch, a gift that accounted for his success as a publisher. Born in Boston in 1706, son of a candle and soap maker, apprenticed to his older brother, a printer, Franklin left home at the age of seventeen. In Philadelphia, before he was twenty-four he owned a print shop where he edited and published the *Pennsylvania Gazette*, and when he was twenty-seven he brought out *Poor Richard's Almanac*, still mined for its

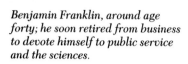
*Benjamin Franklin, around age forty; he soon retired from business to devote himself to public service and the sciences.*

homely maxims on success and happiness. Before he retired from business at the age of forty-two, Franklin, among other achievements, had founded a library, set up a fire company, helped start the academy which became the University of Pennsylvania, and started a debating club which grew into the American Philosophical Society. After his early retirement he intended to devote himself to public affairs and the sciences.

The course of events allowed him less and less time for science, but that was his passion. Franklin's *Experiments and Observations on Electricity* (1751) went through many editions in several languages and established his reputation as a leading thinker and experimenter. His speculations extended widely to the fields of medicine, meteorology, geology, astronomy, physics, and other aspects of science. He invented the Franklin stove, the lighting rod, and a glass harmonica for which Mozart and Beethoven composed. In his travels as colonial agent to London and later American ambassador to France, his insatiable curiosity led to suggestions (some of them later adopted) for improvements in ship design. Franklin's university had been the printshop, and the triumph of this untutored genius further confirmed the Enlightenment trust in the powers of Nature.

EDUCATION IN THE COLONIES   The heights of abstract reasoning, of course, were remote from the everyday concerns of most colonists. For the colonists at large, education in the traditional ideas and manners of society—even literacy itself—remained primarily the responsibility of family and church, and one not always accepted. The modern conception of universal free education as a responsibility of the state was a slow growth and failed to win universal acceptance until the twentieth century. Yet there is evidence of a widespread concern almost from the beginning that steps needed to be taken lest the children of settlers grow up untutored in the wilderness.

Conditions in New England proved most favorable for the establishment of schools. The Puritan emphasis on Scripture reading, which all Protestants shared in some degree, implied an obligation to ensure literacy. The great proportion of highly educated people in Puritan New England (Massachusetts probably had a greater proportion of college graduates in the early seventeenth century than in the twentieth) ensured a common respect for education. And the compact towns of that region made schools more feasible than among the scattered people of the southern colonies. In 1635 the inhabitants of Boston established the Boston Latin Grammar School, which had a distinguished career to the twentieth century, and the same year the General Court voted to establish a college which, begun in 1638, grew into Harvard University. In 1647 the colony enacted the famous "ye olde deluder Satan" Act (designed to thwart the Evil

From the *"Rhymed Alphabet" of* The New England Primer, *first published in America in the 1680s.*

One) which required every town of fifty or more families to set up a grammar school (a Latin school which could prepare a student for college). Although the act was widely evaded, it did signify a serious purpose to promote education. Massachusetts Bay set an example which the rest of New England emulated.

The Dutch in New Netherland were nearly if not equally as active as the New England Puritans, and more active than the English who succeeded them after 1664. In Pennsylvania the Quakers never heeded William Penn's instructions to establish public schools, but did respect the usefulness of education and financed a number of private schools teaching practical as well as academic subjects. In the southern colonies efforts to establish schools were hampered by the more scattered populations, and in parts of the backcountry by indifference and neglect. Some of the wealthiest planters and merchants of the Tidewater sent their children to England or hired tutors, who in some cases would also serve the children of neighbors. In some places wealthy patrons or the people collectively managed to raise some kind of support for "old field" schools and academies at the secondary level.

## THE GREAT AWAKENING

STIRRINGS  In the new currents of learning and the Enlightenment, however, many people seemed to be drifting away from the old moorings of piety. And if the Lord had allowed great Puritan and Quaker merchants of Boston and Philadelphia to prosper, the haunting fear arose that the devil had lured them into the vain pursuit of worldly gain. Intellectually the educated classes were falling into deism and skepticism. And out along the fringes of settlement there grew up a great backwater of the unchurched, people who had no minister to preach or administer sacraments or perform marriages, who fell into a primitive and sinful life, little different from the heathens who lurked in the woods. One Anglican divine called the backcountry preachers in the Carolinas "ignorant wretches, who cannot write." A Baptist communion service was to him like "A Gang of frantic Lunatics broke out of Bedlam." By the 1730s the sense of falling-away had prepared the time for a revival of faith, the Great Awakening, a wave of evangelism that within a few years swept the colonies from one end to the other, America's first mass movement.

In 1734–1735 a rehearsal for the event came in a remarkable spiritual refreshing that occurred in the congregation of Jonathan Edwards, a Congregationalist minister of Northampton in western Massachusetts. Edwards's vivid descriptions of the torments of hell and the delights of heaven inspired his congregants. About the same time William Tennant arrived from Ulster and set up a "Log College" for the education of ministers to serve the Scotch-Irish Presbyterians around Philadelphia. The Log College specialized in turning out zealots who scorned complacency and proclaimed the need for revival.

The catalyst of the Great Awakening, however, was a twenty-seven-year-old Anglican minister, George Whitefield, whose reputation as an evangelist preceded him to the colonies. In the autumn of 1739 he arrived in Philadelphia, and late in that year preached to crowds of as many as 6,000 around Philadelphia. After visiting in Georgia, he made a triumphal procession northward to New England, drawing great crowds and releasing "Gales of Heavenly Wind" that dispersed sparks throughout the colonies. Young and magnetic, possessed of a golden voice, a dramatic actor in the pulpit who impersonated the agonies of the damned and the joys of the regenerate, he swept audiences with his unparalleled eloquence. Even the skeptical Ben Franklin, who went to see the show in Philadelphia, found himself so carried away that he emptied his pockets into the collection plate —perhaps the ultimate tribute to Whitefield's persuasiveness. The core of his message was the need to experience a "new birth"—the need for a sudden and emotional moment of conversion and salvation—and the dangers of an unconverted ministry which had not experienced such rebirth.

Imitators sprang up everywhere, some of whom carried the language and histrionics to extremes. Graduates of the Log College denounced the "pharisaical preachers" who were themselves unconverted. The Rev. James Davenport, an itinerant Congregationalist of New England, set about stomping on the devil. The churched and unchurched flocked to the meetings, and seized of the terror and ecstasy, groveled on the floor or lay unconscious on the benches, to the chagrin of more decorous churchgoers. One never knew, the more traditional clergymen warned, whence came these enthusiasms—perhaps they were delusions sent by the Evil One to discredit the true faith.

PIETY AND REASON Everywhere the Awakening brought splits, especially in the more Calvinistic churches. Presbyterians divided into the "Old Side" and "New Side"; Congregationalists into "Old Lights" and "New Lights." New England would never be the same. The more traditional clergy found its position being

*The Rev. Jonathan Edwards awoke many congregants to their plight in sermons such as "Sinners in the Hands of an Angry God."*

undermined as church members chose sides and either dismissed their ministers or deserted them. Many of the "New Lights" went over to the Baptists, and others flocked to Presbyterian or, later, Methodist groups, which in turn divided and subdivided into new sects.

New England Puritanism was now finally divided. The precarious tension in which the Founders had held the elements of piety and reason was now sundered. Jonathan Edwards, the great theologian of the Awakening and perhaps of all American history, led the movement toward piety and justified the emotional extravagance of the conversion experience as something beyond the ability of the human frame to stand without physical manifestation. But he was an intellectual, himself never given to those excesses nor to the histrionics of Whitefield. Edwards's magnum opus was an elaborate theological reconciliation of Calvinism and the Enlightenment: *Of Freedom of the Will* (1754). Indeed, one curious and paradoxical sequel of the revival was the growth in New England churches of the "New Divinity," which spun out the ramifications of the revival theology in such recondite fashion that whole congregations sometimes got lost in the fog. In consequence New England was infiltrated more and more by Baptists, Presbyterians, Anglicans, and other denominations, but the revival tradition which had its chief theologian in New England scored its most lasting victories along the chaotic frontiers of the middle and southern colonies.

In the more sedate churches of Boston, moreover, the principle of reason got the upper hand in a reaction against the excesses of revival emotion. Bostonian ministers like Charles

Chauncey and Jonathan Mayhew assumed the lead in preaching a doctrine of rationality. They reexamined Calvinist theology and found it too forbidding and irrational that men could be forever damned by predestination. The rationality of Newton and Locke, the idea of natural law, crept more and more into their sermons. They were already on the road to Unitarianism and Universalism.

In reaction to taunts that the "born-again" ministers lacked learning, the Awakening gave rise to the denominational colleges that became so characteristic of American higher education. The three colleges already in existence had grown earlier from religious motives: Harvard, founded in 1636, because the Puritans dreaded "to leave an illiterate ministry to the church when our present ministers shall lie in the dust"; the College of William and Mary, in 1693, to serve James Blair's purpose of strengthening the Anglican ministry; and Yale College, in 1701, set up to serve the Puritans of Connecticut, who felt that Harvard was drifting from the strictest orthodoxy. The Presbyterian College of New Jersey, later Princeton University, was founded in 1746 as successor to William Tennent's Log College. In close succession came King's College (1754) in New York, later Columbia University, an Anglican institution; the College of Rhode Island (1764), later Brown University, Baptist; Queen's College (1766), later Rutgers, Dutch Reformed; and Congregationalist Dartmouth (1769), the outgrowth of an earlier school for Indians. Among the colonial colleges only the University of Pennsylvania, founded as the Philadelphia Academy in 1754, arose from a secular impulse.

The Great Awakening, like the Enlightenment, set in motion currents that still flow in American life. It implanted permanently in American culture the evangelical principle and the endemic style of revivalism. The movement weakened the status of the old-fashioned clergy and encouraged believers to exercise their own judgment, and thereby weakened habits of deference generally. By encouraging the proliferation of denominations it heightened the need for toleration of dissent. But in some respects the counterpoint between the Awakening and the Enlightenment, between the principles of piety and reason, led by different roads to similar ends. Both emphasized the power and right of the individual to judge things for himself, and both aroused millennial hopes that America would become the promised land in which men might attain to the perfection of piety or reason, if not of both.

FURTHER READING

Scholarship in colonial social history is as active as in any historical field. Much recent scholarship is summarized in *Colonial British America* (1984), edited by Jack P. Greene and J. R. Pole. Other useful works include Carl Bridenbaugh's *Early Americans* (1981), Richard F. Hofstadter's *America at 1750: A Social Portrait* (1971),° and James A. Henretta's *The Evolution of American Society, 1700–1815* (1973). Timothy H. Breen's *Puritans and Adventurers: Change and Persistence in Early America* (1980) concentrates on Virginia and Massachusetts. Gary B. Nash examines early race relations in *Red, White, and Black* (2nd ed., 1982).

Until recently Puritan communities received the bulk of scholarly attention. Studies of the New England town include Darrett B. Rutman's *Winthrop's Boston: Portrait of a Puritan Town, 1630–1649* (1965);° Sumner C. Powell's *Puritan Village* (1963),° on the origins and social structure of Sudbury, Massachusetts; Kenneth A. Lockridge's *A New England Town: The First One Hundred Years* (2nd ed., 1985),° which looks at the relationship of family and authority in Dedham, Massachusetts; Philip J. Greven, Jr.'s *Four Generations: Population, Land, and Family in Colonial Andover, Massachusetts* (1970),° a similar study; and Paul S. Boyer and Stephen Nissenbaum's *Salem Possessed* (1974), which connects the notorious witch trials to changes in community structure and economic base. Of the most recent works, see also Christine Heyrman, *Commerce and Culture* (1984)° and Stephen Innes's *Labor in a New Land: Economy and Society in Seventeenth-Century Springfield* (1983).°

Broader in cultural interpretation are Richard S. Dunn's *Puritans and Yankees: The Winthrop Dynasty of New England, 1630–1717* (1962) and E. Digby Baltzell's *Puritan Boston and Quaker Philadelphia* (1979). For an interdisciplinary approach, see John Demos's *Entertaining Satan: Witchcraft and the Culture of Early New England* (1982).° Discussions of women in the New England colonies can be found in Laurel Ulrich's *Good Wives* (1982),° Joy Buel and Richard Buel's *The Way of Duty* (1984),° and Carol Karlsen's *The Devil in the Shape of a Woman: Witchcraft in Colonial New England* (1987). John Demos describes family life in *A Little Commonwealth: Family Life in Plymouth Colony* (1970).°

Later generations of these colonists are described in Michael Zuckerman's *Peaceable Kingdoms: Massachusetts Towns in the Eighteenth Century* (1970), Edward M. Cook, Jr.'s *The Fathers of the Towns: Leadership and Community Structure in Eighteenth Century New England* (1976), Robert A. Gross's *The Minutemen and Their World* (1976),° and Richard L. Bushman's *From Puritan to Yankee: Character and Social Order in Connecticut* (1976).°

For the social history of the southern colonies, see Peter Wood's *Black*

°These books are available in paperback editions.

*Majority: Negroes in Colonial South Carolina from 1670 through the Stono Rebellion* (1975).° Darrett B. Rutman and Anita H. Rutman's *A Place in Time* (2 vols., 1984)° is a community study of life in a Virginia county. Julia Cherry Spruill's *Women's Life and Work in the Southern Colonies* (1938) is the classic in that field. Family life along the Chesapeake is described in Gloria L. Main's *Tobacco Colony* (1982) and Daniel B. Smith's *Inside the Great House* (1980).

The best southern social history is intertwined with analysis of the origins of slavery. Begin with Edmund S. Morgan's *American Slavery, American Freedom: The Ordeal of Colonial Virginia* (1975),° which examines Virginia's social structure, environment, and labor patterns in a biracial context. More specific on the racial nature of the origins of slavery are Winthrop D. Jordan's *White over Black: American Attitudes toward the Negro* (1986)° and David B. Davis's *The Problem of Slavery in Western Culture* (1966).° Philip D. Curtin's *The Atlantic Slave Trade* (1969)° is a valuable quantitative study; Daniel P. Mannix's *Black Cargoes* (1960) is a more descriptive account of the same subject. Black viewpoints are presented in two books on Virginia: Gerald W. Mullin's *Flight and Rebellion: Slave Resistance in Eighteenth Century Virginia* (1972)° and Timothy H. Breen and Stephen Innes's *"Myne Owne Ground": Race and Freedom on Virginia's Eastern Shore, 1640–1676* (1980).° David W. Galenson's *White Servitude in Colonial America* (1981) looks at the indentured labor force.

For patterns of trade during the colonial period, see Gary M. Walton and James F. Shepherd, *The Economic Rise of Early America* (1979). Paul G. E. Clemens's *The Atlantic Economy and Colonial Maryland's Eastern Shore* (1980) is an instructive case study. Trade connections with Europe are stressed in Ralph Davis's *The Rise of the Atlantic Economies* (1973) and Jacob M. Price's *France and the Chesapeake* (2 vols., 1973). The interaction of trade and politics in America's first cities is the subject of Gary B. Nash's *The Urban Crucible* (1979).°

For the role of Indians and settlers in shaping the New World's ecology, see William Cronon's fine work *Changes in the Land* (1983)° and Albert E. Cowdrey's *This Land, This South* (1983). A number of books discuss colonial land policy. James T. Lemon explores land-holding patterns in one county of Pennsylvania in *The Best Poor Man's Country* (1972).° The impact of land pressures and tenancy is explored in Sung Bok Kim's *Landlord and Tenant in Colonial New York* (1978). The political implications of land pressure are documented in Charles S. Grant's *Democracy in the Connecticut Frontier Town of Kent* (1961)° and Patricia U. Bonomi's *A Factious People* (1971),° a study of New York.

Henry F. May's *The Enlightenment in America* (1976) examines intellectual trends in eighteenth-century America. Lawrence A. Cremin's *American Education: The Colonial Experience, 1607–1783* (1970) surveys educational developments, and Joseph J. Ellis's *The New England Mind in Transition: Samuel Johnson of Connecticut, 1696–1772* (1973) examines the role religion played in the development of higher education.

A concise introduction to the events and repercussions of the Great Awakening is J. M. Bumsted and John E. Van de Wetering's *What Must I Do to Be Saved?* (1976), but see also Edwin S. Gaustaad's *The Great Awakening in New England* (1957) and Patricia U. Bonomi's *Under the Cope of Heaven* (1986). The political impact of the new religious enthusiasm is shown in Rhys Isaac's *The Transformation of Virginia, 1740–1790* (1982).° Perry Miller analyzes Jonathan Edwards's theological influence in *Jonathan Edwards* (1949);° Patricia J. Tracy's *Jonathan Edwards, Pastor* (1980)° stresses the Northampton minister's relations to his community.

# 4 ✦

## THE IMPERIAL PERSPECTIVE

In 1757, 150 years after the Jamestown beginnings, Edmund Burke rightly observed: "The settlement of our colonies was never pursued upon any regular plan; but they were formed, grew, and flourished, as accidents, the nature of the climate, or the dispositions of private men happened to operate." For the better part of the seventeenth century England remained too disrupted by the running struggle between Parliament and the Stuart kings ever to perfect either a colonial policy or effective agencies of imperial control. Intervention in colonial affairs was a matter of makeshift commissions, experimentation, and "muddling through," a practice at which the British had a certain skill and not a little luck. Slowly a plan of colonial administration emerged after the Restoration and began to fall into a semblance of order under William III, but even so it fell short of coherence and efficiency.

### English Administration of the Colonies

Throughout the colonial period the king stood as the source of legal authority in America, and land titles derived ultimately from royal grants. All colonies except Georgia got charters from the king before the Glorious Revolution, and thus before the crown lost supremacy to Parliament. The colonies therefore continued to stand as "dependencies of the crown" and the important colonial officials held office at the pleasure of the crown. And Georgia's status conformed to the established practice.

The king exercised his power through the Privy Council, a body of some thirty to forty advisors appointed by and responsible solely to him, and this group became the first agency of colonial supervision. Its actions were commonly designated actions of the King-in-Council. But the Privy Council was too large and too burdened to keep track of the details. So in 1634 Charles I entrusted colonial affairs to eleven of its members, the Lords Commissioners for Plantations in General, with William Laud, archbishop of Canterbury, as its head. The Laud Commission grew in part out of the troubles following the dissolution of the Virginia Company and in part out of Laud's design to impose political and religious conformity on New England. In 1638 his commission ordered Massachusetts to return its charter and answer charges that colonial officials had violated the provisions. Sir Ferdinando Gorges, appointed governor-general of New England, planned to subdue the region by force if necessary, and might have nipped the Puritan experiment in the bud except for the troubles at home which prevented further action.

The Civil War in England, which lasted from 1641 to 1649, was followed by Cromwell's Puritan Commonwealth and Protectorate, and both gave the colonies a respite from efforts at royal control. A Parliamentary Council for the Colonies, set up in 1643, and various Parliamentary committees and commissions, never exercised more than a shadowy power. Puritan New England was naturally well disposed toward the Parliamentary cause, and in 1652 Cromwell dispatched an expedition to the colonies which forced the West Indies, Virginia, and Maryland to recognize Parliamentary authority but left them otherwise unmolested.

THE MERCANTILE SYSTEM   If Cromwell showed little concern for colonial administration, he had a lively concern for colonial trade, which had fallen largely to Dutch shipping during the upheavals in England. Therefore in 1651 Parliament adopted a Navigation Act which excluded nearly all foreign shipping from the English and colonial trade. It required that all goods imported into England or the colonies must arrive on English ships and that the majority of the crew must be English. In all cases colonial ships and crews qualified as English. The act excepted European goods, which might come in ships of the country which produced the goods, but only from the place of origin or the port from which they were usually shipped.

On economic policy, if nothing else, Restoration England under Charles II took its cue from Cromwell. The New Parliament quickly adopted and then elaborated the mercantile system he had effected. The mercantile system, or mercantilism, became in the seventeenth and eighteenth centuries the operative

*This view of eighteenth-century Boston shows the importance of shipping and its regulation in the colonies, especially Massachusetts Bay.*

theory of all major European powers. In a world of national rivalries, the reasoning went, power and wealth went hand in hand. To be strong a state should be wealthy. To be wealthy it should enlarge its stores of gold and silver. To get and keep gold and silver the state should limit foreign imports and preserve a favorable balance of trade. And to accomplish these things the state should encourage manufacturers, through subsidies and monopolies if need be; it should develop and protect its own shipping; and it should make use of colonies as sources of raw materials and markets for its own finished goods. Mercantilists held that the total of the world's wealth, as reflected in the total stock of gold and silver, remained essentially fixed. All that changed was the nation's share of that stock.

The Navigation Act of 1660 amounted to a reenactment of Cromwell's act of 1651, but with a new twist. Ships' crews now had to be not half but three-quarters English, and certain enumerated articles were to be shipped only to England or other

English colonies. These were things needed but not produced by the mother country. The list included at first tobacco, cotton, indigo, ginger, rustick and other dyewoods, and sugar. Later the enumeration expanded to include, among other things, rice, naval stores, hemp, masts and yards, copper ores, and furs. Not only did England (and the colonies) become the only outlet for these colonial exports, but three years later the Navigation Act of 1663 sought to make England the funnel through which all colonial imports had to be routed. The act was sometimes called the Staple Act because it made England the staple (market or trade center) for all goods sent to the colonies. Everything shipped from Europe to America had to stop off in England, be landed, and pay duty before reshipment. There were few exceptions: only servants, horses, and provisions from Scotland; wine from Madeira and the Azores; and salt for fisheries. A third major act rounded out the trade system. The Navigation Act of 1673 (sometimes called the Plantation Duty Act) required that every captain loading enumerated articles give bond to land them in England, or if they were destined for another colony, that he pay on the spot a duty roughly equal to that paid in England.

ENFORCING THE NAVIGATION ACTS    The Navigation Acts set forth policy in provisions that were simple and straightforward enough. And they supplied a convenient rationale for a colonial system: to serve the economic needs of the mother country. Their enforcement in scattered colonies was something else again, however. In the age of Charles II a bureaucracy of colonial administrators began to emerge, but it took shape slowly, and in fact never achieved full delineation. After the Restoration of 1660, supervision of colonial affairs fell once again to the Privy Council, or rather to a succession of its committees. In 1675, however, Charles II introduced some order into the chaos when he designated certain privy councilors the Lords of Trade and Plantations, whose name reflects the overall importance of economic factors. The Lords of Trade were to make the colonies abide by the mercantile system and to seek out ways to make them more profitable to England and the crown. To these ends they served as the clearinghouse for all colonial affairs, building up an archive and a bureaucracy of colonial experts. By advice rather than by direct authority, at least in theory, they named governors, wrote or reviewed the governors' instructions, and handled all reports and correspondence dealing with colonial affairs.

Within five years of the Plantation Duty Act, between 1673 and 1678, collectors of customs appeared in all the colonies and

*England's Navigation Acts affected merchants such as Andrew Brimmer, who imported goods from India and Europe to sell in Boston.*

shortly thereafter a surveyor-general of the customs in the American colonies was named. The most notorious of these, insofar as the colonists were concerned, was Edward Randolph, the first man to make an entire career in the colonial service and the nemesis of insubordinate colonials for a quarter century. Randolph arrived at Boston in June 1676 to demand that Massachusetts answer complaints that it had usurped the proprietary rights in New Hampshire and Maine. More was at stake, however. Since the Restoration the colony had ignored gentle hints that it bring its practices more in line with fundamental elements of the Restoration compromise. Massachusetts had accepted the formality of conducting judicial proceedings in the king's name. It dragged its heels, however, on adopting an Oath of Allegiance, repealing laws counter to English law, allowing use of the Anglican *Book of Common Prayer,* or making property instead of church membership the voting test. The expanding commercial interests of New England counseled prudence and accommodation, but the Puritan leaders harbored a persistent distrust of Stuart designs on their Wilderness Zion.

After a brief stay, Randolph submitted a report bristling with hostility. The Bay Colony had not only ignored royal wishes, it had tolerated violations of the Navigation Acts, refused appeals from its courts to the Privy Council, and had operated a mint in defiance of the king's prerogative. Massachusetts officials had told him, Randolph reported, "that the legislative power is and abides in them solely to act and make laws by virtue" of their charter. Continuing intransigence from Massachusetts led the Lords of Trade to begin legal proceedings against the colonial charter in 1678, although the issue remained in legal snarls for another six years. Meanwhile Randolph returned in 1680 to establish the royal colony of New Hampshire, then set up shop as the king's collector of customs in Boston, whence he dispatched repeated accounts of colonial recalcitrance. Eventually, in 1684, the Lords of Trade won a court decision which annulled the charter of Massachusetts. The Puritan utopia was fast becoming a lost cause.

THE DOMINION OF NEW ENGLAND  Temporarily, its government was placed in the hands of a special royal commission. Then in 1685 Charles II died, to be succeeded by his brother, the duke of York, as James II, the first Catholic sovereign since the death of Queen Mary in 1558. Plans long maturing in the Lords of Trade for a general reorganization of colonial government fitted very well the autocratic notions of James II, who asserted his prerogatives more forcefully than his brother and seemed to have less fear that he might have "to embark on his travels" again. The new king therefore readily approved a proposal to create a Dominion of New England and to place under its sway all colonies down through New Jersey. Something of the sort might have been in store for Pennsylvania and the southern colonies as well if the reign of James II had lasted longer. In that case the English colonies might have found themselves on the same tight leash as the colonies of Spain or France.

The Dominion was to have a government named altogether by royal authority, a governor and council who would rule without any assembly at all. The royal governor, Sir Edmond Andros, who had already served briefly as governor of New York, appeared in Boston in 1686 to establish his rule, which he soon extended over Connecticut and Rhode Island, and in 1688 over New York and the Jerseys. Andros was a soldier, accustomed to taking—and giving—orders. He seems to have been honest, efficient, and loyal to the crown, but totally without tact in circumstances which called for the utmost diplomacy—the uprooting of long-established institutions in the face of popular hostility.

A rising resentment greeted his measures, especially in Massachusetts. Taxation was now levied without the consent of the General Court, and when residents of Ipswich, led by the Rev.

John Wise, protested against taxation without representation, a number of them were imprisoned or fined. Andros suppressed town governments. He proceeded to establish enforcement of the trade laws and subdue smuggling with the help of Edward Randolph, that omnipresent servant of the crown. And most ominous of all, Andros and his lieutenants took over one of the Puritan churches for Anglican worship in Boston. Puritan leaders believed, with good reason, that he proposed to break their power and authority. Andros might have found a moderate party in the prosperous and comfortable merchants, concerned for their businesses perhaps more than for their religion, but his enforcement of the Navigation Acts enraged them as well.

In any case the Dominion was scarcely established before word came of the Glorious Revolution of 1688–1689. James II in the homeland, like Andros in New England, had aroused resentment by arbitrary measures and, what was more, by openly parading his Catholic faith. The birth of a son, sure to be reared a Catholic, put the opposition on notice that James's system would survive him. The Catholic son, rather than the Protestant daughters, Mary and Anne, would be next in line for the throne. Parliamentary leaders, their patience exhausted, invited Mary and her husband, the Dutch stadtholder, William of Orange, to assume the throne as joint monarchs. James, his support dwindling, fled the country.

*King James II (1685–1688).*

THE GLORIOUS REVOLUTION IN AMERICA   When news reached Boston that William had landed in England, Boston staged its own Glorious Revolution, as bloodless as that in England. Andros and his councilors were arrested and Massachusetts reverted to its former government. In rapid sequence the other colonies that had been absorbed into the Dominion followed suit. All were permitted to retain their former status except Massachusetts and Plymouth which, after some delay, were united under a new charter in 1691 as the royal colony of Massachusetts Bay. In New York, however, events took a different course. There, Andros's lieutenant-governor was deposed by a group led by a German immigrant, Jacob Leisler, who assumed the office of governor pending word from England. When ambiguous letters came from William authorizing a continuation of the government, Leisler believed that they gave him power, and for two years he kept the province under his control with the support of the militia. Finally, in 1691, the king appointed a new governor, but an unfortunate tragedy ensued, which turned upon misunderstandings and poor timing. Leisler hesitated to turn over authority, and on this pretext the new governor charged him with treason. Leisler and his son-in-law were hanged on May 16, 1691. Four years too late, in 1695, Parliament exonerated them of all charges. For years to come Leisler and anti-Leisler factions would poison the political atmosphere of New York.

No effort was made to resume the disastrous policy of the Dominion of New England, but the crown salvaged a remnant of that design by bringing more colonies under royal control through the appointment of governors. Massachusetts was first, in 1691. New York kept the status of royal colony it had achieved upon the accession of James II. In Maryland after the Glorious Revolution, a local rebellion against the Catholic proprietor gave the occasion to appoint a royal governor in 1691. Maryland, however, reverted to proprietary status in 1715 after the fourth Lord Baltimore became Anglican. Pennsylvania had an even briefer career as a royal colony, 1692–1694, before reverting to Penn's proprietorship. New Jersey became royal in 1702, South Carolina in 1719, North Carolina in 1729, and Georgia in 1752.

The Glorious Revolution had significant long-term effects on American history in that the Bill of Rights and Toleration Act, passed in England in 1689 (see page 48), influenced attitudes and the course of events in the colonies even though they were not legally binding there. And what was more significant for the future, the overthrow of James II set an example and a precedent for revolution against the monarch. In defense of that action the

*John Locke, author of the influential*
Two Treatises on Government
*(1690).*

philosopher John Locke published his *Two Treatises on Government* (1690), which had an enormous impact on political thought
in the colonies. The *First Treatise* refuted theories of the divine
right of kings. The more important *Second Treatise* set forth
Locke's contract theory of government. People were endowed
with certain natural rights, the reasoning went—basically the
rights to life, liberty, and property. Without government, in a
state of nature, such rights went without safeguard. Hence people came together and by mutual agreement established governments among themselves. Kings were parties to such agreements, and bound by them. When they violated the rights of the
people, therefore, the people had the right—in extreme cases
—to overthrow the monarch and change their government.

The idea that governments emerged by contract out of a primitive state of nature is of course hypothetical, not an account of
actual events. What Locke was seeking, as the historian Carl
Becker put it, was "not the historical origin, but the rational justification, of government." But in the American experience governments had actually grown out of contractual arrangements
such as Locke described: for instance, the Mayflower Compact,
the Cambridge Agreement, the Fundamental Orders of Connecticut. The royal charters themselves constituted a sort of
contract between the crown and the settlers. Locke's writings in
any case appealed to colonial readers, and his philosophy probably had more influence in America than in England. It might be
an overstatement, but a plausible case can be made that Locke's
theories established a tradition, a consensus within which American institutions operated by almost universal consent, at least
from the time of independence and to some extent before.

AN EMERGING COLONIAL SYSTEM  The accession of William and
Mary brought on a restatement and refinement of the existing
Navigation Acts and administrative system. In 1696 two developments created at last the semblance, and to some degree the
reality, of a coherent colonial system. First, the Navigation Act of
1696, "An Act for preventing Frauds and regulating Abuses in
the Plantation Trade," confirmed the existing restrictions on colonial trade but added certain provisions designed to tighten the
enforcement: a special oath by colonial governors to enforce the
Navigation Acts, the use by customs officials of "writs of assistance" (general search warrants which did not have to specify
the place to be searched), and the trial of accused violators in Admiralty Courts, which Edward Randolph had recommended because juries habitually refused to convict. Admiralty cases were
decided by judges whom the governors appointed.

Second, also in 1696, by executive order William III created
the Board of Trade to take the place of the Lords of Trade and
Plantations. The new board included eight privy councilors and
additional members from outside. Colonial officials were required to report to the board, and its archives constitute the largest single collection of materials on colonial relations with the
mother country from that time on.

The functions of the Board of Trade, which continued through
the remainder of the colonial period, were again primarily advice and policy-making. Since its main purpose was to make the
colonies serve the mother country's economy, the board investi-
gated the enforcement of the Navigation Acts, and recommended ways to limit colonial manufactures and to encourage
the production of raw materials. At the board's behest Parliament enacted a bounty for the production of naval stores, ship
timber, masts, and hemp. Similar payments were later extended
to encourage the production of rice, indigo, and other commodities. The board examined all colonial laws and made recommendations for their disallowance by the crown. In all, 8,563 colonial
laws eventually were examined and 469 of them were actually
disallowed. The board also made recommendations for official
appointments in the colonies.

SALUTARY NEGLECT  From 1696 to 1725 the board met regularly
and worked vigorously toward subjecting the colonies to a more
efficient royal control. After 1725, however, the board entered a
period of relative inactivity. After the death of Queen Anne the
throne went in turn to the Hanoverian monarchs, George I
(1714–1727) and George II (1727–1760), German princes who
were next in the Protestant line of succession by virtue of de-

scent from James I. Under these monarchs, the cabinet (a kind of executive committee in the Privy Council) emerged as the central agency of administration. Robert Walpole, as first minister (1721–1742), deliberately followed a policy of not rocking the boat lest he endanger the Hanoverian settlement, a policy which Edmund Burke later called "a wise and salutary neglect." The board became chiefly an agency of political patronage, studded with officials who took an interest mainly in their salaries. The board experienced a revival after 1748, and from 1752 to 1761 actually had power to appoint colonial governors, but generally decreased in significance thereafter.

In the course of the eighteenth century other administrative agencies and offices became involved in certain aspects of colonial government. The most important of these was the secretary of state for the Southern Department. After about 1700 he was the chief administrative official with supervision over colonial matters. Royal governors were responsible to him for colonial defense and military matters. At the same time the secretary had responsibility for Mediterranean affairs and relations with France and Spain, which of course often involved colonial matters—and colonial wars. But the secretary was too busy with diplomacy to give sustained attention to the colonies, and indeed none showed much energy, except the elder William Pitt, who held the office while also first minister. The duke of Newcastle, who served (1727–1748) during the decades of salutary neglect, was, according to a contemporary, a man who lost an hour in the morning every day and spent the rest of the day running around trying to find it.

## Colonial Governments

Government within the colonies, like colonial policy, evolved without plan, but colonial governments at least had in the English government a body of precedent to fall back on. In broad outline the governor, council, and assembly in each colony corresponded to the king, lords, and commons of the mother country. At the outset all the colonies except Georgia had begun as projects of trading companies or feudal proprietors holding charters from the crown, but eight colonies eventually relinquished or forfeited their charters and became royal provinces. In these the governor was named by the crown. In Maryland, Pennsylvania, and Delaware the governor remained the choice of a proprietor, although each had an interim period of royal government. Connecticut and Rhode Island were the last of the corporate colonies; they elected their own governors to the end of the colonial period. In the corporate and proprietary colonies, and in Massachusetts, the charter served as a rough equivalent to a written constitution. Rhode Island and Connecticut in fact kept their charters as state constitutions after independence. Over the years certain anomalies appeared, as colonial governments diverged from that of England. On the one hand the governors retained powers and prerogatives which the king had lost in the course of the seventeenth century. On the other hand the assemblies acquired powers, particularly with respect to appointments, which Parliament had yet to gain.

POWERS OF THE GOVERNORS   The crown never vetoed acts of Parliament after 1707, but the colonial governors still held an absolute veto and the crown could disallow (in effect, veto) colonial legislation on advice of the Board of Trade. With respect to the assembly, the governor still had the power to determine when and where it would meet, to prorogue (adjourn or recess) sessions, and to dissolve the assembly for new elections or to postpone elections indefinitely at his pleasure. The crown, however, was pledged to summon Parliament every three tyears and call elections at least every seven, and could not prorogue sessions. The royal or proprietary governor, moreover, nominated for life appointment the members of his council (except in Massachusetts, where they were chosen by the lower house) and the council functioned as both the upper house of the legislature and the highest court of appeal within the colony. With respect to the judiciary, in all but the charter colonies the governor still held the prerogative of creating courts and of naming and dismissing judges, powers explicitly denied the king in England. The assemblies, however, generally made good their claim that courts should be created only by legislative authority, although the crown repeatedly disallowed acts to grant judges life tenure in order to make them more independent.

As chief executive the governor could appoint and remove officials, command the militia and naval forces, grant pardons, and as his commission often put it, "execute everything which doth and of right ought to belong to the governor"—which might cover a multitude of powers. In these things his authority resembled the crown's, for the king still exercised executive authority and had the power generally to name all administrative officials. This often served as a powerful means of royal influence in Parliament, since the king could appoint members or their friends to lucrative offices. And while the arrangement might seem to another age a breeding ground for corruption or tyranny, it was

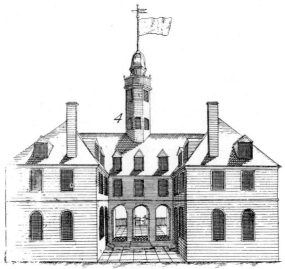

*The Virginia Capitol, depicted here in the eighteenth century, "was an architectural representation of the British constitution as adapted for use in the colonies." In the upper story of one wing sat the King's Council, the upper legislative house. Immediately below, the governor and council sat as the General Court, the highest judicial body. Across from the Court sat the House of Burgesses, the body of elected representatives.*

often viewed in the eighteenth century as a stabilizing influence, especially by the king's friends. But it was an influence less and less available to the governors. On the one hand colonial assemblies nibbled away at their power of appointment; on the other hand the authorities in England more and more drew the control of colonial patronage into their own hands.

POWERS OF THE ASSEMBLIES   Unlike the governor and council, appointed by an outside authority, either king or proprietor, the colonial assembly was elected. Whether called the House of Burgesses (Virginia), of Delegates (Maryland), of Representatives (Massachusetts), or simply Assembly, the lower houses were chosen by popular vote in counties or towns or, in South Carolina, parishes. Although the English Toleration Act of 1689 did not apply to the colonies, religious tests for voting tended to be abandoned thereafter (the Massachusetts charter of 1691 so specified) and the chief restriction left was a property qualification, based on the notion that only men who held a "stake in society" could vote responsibly. Yet the property qualifications generally set low hurdles in the way of potential voters. Property holding was widespread, and a greater proportion of the population could vote in the colonies than anywhere else in the world of the eighteenth century.

Women, children, and blacks were excluded—as a matter of course—and continued to be excluded for the most part into the twentieth century, but the qualifications excluded few adult free white males. Virginia, which at one time permitted all freemen to vote, in the eighteenth century required only the ownership of 25 acres of improved land or 100 acres of wild land (available from speculators for a total of about £3), or the ownership of a "house" and part of a lot in town, the ownership of a £50 estate, or a service in a five-year apprenticeship in Williamsburg or Norfolk. Qualifications for membership in the assembly ran somewhat higher, and in an age which still held to habits of deference, officeholders tended to come from the more well-to-do —a phenomenon not unknown today—but there were exceptions. One unsympathetic colonist observed in 1744 that the New Jersey Assembly "was chiefly composed of mechanicks and ignorant wretches; obstinate to the last degree." In any case, gentlefolk who ran for office found then as now that a certain respect for the sensibilities of humbler men paid off in votes.

Colonial politics of the eighteenth century recapitulated English politics of the seventeenth. In one case there had been a tug of war between king and Parliament, ending with the supremacy of Parliament, confirmed by the Glorious Revolution. In the other case colonial governors were still trying to wield prerogatives which the king had lost in England, a fact of which the assemblies were fully informed. They also knew all the arguments for the "rights" and "liberties" of the people and their legislative bodies, and against the dangers of despotic power. A further anomaly in the situation was the undefined relationship of the colonies to Parliament. The colonies had been created by authority of the crown and their governmental connections ran to the crown, yet Parliament on occasion passed laws which applied to the colonies, and were tacitly accepted by the colonies.

By the early eighteenth century the assemblies, like Parliament, held two important strands of power—and they were perfectly aware of the parallel. First, they held the power of the purse string in their right to vote on taxes and expenditures. Second, they held the power to initiate legislation and not merely, as in the early history of some colonies, the right to act on proposals from the governor and council. These powers they used to pull other strands of power into their hands when the chance presented itself. Governors were held on a tight leash by the assembly's control of salaries, his and others, which were voted annually and sometimes not at all. Only in four southern colonies did governors have some freedom from this coercion. In South Carolina and Georgia they were paid from crown funds, and in North Carolina and Virginia out of permanent funds drawn from colonial revenues: an export tax of two pence per hogshead of tobacco in Virginia and the more uncertain returns from quit-rents in North Carolina.

But even in those colonies the assemblies controlled other appropriations, and by refusing to vote money forced governors to yield up parts of the traditional executive powers. Assemblies, because they controlled finance, demanded and often got the right to name tax collectors and treasurers. Then they stretched the claim to cover public printers, Indian agents, supervisors of public works and services, and other officers of the government. By specifying how appropriations should be spent they played an important role even in military affairs and Indian relations, as well as other matters. Indeed in the choice of certain administrative officers they pushed their power beyond that of Parliament in England, where appointment remained a crown prerogative.

All through the eighteenth century the assemblies expanded their power and influence, sometimes in conflict with the governors, sometimes in harmony with them, and often in the course of routine business, passing laws and setting precedents the collective significance of which neither they nor the imperial authorities fully recognized. Once established, however, these laws and practices became fixed principles, parts of the "constitution" of the colonies. Self-government became first a habit, then a "right."

### TROUBLED NEIGHBORS

The English invasion of North America would have been a different story, maybe a shorter and simpler story, had the English first encountered a stronger Indian presence. Instead, in the coastal regions they found scattered and mutually hostile groups which were subject to a policy of divide and conquer. Some, perhaps most, of the Indians guessed at the settlers' purpose quickly, like those, Powhatan told John Smith, "who do inform me your coming is not for trade, but to invade my people and

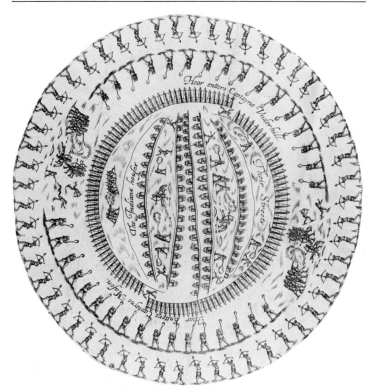

*The Puritans and their Indian allies, the Narragansetts, mount a ferocious attack on the Pequots at Mystic, Connecticut (1637).*

possess my country." But tempted by trade goods or the promise of alliances, or intimidated by a show of force, they let things drift until the English were too entrenched to push back into the sea.

During the first half of the seventeenth century the most severe tests of the colonists' will to prevail came with the Virginia troubles of 1622 and 1644 and Connecticut's Pequot War of 1637. In both colonies Indian leaders had a desperate sense of last-chance efforts to save their lands; in both they failed. For the Pequots the result was virtual extermination—Puritan savagery in killing and enslaving Pequots was so great as to offend even the Englishmen's allies, the Narrangansetts, who had never seen such total war. In Virginia, according to a census taken in 1669, only eleven of twenty-eight tribes described by John Smith in

1608, and only about 2,000 of some 30,000 Indians, remained in the colony. Indian resistance had been broken for the time.

Then in the mid-1670s both New England and Virginia went through another time of troubles: an Indian war in New England, and in Virginia a civil war masquerading as an Indian war. For a long time in New England the Indian fur trade had contributed to peaceful relations, but the growth of settlement and the decline of the animal population was reducing the eastern tribes to relative poverty. Colonial government encroached repeatedly, forcing Indians to acknowledge English laws and customs, including Puritan codes of behavior, and to permit English arbitration of disputes. On occasion colonial justice imposed fines, whippings, and worse. At the same time Puritan missionaries reached out to the tribes and one, John Eliot, translated the Bible into the Algonquian language. By 1675 several thousand converts had settled in special "praying Indian" towns.

CONFLICTS WITH THE INDIANS    The spark that set New England ablaze was struck by the murder of one Sassamon, a "praying Indian" who had attended Harvard, later strayed from the faith while serving King Philip of the Wampanoag tribe, and then returned to the Christian fold. King Philip (Metacomet to the Wampanoags) was a son of Chief Massasoit, who had early befriended the Pilgrims. Now King Philip became their enemy when Plymouth Colony tried and executed three Wampanoags for the murder of Sassamon. In retaliation the tribesmen attacked the settlement of Swansea on the fringes of Plymouth.

Thus began "King Philip's War," which the land-hungry leaders of Connecticut and Massachusetts quickly enlarged by attacking the peaceful Narragansetts at their chief refuge in Rhode Island—a massacre the Rhode Island authorities were helpless to prevent. From June to December 1675 Indian attacks ravaged the interior of Massachusetts and Plymouth, and guerrilla war continued through 1676. At one point Indians put to the torch a town within twenty miles of Boston. Finally, depleted supplies and the casualty toll wore down Indian resistance. In August Philip himself was tracked down and killed. The rest was a matter of mopping up pockets of resistance, but fighting went on until 1678 in New Hampshire and Maine. New England might have perished if King Philip had formed an effective coalition, but his failure to do so was typical of Indian wars. Indians who survived the slaughter had to submit to colonial authority and accept confinement to ever-dwindling plots of land.

BACON'S REBELLION  The news from New England added to tensions among settlers strung out into the interior of Virginia, and contributed to the tangled events thereafter known as Bacon's Rebellion. Virginia had the makings of trouble at the time in depressed tobacco prices and in the crowds of freed servants who found the best lands already taken. Just before the outbreak, Gov. William Berkeley had remarked in a letter: "How miserable that man is that Governes a People where six parts of seaven at least are Poore, Endebted, Discontented and Armed." And, he might have added, greedily eyeing lands north of the York River guaranteed to the Chesapeake tribes in 1646.

The discontent turned to violence in July 1675 when a petty squabble between a frontier planter and the Doeg Indians on the Potomac led to the murder of the planter's herdsman, and in turn to retaliation by frontiersmen who killed ten or more Doegs and, by mistake, fourteen Susquehannocks. Soon a force of Virginia and Maryland militiamen laid siege to the Susquehannocks, murdered in cold blood five chieftains who came out for a parley, and then let the enraged survivors get away to take their revenge on frontier settlements. Scattered attacks continued on down to the James, where Nathaniel Bacon's overseer was killed.

By then, their revenge accomplished, the Susquehannocks pulled back. What followed had less to do with a state of war than with a state of hysteria. Berkeley proposed that the assembly support a series of forts along the frontier. But that would not slake the thirst for revenge—nor would it open new lands to set-

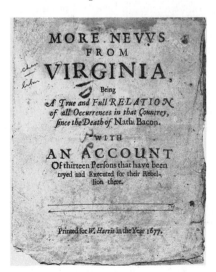

*A 1677 report to Londoners of Bacon's Rebellion.*

MORE NEVVS FROM VIRGINIA,

Being

A True and Full RELATION of all Occurrences in that Countrey, since the Death of Nath. Bacon.

WITH

AN ACCOUNT

Of thirteen Persons that have been tryed and Executed for their Rebellion there.

Printed for W. Harris in the Year 1677.

tlement. Besides, it would be expensive. Some thought Berkeley was out to preserve a profitable fur trade, although there is no evidence that he was deeply involved personally. At this point in May 1676 Nathaniel Bacon assumed command of a group of frontier vigilantes. The twenty-nine-year-old Bacon had been in Virginia only two years, but he had been well set up by an English father relieved to get him out of the country. He was also a member of the governor's council. Later historians would praise him as "The Torchbearer of the Revolution" and leader of the first struggle of common man versus aristocrat, of frontier versus tidewater. These things, to a degree, he was. The rebellion he led was a battle of the "outs" versus the "ins," in defiance of duly constituted authority. It drew into its ranks numbers of indentured servants, poor freemen, and even slaves, who held out to the end. But Bacon was also the spoiled son of a rich squire who had a talent for trouble, who led punitive expeditions against peaceful Indians, and whose main achievement was to persuade the friendly Occaneechees to destroy a small band of Susquehannocks just before he treacherously slaughtered the Occaneechees themselves.

After that the events had little to do with Indians, except some friendly Pamunkeys, who also felt Bacon's wrath. Bacon was early in the line of one hoary American tradition. Indians, he said, were "all alike," and therefore apparently fair game. Hoping to rally support against Bacon, Governor Berkeley called elections for a new assembly, which met in June 1676. Bacon was elected, had a brief reconciliation with Berkeley, and rejoined the governor's council, but failed to get the commission he demanded as commander of the militia. He fled Jamestown, aroused his own men to intimidate Berkeley, and eventually attacked and burned Jamestown in September, only to fall ill and die of swamp fever a month later.

Berkeley quickly regained control and subdued the leaderless rebels. In the process he hanged twenty-three of them and confiscated several estates. In London, report had it, King Charles II said: "That old fool has hang'd more men in that naked Country than he had done for the Murther of his Father." For such severity the king recalled Berkeley to England and a royal commission made treaties of pacification with the remaining Indians, some of whose descendants still live on tiny reservations guaranteed them in 1677. The fighting, however, opened new lands to the colonists and confirmed the power of an inner group of established landholders who sat in the council.

The battles of the mid-1670s may also have marked a turning point in colonial history. One historian, Stephen Saunders

Webb, has noted that these battles cost proportionately more casualties than any other American war. They devastated the frontier regions of both New England and Virginia, which took years to recover. The colonies involved were so weakened, Webb argues, that 1676 actually marked the "End of American Independence." A British military force was dispatched to Virginia and the crown thenceforth worked to tighten the system of imperial administration over colonies that had long been pretty much left alone.

The Middle Colonies, untouched by the troubles, flourished, along with the Iroquois Confederation, which had long conspired to weaken the rival Algonquin tribes to the east. The more powerful tribes all along had been back in the interior: mainly the Iroquois Confederation of the Hudson and Mohawk Valleys, the Cherokees of the southern Appalachians and foothills, and the Creeks farther south. By the time settlement pressed against these lands the English beachheads had grown into a formidable power. But the Indians had grown in strength too. Thrust suddenly by European traders into the Iron Age, they had adopted into their cultures firearms, steel knives, iron utensils, and alchohol, and into their populations survivors of the eastern tribes. During the first century of settlement they had also learned the subtleties of international diplomacy, weighing the relative advantages of English, French, and Spanish trade goods and alliances, and learning to play the balance-of-power games that the great powers played in Europe.

NEW FRANCE   Permanent French settlement in the New World began the year after the Jamestown landing, far away in Québec where the explorer Samuel de Champlain unfurled the *fleur-de-lis* on the shores of the St. Lawrence River in 1608, and three years later at Port Royal, Acadia (later Nova Scotia). While Acadia remained a remote outpost, New France expanded well beyond Québec, from which Champlain pushed his explorations up the great river and into the Great Lakes as far as Lake Huron, and southward to the lake which still bears his name. There, in 1609, he joined a band of Huron and Ottawa allies in a fateful encounter, fired his arquebus into the ranks of their Iroquois foes, and kindled an enmity which pursued New France to the end. Shortly afterward the Iroquois had a more friendly meeting with Henry Hudson near Albany, and soon acquired their own firearms from Dutch, and later English, traders. Thenceforth the Iroquois stood as a buffer against any French designs to move toward the English of the Middle Colonies, and as a constant menace on the flank of the French waterways to the interior.

Until his death in 1653 Champlain governed New France under a sequence of trading companies, the last being the Company of a Hundred Associates which the king's minister, Cardinal Richlieu, formed in 1627 of men chosen for their close loyalty to the crown. The charter imposed a fatal weakness that hobbled New France to its end. The company won a profitable monopoly of the fur trade, but it had to limit the population to French Catholics. Neither the enterprising, seafaring Huguenots of coastal France nor foreigners of any faith could populate the country. Great seigneurial land grants went to persons who promised to bring settlers to work the land under feudal tenure. The colony therefore remained a scattered patchwork of dependent peasants, Jesuit missionaries, priests, soldiers, officials, and *coureurs de bois* (literally, runners of the woods) who ranged the interior in quest of furs.

In 1663 King Louis XIV and his chief minister, Jean Baptiste Colbert, changed New France into a royal colony and pursued a plan of consolidation and stabilization. Colbert dispatched new settlers, including shiploads of young women to lure disbanded soldiers and *coureurs de bois* into settled matrimony. He sent out tools and animals for farmers, nets for fishermen, and tried to make New France self-sufficient in foodstuffs. The population grew from about 4,000 in 1665 to about 15,000 in 1690. Still, Louis de Baude, Count Frontenac, who was governor from 1672 to 1682 and 1689 to 1698, held to a grand vision of French empire in the interior, spurring on the fur traders and missionaries and converting their outposts into military stations in the wilderness: Fort Detroit appeared at the far end of Lake Erie, Fort Michilimackinac at the far end of Lake Huron.

FRENCH LOUISIANA From the Great Lakes explorers moved southward. In 1673 Louis Joliet and Père Marquette, a Jesuit priest, ventured into Lake Michigan, up the Fox River from Green Bay, then down the Wisconsin to the Mississippi, and on as far as the Arkansas River. Satisfied that the great river flowed to the Gulf of Mexico, they turned back for fear of meeting with Spaniards. Nine years later Robert Cavalier, sieur de la Salle, went all the way to the Gulf and named the country Louisiana after the king.

Settlement of the Louisiana country finally began in 1699 when Pierre le Moyne, sieur d'Iberville, landed a colony at Biloxi, Mississippi. The main settlement then moved to Mobile Bay and in 1710 to the present site of Mobile, Alabama. For nearly half a century the chief mover and shaker in Louisiana was Jean Baptiste le Moyne, sieur de Bienville, a younger brother of

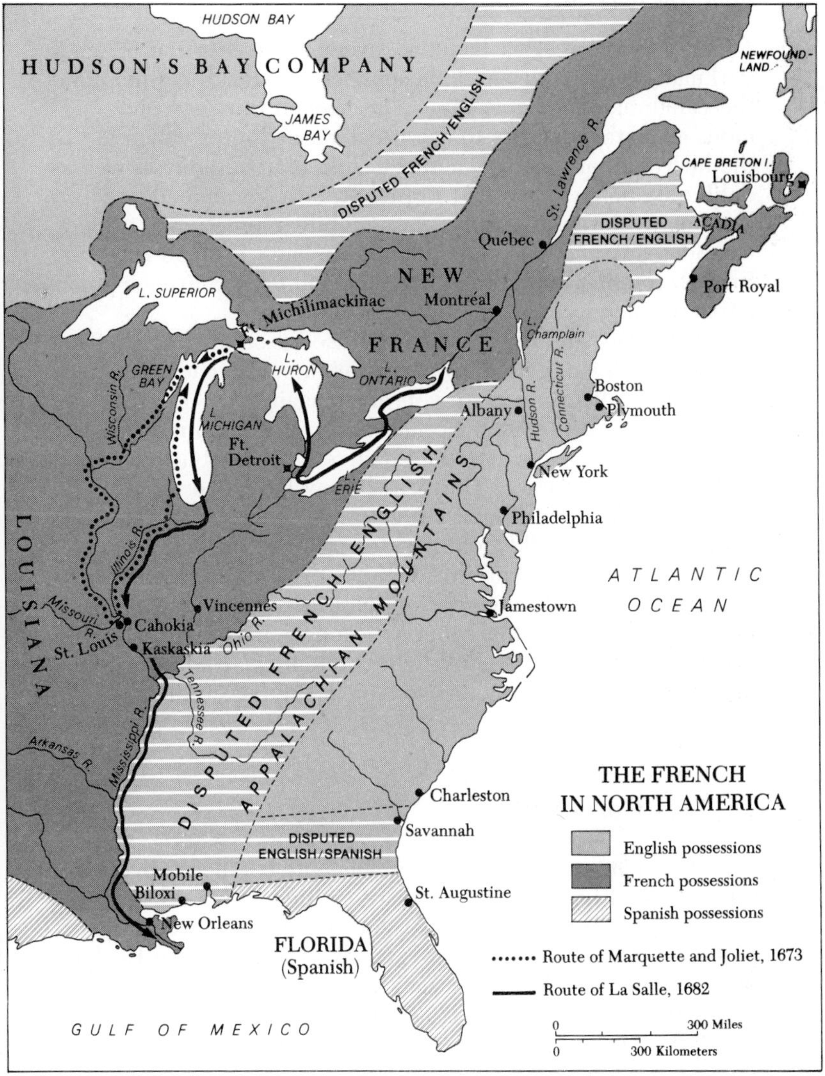
HUDSON BAY
HUDSON'S BAY COMPANY
JAMES BAY
NEWFOUNDLAND
DISPUTED FRENCH/ENGLISH
St. Lawrence R.
CAPE BRETON I.
Louisbourg
ACADIA
DISPUTED FRENCH/ENGLISH
Québec
Port Royal
NEW FRANCE
Montréal
L. SUPERIOR
Ft. Michilimackinac
L. Champlain
GREEN BAY
L. HURON
L. ONTARIO
Wisconsin R.
L. MICHIGAN
Ft. Detroit
L. ERIE
Albany
Hudson R.
Connecticut R.
Boston
Plymouth
New York
Philadelphia
LOUISIANA
Illinois R.
DISPUTED FRENCH/ENGLISH
APPALACHIAN MOUNTAINS
ATLANTIC OCEAN
Missouri R.
Vincennes
Cahokia
St. Louis
Kaskaskia
Ohio R.
Jamestown
Tennessee R.
Arkansas R.
Mississippi R.
Charleston
Savannah
DISPUTED ENGLISH/SPANISH
Mobile
Biloxi
New Orleans
St. Augustine
FLORIDA (Spanish)
GULF OF MEXICO
English possessions
French possessions
Spanish possessions
Route of Marquette and Joliet, 1673
Route of La Salle, 1682
0 300 Miles
0 300 Kilometers
THE FRENCH IN NORTH AMERICA

d'Iberville. Bienville arrived with the first settlers in 1699, when he was only eighteen, and left the colony for the last time in 1743, when he was sixty-two. Sometimes called the "Father of Louisiana," he served periodically as governor or acting governor and always as advisor during those years. In 1718 he founded New Orleans, which shortly thereafter became the capital. Louisiana, first a proprietary and then a corporate colony, became a royal province in 1732.

"France in America had two heads," the historian Francis Parkman wrote, "one amid the snows of Canada, the other amid the canebrakes of Louisiana." The French thus had one enormous advantage: access to the great water routes which led to the heartland of the continent. Because of geography as well as deliberate policy, however, French America remained largely a howling wilderness traversed by a mobile population of traders, trappers, missionaries—and, mainly, Indians. In 1750 when the English colonies numbered about 1.5 million, the French population was no more than 80,000.

Yet in some ways the French had the edge on the British. They offered European goods in return for furs, encroached far less upon Indian lands, and so won allies against the English who came to possess the land. French governors could mobilize for action without any worry about quarreling assemblies or ethnic and religious diversity. The British may have had the edge in population, but their separate colonies often worked at cross purposes. The Middle Colonies, for instance, protected by the Iroquois buffer, could afford to ignore the French threat—for a long time at least. Whenever conflict threatened, colonial assemblies seized the time to extract new concessions from their governors. Colonial merchants, who built up a trade supplying foodstuffs to the French, persisted in smuggling supplies even in wartime.

## THE COLONIAL WARS

Colonists of the two nations came into conflict from the beginning of settlement. The Acadians clashed with Englishmen in Maine, across the Bay of Fundy, and suspiciously eyed the *Bostonnais.* Only a thin stretch of woods separated New England from Québec and Montréal, and an English force briefly occupied Québec from 1629 to 1632. Between New York and Québec, Lake Champlain supplied an easy water route for invasion in either direction, but the Iroquois stood athwart the path. Farther south the mountainous wilderness widened into an almost impenetrable buffer. On the northernmost flank, the isolated Hudson Bay Company offered British competition for the fur trade of the interior, and both countries laid claim to Newfoundland. On the southernmost flank, the British and French jockeyed for position in the Caribbean sugar islands.

But for most of the seventeenth century the two continental empires developed in relative isolation from each other, and for most of that century the homelands remained at peace with each other. After the Restoration, Charles II and James II pursued a policy of friendship with Louis XIV—and secretly took pensions from His Catholic Majesty. The Glorious Revolution of 1688, however, worked an abrupt reversal in English diplomacy. William III, the new king, as stadtholder of the Dutch Republic, had fought a running conflict against the ambitions of Louis XIV in the Netherlands and the German Palatinate. His ascent to the throne brought England almost immediately into a Grand Coalition against Louis in the War of the League of Augsburg, sometimes called the War of the Palatinate and known in the colonies simply as King William's War (1689–1697). This was the first of four great European and intercolonial wars over the next sixty-four years: the War of the Spanish Succession (Queen Anne's War, 1701–1713), the War of the Austrian Succession (King George's War, 1744–1748), and the Seven Years' War (the French and Indian War, which lasted nine years in America, 1754–1763). In all except the last, which the historian Lawrence Gipson called the "Great War for Empire," the battles in America were but a sideshow to greater battles in Europe, where British policy riveted on keeping a balance of power against the French. The alliances shifted from one fight to the next, but Britain and France were pitted against each other every time.

Thus for much of the century after the great Indian conflicts of 1676 the colonies were embroiled in wars and rumors of wars. Some war contractors got rich, but the effect on much of the population was devastating. New England, especially Massachusetts, suffered probably more than the rest for it was closest to the centers of French population. One historian estimated that about 8 percent of the men of the Bay Colony fell in 1745–1746 alone. One result was that Boston's population stagnated through the eighteenth century while Philadelphia and New York continued to grow. Boston had to struggle to support a large population of indigent widows and orphans. Eventually, the economic impact of the wars left increasing numbers of the indigent in New England.

KING WILLIAM'S WAR    In King William's War scattered fighting occurred in the Hudson Bay posts, most of which fell to the French, and in Newfoundland, which fell to a French force under d'Iberville, soon to be the founder of Louisiana. The French aroused their Indian allies to join in scattered raids along the northern frontier, beginning with a surprise attack which destroyed Schenectady, New York, in the winter of 1690. In Mas-

## EUROPEAN WARS ALSO FOUGHT IN NORTH AMERICA

| European War | Major Participants | Colonial War | Dates | Treaty |
|---|---|---|---|---|
| War of the League of Augsburg (War of the Palatinate) | England and Holland *vs.* France | King William's War | 1689–1697 | Treaty of Ryswick (1697) |
| War of the Spanish Succession | England, Austria, and Holland *vs.* France and Spain | Queen Anne's War | 1701–1713 | Peace of Utrecht (1713) |
| War of the Austrian Succession | England and Austria *vs.* France and Prussia | King George's War | 1744–1748 | Treaty of Aix-la-Chapelle (1748) |
| Seven Years' War | England and Prussia *vs.* France, Spain, Austria, and Russia | French and Indian War | 1754–1763 | Peace of Paris (1763) |

sachusetts, Capt. William Phips, about to become the first royal governor, got up an expedition which took Acadia. New York's acting governor, Jacob Leisler, laid plans with agents from Massachusetts, Plymouth, and Connecticut for concerted attacks on Québec. But a New England expedition via the St. Lawrence bogged down in futility when the New York contingent failed to show up. The New York expedition via Lake Champlain never got under way for want of support from other colonies or the Iroquois allies, who refused to move in the face of a smallpox outbreak. The war finally degenerated into a series of frontier raids and ended ingloriously with the Treaty of Ryswick (1697), which returned the colonies to their prewar status.

QUEEN ANNE'S WAR   But fighting resumed only five years later. In 1700 the Spanish crown passed to Philip of Anjou, grandson of Louis XIV and potential heir to the throne of France. Against this new threat to the balance of power—a possible union of France and Spain—William III organized a new alliance, but the War of the Spanish Succession began after his death and was known to the colonists as Queen Anne's War. This time the Iroquois, tired of fighting the French, remained neutral and the French respected New York's immunity from attack. The brunt of this war therefore fell on New England and South Carolina. In Charleston the colonists raised a force which destroyed the Spanish town of St. Augustine in 1702, but withdrew after failing to reduce its fort of San Marcos. In 1706 Charleston fought off a counterattack, and for the next seven years a sporadic border war raged between South Carolina and Florida, the English with Yemassee and Creek allies taking the war nearly to St. Augustine.

South Carolina's Indian allies in fact constituted most of a force which responded to North Carolina's call for help in the Tuscarora War (1711–1713). The Tuscaroras, a numerous people who had long led a settled life in the Tidewater, suddenly found their lands invaded in 1709 by German and Swiss settlers. The war began when the Tuscaroras fell upon the new settlements with devastating effect. It ended with even more devastating effect when slave merchants of South Carolina mobilized their Indian allies to kill about 1,000 Tuscaroras and enslave another 700. The survivors found refuge in the north, where they became the sixth nation of the Iroquois Confederacy.

In New England the exposed frontier from Maine to Massachusetts suffered repeated raids during Queen Anne's War. In the winter of 1704 the villages of Wells, Maine, and Deerfield, Massachusetts, were sacked by French and Indian forces, and the settlers were either slaughtered or taken on desperate marches through the snow to captivity among the Indians or the Canadians. Once again Port Royal fell in 1710, and once again a British force moved upriver toward Québec, but gave up the effort after eight transports ran aground. Things went better for the English in the Caribbean, where they took control of St. Christopher, and in Europe, where John Churchill, duke of Marlborough, led allied forces to brilliant victories in Germany and the Netherlands.

In the complex Peace of Utrecht (1713) England accepted Philip of Anjou as king of Spain, but only with the proviso that he renounce the throne of France. England also took from Spain the stronghold of Gibraltar and the island of Minorca. Louis XIV gave up most of his claims in Germany and recognized British title to the Hudson Bay, Newfoundland, Acadia (now Nova Scotia), and St. Christopher, as well as the British claim to sovereignty over the Iroquois (nobody consulted the Iroquois). The French renounced any claim to special privileges in the commerce of Spanish or Portuguese America. Spain agreed not to transfer any of its American territory to a third party, and granted to the British the *asiento,* a contract for supplying Spanish America 4,800 slaves annually over a period of thirty years and the right to send one ship a year to the great fair at Porto Bello in Panama—concessions which opened the door for British smuggling, a practice which grew into a major cause of friction and, eventually, of renewed warfare.

In the South the frontier flared up once more shortly after the war. The former Yemassee and Creek allies, outraged by the continuing advance of settlement, attacked the Charleston colony. The Yemassee War of 1715 was the southern equivalent of King Philip's War in New England, a desperate struggle which threatened the colony's very existence. Once again, however, the Indians were unable to present a united front. The Cherokees remained neutral for the sake of their fur trade and the defeated Yemassees retired into Florida or mingled with the Creeks who retreated beyond the Chattahoochee River, leaving open the country in which the new colony of Georgia appeared eighteen years later.

KING GEORGE'S WAR    In the generation of nominal peace after Queen Anne's War the European colonists jockeyed for position, intrigued with the Indians, and set up fortified posts at strategic points in the wilderness. The third great international war began in 1739 with a preliminary bout between England and Spain, called the War of Jenkins' Ear in honor of an English seaman who lost an ear to a Spanish *guardacosta* and exhibited the shriveled member as part of a campaign to arouse London against Spain's rudeness to smugglers. The war began with a great British disaster, a grand expedition against Porto Bello in Panama, for which thousands of colonists volunteered and in which many died of yellow fever. One of the survivors, Lawrence Washington of Virginia, memorialized the event by naming his estate Mount Vernon, after the ill-starred but popular admiral in command. Along the southern frontier the new colony of Georgia, less than a decade old, now served its purpose as a military buffer. Gen. James Oglethorpe staged a raid on St. Augustine and later fought off Spanish counterattacks, but Charleston remained secure.

In 1744 France entered the war, which merged with another general European conflict, the War of the Austrian Succession, or King George's War in the colonies. Once again border raids flared along the northern frontier. Gov. William Shirley of Massachusetts mounted an expedition under William Pepperell of Maine, a prominent merchant with a genius for management, and reduced the French Fort Louisbourg on Cape Breton after a lengthy siege. It was a costly conquest, but the war ended in stalemate. In the Treaty of Aix-la-Chapelle (1748) the British exchanged Louisbourg for Madras, which the French had taken in India.

In the brief respite that followed before the climactic struggle, the focus of attention turned to the Ohio Valley. French penetration had moved westward by the Great Lakes and down the Mississippi, but the Ohio, with short portages from Lake Erie to its headwaters, would make a shorter connecting link for French America. But during the 1740s fur traders from Virginia and Pennsylvania had begun to penetrate into that disputed region. Some 300 of them operated in the country by 1749, according to the French commander of Fort Miami, south of Detroit. Not far behind were the Pennsylvania and Virginia land speculators. "The English," one French agent warned the Indians, "are much less anxious to take away your peltries than to become masters of your lands." Pennsylvania, because of the Quaker impulse, gave less support to its speculators than Virginia, which laid claim to the country through a quirk in the 1609 charter which described boundaries leading "westward and Northwestward" to the South Sea; it was their northern boundary, they said, which led "Northwestward." Virginians had organized several land companies, most conspicuously the Ohio Company, to which the king granted 200,000 acres along the upper Ohio in 1749, with a promise of 300,000 more. The company forthwith dispatched a Pennsylvania frontiersman to seek out the best lands.

The French resolved to act before the British advance became a dagger pointed at the continental heartland. In 1749 French scouts proceeded down the Allegheny and Ohio Rivers to spy out the land, woo the Indians, and bury leaden plates with inscriptions stating the French claim. Magic engravings hardly made the soil French, but in 1753 a new governor, the Marquis Duquesne, arrived in Canada and set about making good on the claim with a chain of forts in the region.

THE FRENCH AND INDIAN WAR   When news of these trespasses reached Williamsburg, Governor Dinwiddie sent out an emissary to warn off the French. An ambitious young adjutant-general of the Virginia militia, Maj. George Washington, whose older brothers owned a part of the Ohio Company, volunteered for the mission. With a few companions, Washington made his way to Fort LeBoeuf and returned with a polite but firm refusal. Dinwiddie then sent one Capt. William Trent with a small force to erect a fort at the strategic fork where the Allegheny and Monongahela Rivers meet to form the great Ohio. No sooner was Trent started than a larger French force appeared, ousted him, and proceeded to build Fort Duquesne on the same strategic site. Meanwhile Washington had been organizing a force of volunteers, and in the spring of 1754 he went out with an advance guard and a few Indian allies. Near Great Meadows they fell into a skirmish with a French detachment. Who fired first is unknown, and perhaps irrelevant, but it marked the first bloodshed of a long—and finally decisive—war which reached far beyond America. Washington fell back with his prisoners and hastily constructed a stockade, Fort Necessity, which soon fell under siege by a larger force from Fort Duquesne. On July 4, 1754, Washington surrendered and was permitted to withdraw with his survivors. With that disaster in the backwoods a great world war had begun, but Washington came out of it with his reputation intact—and he was world-famous at the age of twenty-two.

Back in London the Board of Trade already had taken notice of the growing conflict in the backwoods, and had called a meeting in Albany, New York, of commissioners from all the colonies as far south as Maryland to confer on precautions. The Albany Congress (June 19 to July 10, 1754), which was sitting when the first shots sounded at Great Meadows, ended with little accomplished. The delegates conferred with Iroquois chieftains and

*Benjamin Franklin's symbol of the need to unite
the colonies against the French in 1754 would
become popular again twenty years later, when the
colonies faced a different threat.*

sent them away loaded with gifts in return for some half-hearted
promises of support. The congress is remembered mainly for the
Plan of Union worked out by a committee under Benjamin
Franklin and adopted by unanimous vote of the commissioners.
The plan called for a chief executive, a kind of supreme governor
to be called the President-General of the United Colonies, appointed and supported by the crown, and a supreme assembly
called the Grand Council, with forty-eight members chosen by
the colonial assemblies. This federal body would oversee matters
of defense, Indian relations, and trade and settlement in the
west, and would levy taxes to support its programs.

It must have been a good plan, Franklin reasoned, since the assemblies thought it gave too much power to the crown and the
crown thought it gave too much to the colonies. At any rate the
assemblies either rejected or ignored the plan, and the Board of
Trade never had to face a decision. Only two substantive results
came out of the congress. Its idea of a supreme commander for
British forces in America was adopted, as was its advice that a
New Yorker who was a friend of the Iroquois be made British superintendent of the northern Indians.

In London the government decided to force a showdown in
America, but things went badly at first. In 1755 the British fleet
failed to halt the landing of reinforcements in Canada, but scored
one success in Nova Scotia with the capture of Fort Beauséjour
and then buttressed their hold on the country by expelling most

of its French population. Some 5,000–7,000 Acadians who refused to take an oath of allegiance were scattered through the colonies from Maine to Georgia. Impoverished and homeless, many of them desperately found their way to French Louisiana, where they became the "Cajuns" (a corruption of "Acadians") whose descendants still preserve the language of Molière along the remote bayous.

The backwoods, however, became the scene of one British disaster after another over the next three years. In 1755 a new British commander-in-chief, Gen. Edward Braddock, arrived in Virginia with two regiments of regulars. With the addition of some colonial troops, including Washington as a volunteer staff officer, Braddock hacked a road through the wildernesses from the upper Potomac to the vicinity of Fort Duquesne. Hauling heavy artillery to invest the French fort, along with a wagon train of supplies, Braddock's men achieved a great feat of military logistics, and were on the verge of success when, seven miles from

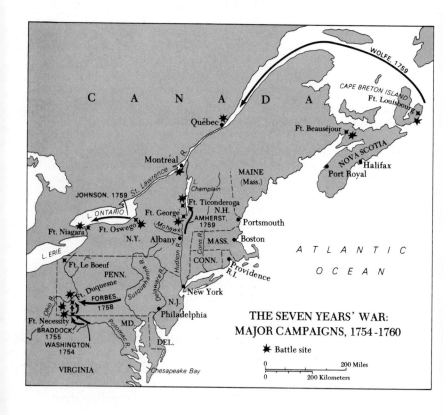

THE SEVEN YEARS' WAR:
MAJOR CAMPAIGNS, 1754-1760

✳ Battle site

Fort Duquesne, the surrounding woods suddenly came alive with Indians and Frenchmen in Indian costume. Beset on three sides by concealed enemies, the wagon train broke down in blind panic and the British forces retreated in disarray, abandoning most of their artillery and supplies. Braddock lost his life in the encounter, and his second in command retreated with the remaining British regulars to the safety of Philadelphia.

After that, Indian attacks flared up along the frontier. Among the first to seize the chance to even old scores were the Delawares, once befriended by Penn but later cheated out of their lands by his successors. Scotch-Irish and German refugees fled eastward as the Delawares burned, killed, and pillaged in their settlements. Pennsylvania Quakers, stubbornly pacifist, insisted that compromise was still possible, but finally, under British pressure, bent their principles only to the extent of withdrawing from the Pennsylvania Assembly and letting the war party vote the money and measures needed to fight back.

A WORLD WAR  For two years war raged along the frontier without becoming the cause of war in Europe. In 1756, however, the colonial war merged with what became the Seven Year's War in Europe. There, Empress Maria Theresa of Austria, still brooding over the loss of territory in the last conflict, worked a diplomatic revolution by bringing Austria's old enemy France, as well as Russia, into an alliance against Frederick the Great of Prussia. Britain, ever mindful of the European balance of power, now deserted Austria to ally with Frederick. The onset of war brought into office a new British government with the popular and eloquent William Pitt as war minister. Pitt's ability and assurance ("I know that I can save England and no one else can") instilled confidence at home and abroad. The grandson of "Diamond" Pitt, once governor of Madras in India, Pitt committed his main forces to the war for overseas empire while providing subsidies to Frederick, who was desperately fighting off attacks from three sides.

Soon the force of British sea power began to cut off French reinforcements and supplies to the New World—and the trading goods with which they bought Indian allies. Pitt improved the British forces, gave command to young men of ability, and carried the battle to the enemy. In 1758 the tides began to turn. Fort Louisbourg fell. The Iroquois, sensing the turn of fortunes, pressed their dependents, the Delawares, to call off the frontier attacks. Gen. John Forbes organized a new expedition against Fort Duquesne and pushed a new wilderness road directly west-

ward from Philadelphia. Having learned caution from Braddock's defeat, he kept his scouts alert on his flanks and
proceeded slowly to set up supply posts along the way and send
out emissaries to court the Indians. When he finally reached his
goal, the outnumbered French chose discretion as the better
part of valor, burned Fort Duquesne, and deserted the scene. On
the site arose the British Fort Pitt, and later the city of Pitts-
burgh.

In 1759 the war reached its climax in a three-pronged offensive against Canada, along what had become the classic invasion
routes: via Niagara, Lake Champlain, and up the St. Lawrence.
British forces were earmarked for each. On the Niagara expedition British forces were joined by a group of Iroquois under a
New Yorker, William Johnson, who commanded the capture of
Fort Niagara after the British commander fell in the field. The
loss of Niagara virtually cut the French lifeline to the interior.
On Lake Champlain Gen. Jeffrey Amherst took Fort George and
Fort Ticonderoga, then paused to refortify and await reinforce-
ments for an advance northward.

Meanwhile the most decisive battle was shaping up at Québec.
Commanding the expedition up the St. Lawrence was Gen.
James Wolfe, a dedicated professional soldier who at the age of
thirty-three had already spent more than half his life in military
service. For two months Wolfe probed the defenses of Québec,
seemingly impregnable on its fortified heights and defended by
alert forces under Gen. Louis Joseph de Montcalm. Finally

*The decisive British assault on Québec (1759).*

The Death of Wolfe, *painted in 1770 by the American artist Benjamin West.*

Wolfe found a path by which he led his force up the cliffs behind Québec under cover of darkness on the night of September 12–13 and emerged on the Plains of Abraham, athwart the main roads to the city. There, in a set battle more like the warfare of Europe than the skirmishes of the backwoods, his forces waited out the French advance until it was within close range, then loosed a simultaneous volley followed by one more which devastated the French ranks—and ended French power in North America for all time. News of the victory was clouded by the word of Wolfe's—and Montcalm's—death in the battle, but it reached London along with similar reports from India, where Gen. Robert Clive of the East Indian Company had reduced French outposts one by one, secured Bengal, and established the base for an expanding British control of India. It was the *annus mirabilis,* the miraculous year 1759, during which Great Britain secured an empire on which the sun never set.

The war dragged on until 1763, but the rest was a process of mopping up. Montréal, the last important vestige of French control in North America, fell in 1760, and while the frontiers remained active with the scattered Indian raids, the game was up for the French. In the South, where little significant action had occurred, the Cherokee nation flared into belated hostility, but Jeffrey Amherst, dispatched now to Charleston, moved toward the mountains with a force of British regulars and provincials and broke Cherokee resistance in 1761. In the North, just as peace was signed, a chieftain of the Ottawas, Pontiac, conspired to confederate all the Indians of the frontier and launched a series of attacks that were not finally suppressed until 1764, after the backwoods had been ablaze for ten years.

Just six weeks after the capture of Montréal in 1760 King George II died and his grandson ascended to the throne as George III. George III resolved to take a more active role than his Hanoverian predecessors. Under the guidance of his former tutor and chief advisor, the Scottish earl of Bute, he resolved to seek peace and forced Pitt out of office. Pitt had wanted to carry

NORTH AMERICA, 1713

the fight to the enemy by declaring war on Spain before the French could bring that other Bourbon monarchy into the conflict. He was forestalled, but Spain belatedly entered in 1761 and during the next year met the same fate as the French: in 1762 British forces took Manila in the Philippines and Havana in Cuba.

THE PEACE OF PARIS   An end to war came in the Peace of Paris of 1763. Bute as first minister accepted a more generous settlement than Pitt was willing to do, but nevertheless it was a peace that ended French power in North America and all but eliminated it in India, where France retained only a few trading posts. In America Britain took all French North American possessions east

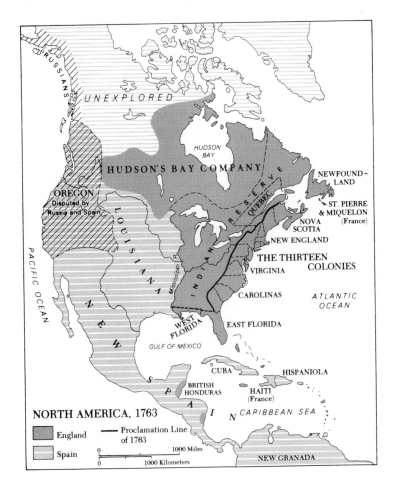

NORTH AMERICA, 1763

of the Mississippi River, and all of Spanish Florida, east and west. France ceded Louisiana to Spain in compensation for Spain's loss of the Floridas. This left France no territory on the continent of North America. In the West Indies France gave up Tobago, Dominica, Grenada, and St. Vincent. British power reigned supreme over North America east of the Mississippi, but a fatal irony would pursue the British victory.

In gaining Canada the British government put in motion a train of events that would end twenty years later with the loss of all the rest of British North America. France, humiliated in 1763, thirsted for revenge. In London, Benjamin Franklin, agent for the colony of Pennsylvania (1764–1775), found the French minister inordinately curious about America and suspected him of wanting to ignite the coals of controversy. Less than three years after Franklin left London, and only fifteen years after the conquest of New France, he would be in Paris arranging an alliance on behalf of Britain's rebellious colonists.

## FURTHER READING

For greater depth on the structure of colonial government and the global context of colonial development, see the fourth volume of Charles M. Andrews's *The Colonial Period of American History* (4 vols., 1934–1938), which details the evolution of the British imperial system. Lawrence H. Gipson's *The British Empire before the American Revolution* (15 vols., 1936–1970) places the British colonies in the context of European imperial politics.

The economics motivating colonial policies are covered in John J. McCusker and Russell R. Menard's *The Economy of British America, 1607–1789* (1985).° The problems of colonial customs administration are explored in Michael G. Hall's *Edward Randolph and the American Colonies, 1676–1703* (1960).

The effect of imperial policies on colonial politics is covered in Alison G. Olson's *Anglo-American Politics, 1600–1775* (1973), which traces the rise of party-like factions on the provincial level. Jack P. Greene's *The Quest for Power* (1963)° describes the politics of the southern colonies, and Richard P. Johnson's *Adjustment to Empire* (1981) examines New England. A good account of Bacon's Rebellion is found in Wilcomb E. Washburn's *The Governor and the Rebel* (1957). The Andros crisis and related topics are treated in David S. Lovejoy's *The Glorious Revolution in America* (1972) and Jack M. Sosin's *English America and the Revolution of 1688* (1982). Stephen S. Webb's *The Governors-General* (1979) argues that the crown was more concerned with military administration than with commercial regulation, and Webb's *1676: The End of Ameri-*

° These books are available in paperback editions.

*can Independence* (1984)° shows how Bacon's Rebellion and the Indian wars undermined the autonomy of colonial governments.

Historians of early Indian wars have taken several different approaches to the topic. Richard Slotkin's *Regeneration through Violence* (1973)° links the colonists' treatment of Indians with later national character traits. Alden T. Vaughan defends the treatment of Indians by the Puritans in *New England Frontier: Puritans and Indians, 1620–1675* (1965).° Francis Jennings counters this thesis in *The Invasion of America* (1975).° See also Jennings's *The Ambiguous Iroquois Empire* (1984).°

A good introduction to the imperial phase of the colonial conflicts is Howard H. Peckham's *The Colonial Wars, 1689–1762* (1964). More analytical is Douglas Leach's *Arms for Empire: A Military History of the British Colonies in North America* (1973). Fred Anderson's *A People's Army* (1984)° is a social history of the Seven Years' War. See also the majestic works of Francis Parkman, *France and England in North America;* the most rewarding single part is *Montcalm and Wolfe* (2 vols., 1884).

# 5

## FROM EMPIRE TO INDEPENDENCE

### THE HERITAGE OF WAR

Seldom if ever since the days of Elizabeth had England thrilled with such pride as in the closing years of the Great War for Empire. The victories of 1759 had delivered Canada and India to British control. In 1760 the young and vigorous George III ascended to the throne and confirmed once again the Hanoverian succession. Even the downfall of Pitt, who lost favor in 1761, failed to check the momentum of his war machine. And in 1763 the Peace of Paris, even though it brought England less than Pitt would have liked, confirmed the possession of a great new empire.

The colonists shared in the ebullience of patriotism. But the moment of euphoria was all too brief. It served to mask festering resentments and new problems which were the heritage of the war. Underneath the pride in the British Empire an American nationalism was maturing. Ben Franklin foresaw a time, he said, when the capital of the British Empire would be on the Hudson instead of the Thames. Americans were beginning to think and speak of themselves more as Americans than as English or British. With a great new land to exploit, they could look to the future with confidence.

They had a new sense of importance after starting and fighting a vast world war with such success. Some harbored resentment, justified or not, at the haughty air of British soldiers and slights received at their hands, and many in the early stages of the war lost their awe of British soldiers who were at such a loss in frontier fighting. One Massachusetts soldier expressed some puzzle-

*George III, at age thirty-three, the young king of a victorious empire.*

ment that he should be expected to "stand still to be shot at" in the field rather than take cover.

In a recent social history of Massachusetts soldiers in the war, the historian Fred Anderson argues that they became convinced as well of their moral superiority to the British. The British army upheld extremely sharp social distinctions between officers and men, and imposed a harsh discipline, neither of which colonial militias were accustomed to. The Bay Colony men, moreover, expressed shock at the degree of cursing, whoring, and Sabbath breaking they observed among British regulars. The war heightened the New Englanders' sense of their separate identity and of their greater worthiness to be God's people. The Puritan utopia might be a lost cause, but the Puritan ideal was resilient.

Imperial forces, nevertheless, had borne the brunt of the war and had won it for the colonists, who had supplied men and materials reluctantly, and who persisted in trading with the enemy. Molasses in the French West Indies, for instance, continued to draw New England ships like flies. The trade was too important for the colonists to give up, but more than Pitt could tolerate, although he put up with the colonies' reluctance to support even their own forces. Along with patrols, one important means of disrupting this trade was the use of "writs of assistance," general search warrants that allowed officers to enter any place during daylight hours to seek evidence of illegal trade. When the death of George II invalidated the writs in 1760, Boston merchants hired James Otis to fight in the courts against renewal. He lost, but in the process advanced the radical precept that any act of Parliament which authorized such "instruments of slavery" was against the British Constitution, against natural equity, and therefore void.

Neither at Albany in 1754 nor later in the war had the colonies been able, or even seriously sought, to form a concerted plan of action. They had relied on the imperial authorities to name a commander-in-chief, to formulate strategy, to bear most of the cost, and to set up superintendents of Indian affairs north and south. The assemblies had used the exigencies of war, though, to extract still more power from the governors and turn themselves more than ever into little parliaments. When the war ended Virginia was still embroiled in what came to be called the "parson's cause." Since the seventeenth century the Virginia clergy had been paid in tobacco, but after a crop failure in 1755 the legislature converted payment to cash at two pence per pound of tobacco—well below the market price of about six pence. After the Privy Council disallowed the Two Penny Act in 1759, several clergymen brought suit for full payment at market value. In the most celebrated suit a young lawyer named Patrick Henry swayed the jury with his logic that the king's disallowing a beneficial law had broken the compact with his people and had forfeited all right to obedience. The jury awarded the plaintiff but one pence.

*Patrick Henry, a young attorney in the burgeoning American colonies.*

The peace which secured an empire laid upon the British ministry a burden of new problems. How should they manage the defense and governance of the new possessions? What disposition should they make of the western lands? How were they to service an unprecedented debt of nearly £140 million built up during the war, and bear the new burdens of administration and defense? And—the thorniest problem of all, as it turned out—what role should the colonies play in all this? The problems were of a magnitude and complexity to challenge men of the greatest statemanship and vision, but those qualities were rare among the ministers of George III.

## BRITISH POLITICS

In the British politics of the day nearly everybody who was anybody called himself a Whig, even King George. Whig had been the name given to those who opposed James II, led the Glorious Revolution of 1688, and secured the Protestant Hanoverian succession in 1714. By the time of the Glorious Revolution even their Tory adversaries had had enough of James II, but the Tories continued to bear the stigma of support for the Stuart cause and their influence waned. The Whigs were the champions of liberty and parliamentary supremacy, but with the passage of time Whiggism had drifted into complacency and leadership settled upon an aristocratic elite of the Whig gentry. This dominant group of landholding families was concerned mostly with the pursuit of personal place and advantage, and with local questions rather than great issues of statecraft. In the absence of party organization, parliamentary politics hinged on factions bound together by personal loyalties, family connections, and local interests, and on the pursuit of royal patronage.

In the administration of government an inner "Cabinet" of the king's ministers had been supplanting the unwieldy Privy Council as the center of power ever since the Hanoverian succession. The kings still had the prerogative of naming their ministers, and they used this prerogative to form coalitions of men who controlled enough factions in the House of Commons to command majorities for the government's measures, though the king's ministers were still technically responsible to the king rather than to parliamentary majorities. George III resolved to take a more active role in the process than the first two Georges, who had abandoned initiative to the great Whig families—George I in part because he barely spoke English.

In 1761 the new king made the earl of Bute, a Scottish lord, his first minister. Bute held the trust of the king as a longtime confidant and political mentor, but as a lord he was disqualified from the House of Commons and had little influence there. In 1763, moreover, just as the great war came to an end, Bute wearied of parliamentary intrigues and stepped aside. For the remainder of that decade the king turned first to one and then to another leader, ministries came and went, and the government fell into instability just as the new problems of empire required solutions. Ministries rose and fell because somebody offended the king, or because somebody's friend failed to get a job. Colonial policy remained marginal to the chief concerns of British politics. The result was first inconsistency and vacillation, followed by stubborn inflexibility.

## Western Lands

No sooner was peace arranged in 1763 than events thrust the problem of the western lands upon the government in an acute form. The Indians of the Ohio region, half unable to believe that their French friends were helpless and fully expecting the reentry of English settlers, grew restless and receptive to the warnings of the visionary Delaware Prophet and his disciple, Pontiac, chief of the Ottawa. In May 1763 Pontiac's effort to seize Fort Detroit was betrayed and failed, but the western tribes joined Pontiac's conspiracy to reopen frontier warfare and within a few months wiped out every British post in the Ohio region except Detroit and Fort Pitt. A relief force lifted the siege of Fort Pitt in August and Pontiac abandoned the attack on Detroit in November, but the outlying settlements suffered heavy losses before British forces could stop the attacks. Pontiac himself did not agree to peace until 1766.

THE PROCLAMATION OF 1763  To keep the peace, the ministers in London reasoned, further settlement could wait another day. The immediate need was to stop Pontiac's warriors and reassure the Indians. There were influential fur traders, moreover, who preferred to keep the wilderness as a game preserve. The pressure for expansion might ultimately prove irresistible—British and American speculators were already dazzled by the prospects—but there would be no harm in a pause while things settled down and a new policy evolved. The king's ministers therefore brought forward, and in October the king signed, the

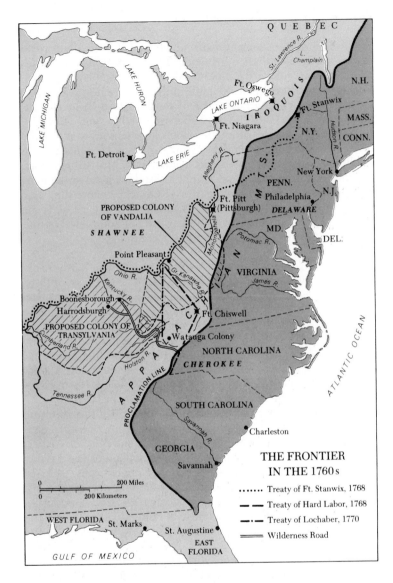

THE FRONTIER
IN THE 1760s

...... Treaty of Ft. Stanwix, 1768
— — — Treaty of Hard Labor, 1768
— · — · Treaty of Lochaber, 1770
═══ Wilderness Road

Royal Proclamation of 1763. The order drew a Proclamation Line along the crest of the Appalachians beyond which settlers were forbidden to go and colonial governors were forbidden to authorize surveys or issue land grants. It also established the new British colonies of Quebec and East and West Florida, the last two consisting mainly of small settlements at St. Augustine and St. Marks respectively, now peopled mainly by British garrisons.

The line did not long remain intact. In 1768 the chief royal agents for Indian affairs north and south negotiated two treaties (Fort Stanwix and Hard Labor) by which the Iroquois and Chero-kees gave up their claims to lands in the Ohio region—a strip in western New York, a large area of southwestern Pennsylvania, and between the Ohio and the Tennessee farther south. In 1770, by the Treaty of Lochaber, the Cherokees agreed to move the line below the Ohio still farther westward. Land speculators, in-cluding Benjamin Franklin and a number of British investors, soon formed a syndicate and sought a vast domain covering most of present West Virginia and eastern Kentucky, where they pro-posed to establish the colony of Vandalia. The Board of Trade lent its support, but the formalities were not completed before Vandalia vanished in the revolutionary crisis.

SETTLERS PUSH WEST Regardless of the formalities, hardy back-woodsmen pushed on over the ridges; by 1770 the town of Pitts-burgh had twenty log houses, and a small village had appeared on the site of Wheeling. In 1769 another colony was settled on the Watauga River by immigrants from southwestern Virginia, soon joined by settlers from North Carolina. The Watauga colony turned out to be within the limits of North Carolina, but so far removed from other settlements that it became virtually a sepa-rate republic under the Watauga Compact of 1772; North Caro-lina took it into the new district of Washington in 1776.

Another opening came south of the Ohio into the dark and bloody ground of Kentucky, which had been something of a neu-tral hunting ground shared by the northern and southern tribes. The Shawnees, who lived north of the Ohio, still claimed rights there despite the Iroquois and Cherokee concessions. In 1774 conflicts on the northwestern frontier of Virginia led the last royal governor, Lord Dunmore, to organize two expeditions against the Shawnees. After a battle at Point Pleasant, where the Kanawha empties into the Ohio, the defeated war chiefs of the Shawnees forced their leader, Cornstalk, to surrender their claims. James Harrod of Pennsylvania soon rebuilt his settlement at Harrodsburg which had been destroyed during the fighting, and Judge Richard Henderson of North Carolina formed a plan to settle the area on a larger scale. He organized the Transylvania Company in 1774, and in 1775 bought from the Cherokees a du-bious title to the land between the Kentucky and Cumberland Rivers. Next he sent out a band of men under the most famous frontiersman of them all, Daniel Boone, to cut the Wilderness Road from the upper Holston River via the Cumberland Gap in

Daniel Boone Escorting Settlers through the Cumberland Gap, *by George Caleb Bingham.*

southwestern Virginia on up to the Kentucky River. Along this road settlers moved up to Boonesborough, and Henderson set about organizing a government for his colony of Transylvania. But his claim was weak. Transylvania sent a delegation to the Continental Congress, which refused to receive it, and in 1776 Virginia responded to a petition from the Harrodsburg settlers and organized much of present Kentucky into a county of Virginia.

## GRENVILLE AND THE STAMP ACT

GRENVILLE'S COLONIAL POLICY    Just as the Proclamation of 1763 was being drafted, a new ministry had begun to grapple with the problems of imperial finances. The new chief minister, George Grenville, first lord of the Treasury, was a man much like the king: industrious, honest, meticulous, and obtuse. His opinions, the king himself observed, were "seldom formed from any other motives than such as may be expected to originate in the mind of a clerk in a counting house." Grenville apparently took without question the need for redcoats to defend the frontier, although the colonies had been left mostly to their own devices before 1754. But he faced estimates of £300,000 annually for American defense, on top of an already staggering debt. He had already tried to find new revenues at home, one result being a cider tax

*George Grenville, first lord of the treasury, whose tax policy aroused colonial opposition.*

so unpopular that it helped to drive him briefly out of office. It would not be the last time that British or American officials would learn that taxes on drink, fortified or otherwise, stirred deadly passions.

With the large tax burden at home and a much lighter one in the colonies, Grenville reasoned that the Americans were obligated to share the cost of their own defense. As he began to tot up the accounts he learned that the American customs service spent £8,000 to collect only a fourth that amount in revenue. Clearly evasion and inefficiency, not to mention corruption, were rampant, and the service needed tightening. Grenville directed absentee customs agents to pack themselves off to America and cease hiring deputies. He issued stern orders to colonial officials and set the navy to patrolling the coasts. In Parliament he secured an Act for the Encouragement of Officers Making Seizures (1763) which set up a new vice-admiralty court in Halifax with jurisdiction over all the colonies, a court which had no juries of colonists sympathetic to smugglers. The old habits of salutary neglect in the enforcement of the Navigation Acts were coming to an end, causing no little annoyance to American shippers.

Strict enforcement of the old Molasses Act of 1733 posed a serious threat to New England's mercantile prosperity, which in turn created markets for British goods. The sixpence-per-gallon duty had been set prohibitively high, not for purposes of revenue but to prevent trade with the French sugar islands. Yet the rum distilleries consumed more molasses than the British West Indies provided, and as Gov. Francis Bernard of Massachusetts wrote to the king: "Even illegal trade, where the balance is in favor of British subjects, makes its final return to Great Britain." Grenville recognized that the sixpence duty, if enforced, would be ruinous to a major colonial enterprise, and put through a new Revenue Act of 1764, commonly known as the Sugar Act, which cut the duty in half, from sixpence to three pence per gallon. This, he reasoned, would reduce the temptation to smuggle or to bribe the customs officers. In addition the Sugar Act levied new duties on imports of foreign textiles, wines, coffee, indigo, and sugar. The act, Grenville estimated, would bring in about £45,000 a year which would go "toward defraying the necessary expenses of defending, protecting, and securing, the said colonies and plantations." For the first time Parliament had adopted duties frankly designed to raise revenues in the colonies and not merely incidental to regulation of trade.

One other measure in Grenville's new design of colonial policy had an important impact on the colonies: the Currency Act of 1764. The colonies faced a chronic shortage of hard money, which kept going out to pay debts in England. To meet the shortage they resorted to issuing their own paper money. British creditors, however, feared payment in a depreciated currency. To

The Great Financier, or British Economy for the Years 1763, 1764, 1765. *A cartoon critical of Grenville's tax policies. America, depicted as an Indian (at left), groans under the burden of new taxes.*

alleviate their fears, Parliament in 1751 had forbidden the New England colonies to make their currency legal tender. Now Grenville extended the prohibition to all the colonies. The result was a decline in the value of existing paper money, since nobody was obligated to accept it in payment of debts, even in the colonies. The deflationary impact of the Currency Act, combined with new duties and stricter enforcement, delivered a severe shock to a colonial economy already suffering a postwar business decline.

THE STAMP ACT   But Grenville's new design was still incomplete. The Sugar Act would defray only a fraction of the cost of maintaining the 10,000 troops to be stationed in the colonies. Grenville announced when he introduced the act that he had in mind still another measure to raise money in America, a stamp tax. Early in 1765 he presented his plan to agents of the colonies in London. They protested unanimously, but had no response to his request for an alternative. And neither he nor they seemed to have any inkling of the storm it would arouse. Benjamin Franklin, representing four colonies, even proposed one of his friends as a stamp agent.

On February 13, 1765, Grenville laid his proposal before Parliament. It aroused little interest or debate. Only three speeches were delivered in opposition, but one of them included a fateful phrase. Col. Isaac Barré, who had served with Wolfe at Québec, said that British agents sent out to the colonies had "caused the blood of these sons of liberty to recoil within them." Nevertheless the act passed the Commons easily. The act created revenue stamps ranging in cost from three pence to £6, and required that they be fixed to printed matter and legal documents of all kinds: newspapers, pamphlets, broadsides, almanacs, bonds, leases, deeds, licenses, insurance policies, ship clearances, college diplomas, even dice and playing cards. The requirement would go into effect on November 1, 1765.

In March 1765 Grenville put through the measure that completed his design, the Quartering Act, in effect still another tax. This act required the colonies to supply British troops with provisions and to provide them barracks or submit to their use of inns and vacant buildings. It applied to all colonies, but affected mainly New York, headquarters of the British forces.

WHIG IDEOLOGY IN THE COLONIES   The cumulative effect of Grenville's measures raised colonial suspicions to a fever. Unwittingly this plodding minister of a plodding king had stirred up a storm of protest and set in train a profound and searching exploration of English traditions and imperial relations. The radical ideas of the minority "Real Whigs" were widespread in the colonies. They had absorbed these ideas from the polemics of John Trenchard and Thomas Gordon, authors of *Cato's Letters* (1720–1723), Joseph Addison's play *Cato* (1713), Viscount Bolingbroke, Algernon Sidney, the histories of Paul Rapin and Catherine Macaulay, and above all from John Locke's justification of the Glorious Revolution, his *Two Treatises on Government* (1690). They knew that English history had been a struggle by Parliament to preserve life, liberty, and property against royal tyranny.

They also knew from their religious heritage and by what Patrick Henry called "the lamp of experience" that human nature is corruptible and lusts after power. The safeguard against abuses, in the view of those who called themselves "Real Whigs," was not to rely on human goodness but to check power with power. And the British Constitution had embodied these principles in a mixed government of kings, lords, and commons, each serving as a check on the others. Even on the continent of Europe enlightened philosophers looked with admiration upon English liberties. A character in a Mozart opera announced: "I am an Englishwoman, born to freedom." The French writer Montesquieu, in his *Spirit of the Laws*, mingled the idea of a mixed government (king, lords, commons) with his own notion of the separation of powers (executive, legislative, judicial). The colonists, like Montesquieu, embraced the Enlightenment philosophy of natural law and natural rights. But if the Enlightenment found lodgment in their minds, the Real Whig interpretation of history and human nature was built into their bones. In the end it saved them from the facile optimism and the pursuit of utopia which would lure the French revolutionaries into the horrors of the Terror.

But in 1764 and 1765 it seemed to the colonists that Grenville had loosed upon them the very engines of tyranny from which Parliament had rescued England in the seventeenth century, and by imposition of that very Parliament! A standing army was the historic ally of despots, and now with the French gone and Pontiac subdued, several thousand soldiers remained in the colonies: to protect the colonists or to subdue them? It was beginning to seem clear that it was the latter. Among the fundamental rights of Englishmen were trial by jury and the presumption of innocence, but vice-admiralty courts excluded juries and put the burden of proof on the defendant. Most important, Englishmen had the right to be taxed only by their elected representatives. Parliament claimed that privilege in England, and the colonial assemblies had long exercised it in America. Now Parliament was out to usurp the assemblies' power of the purse strings.

THE QUESTION OF REPRESENTATION   In a flood of colonial pamphlets, speeches, and resolutions, debate on the Stamp Tax turned mainly on the point expressed in a slogan familiar to all Americans: "no taxation without representation," a cry that had been raised years before in response to the Molasses Act of 1733. In 1764 James Otis, now a popular leader in the Massachusetts assembly, set forth the argument in a pamphlet, *The Rights of the British Colonists Asserted and Proved.* Grenville had one of his subordinates prepare an answer which developed the ingenious theory of "virtual representation." If the colonies had no vote in Parliament, neither did most Englishmen who lived in boroughs that had developed since the last apportionment. Large cities had grown up which had no right to elect a member, while old boroughs with little or no population still returned members. Nevertheless each member of Parliament represented the interests of the whole country and indeed the whole empire. Charleston, for instance, had fully as much representation as Manchester, England.

To the colonists virtual representation was nonsense, justified neither by logic nor by their own experience. In America, to be sure, the apportionment of assemblies failed to keep pace with the westward movement of population, but it was based more nearly on population and—in contrast to British practice—each member was expected to live in the district he represented. In a pamphlet widely circulated during 1765 Daniel Dulany, a young lawyer of Maryland, suggested that even if the theory had any validity for England, where the interests of electors might be closely tied to those of nonelectors, it had none for colonists 3,000 miles away, whose interests differed and whose distance from Westminster made it impossible for them to influence members. James Otis went more to the heart of the matter. If such considerable places as Manchester, Birmingham, and Sheffield were not represented, he said, "they ought to be."

PROTEST IN THE COLONIES   Soon after passage of the Stamp Act, Benjamin Franklin wrote back to a radical friend in Philadelphia: "We might as well have hindered the sun's setting. But since 'tis down . . . let us make as good a night of it as we can." In reply his friend predicted "the works of darkness" in the night. The

Stamp Act became the chief target of colonial protest. The Sugar Act affected mainly New England, but the Stamp Act imposed a burden on all the colonists who did any kind of business. And it affected most of all the articulate elements in the community: merchants, planters, lawyers, printer-editors—all strategically placed to influence opinion.

Through the spring and summer of 1765 popular resentment found outlet in mass meetings, parades, bonfires, and other demonstrations. The protest enlisted farmers, artisans, laborers, businessmen, dock workers, and seamen alarmed at the disruption of business. Lawyers, editors, and merchants like Christopher Gadsden of Charleston and John Hancock of Boston took the lead or lent support. In North Carolina the governor reported the mobs to be composed of "gentlemen and planters." They began to assume a name adopted from Colonel Barré's speech: Sons of Liberty. They met underneath "Liberty Trees"—in Boston a great elm on Hanover Square, in Charleston a live oak in Mr. Mazyck's pasture. They erected "Liberty poles" topped by the Phrygian liberty cap, the ancient Roman *pileus* which was presented to freed slaves. One day in mid-August, nearly three months before the effective date of the Stamp Act, an effigy of Boston's stamp agent swung from the Liberty Tree and in the evening a mob carried it through the streets, destroyed the stamp office, and used the wood to burn the effigy. Somewhat

*In protest of the Stamp Act, which was to take effect the next day, the* Pennsylvania Journal *appeared with the skull and crossbones on its masthead.*

later another mob sacked the home of Lt.-Gov. Thomas Hutchinson and the local customs officer. Thoroughly shaken, the Boston stamp agent resigned his commission and stamp agents throughout the colonies felt impelled to follow his example.

By November 1, its effective date, the Stamp Act was a dead letter. Business went on without the stamps. Newspapers appeared with the skull and crossbones in the corner where the stamp belonged. After passage of the Sugar Act a movement had begun to boycott British goods. Now the adoption of non-importation agreements became a universal device of propaganda and pressure on British merchants. Sage and sassafras took the place of tea. Homespun garments became the fashion as symbols of colonial defiance.

The general revolt gave impulse to the idea of colonial unity, as colonists discovered that they had more in common with each other than with London. In May, long before the mobs went into action, the Virginia House of Burgesses had struck the first blow against the Stamp Act in the Virginia Resolves, a series of resolutions inspired by young Patrick Henry's "torrents of sublime eloquence." Virginians, the burgesses declared, were entitled to the rights of Englishmen, and Englishmen could be taxed only by their own representatives. Virginians, moreover, had always been governed by laws passed with their own consent. Newspapers spread the resolutions throughout the colonies, along with even more radical statements that were kept out of the final version, and other assemblies hastened to copy Virginia's example. On June 8, 1765, the Massachusetts House of Representatives issued a circular letter inviting the various assemblies to send delegates to confer in New York on appeals for relief from the king and Parliament.

Nine responded, and from October 7 to 25 the Stamp Act Congress of twenty-seven delegates conferred and issued expressions of colonial sentiment: a Declaration of the Rights and Grievances of the Colonies, a petition to the king for relief, and a petition to Parliament for repeal of the Stamp Act. The delegates acknowledged that the colonies owed a "due subordination" to Parliament, but they questioned "whether there be not a material distinction . . . between the necessary exercise of Parliamentary jurisdiction in general Acts, for the amendment of the Common Law and the regulation of trade and commerce throughout the whole empire, and the exercise of that jurisdiction by imposing taxes on the colonies." Parliament, in short, might have powers to legislate for the regulation of the empire, but it had no right to levy taxes, which were a free gift granted by the people through their representatives.

REPEAL OF THE ACT   The storm had scarcely broken before Grenville's ministry was out of office, dismissed not because of the colonial turmoil but because they had fallen out with the king over the distribution of offices. In July 1765 the king installed a new minister, the marquis of Rockingham, leader of the "Rockingham Whigs," the "old Whig" faction which included men like Barré and Edmund Burke who sympathized with the colonists' views. Rockingham resolved to end the quarrel by repealing the Stamp Act, but he needed to move carefully in order to win a majority. Simple repeal was politically impossible without some affirmation of parliamentary authority. When Parliament assembled early in the year, William Pitt demanded that the Stamp Act be repealed "absolutely, totally, and immediately," but urged that Britain's authority over the colonies "be asserted in as strong terms as possible," except on the point of taxation. Rockingham steered a cautious course, and seized upon the widespread but false impression that Pitt accepted the principle of "external" taxes on trade but rejected "internal" taxes within the colonies. Benjamin Franklin, summoned before Parliament for interrogation in what was probably a rehearsed performance, helped to further the false impression that this was the colonists'

The Repeal, or the Funeral Procession of Miss Americ-Stamp *(1766)*. *Grenville carries the dead Stamp Act in its coffin. In the background, trade with America starts up again.*

view as well, an impression easily refuted by reference to the colonial resolutions of the previous year.

In March 1766 Parliament passed the repeal, but in order to pacify Grenville's following without offending the Pitt supporters, Rockingham accepted the Declaratory Act, which asserted the full power of Parliament to make laws binding the colonies "in all cases whatsoever." It was a cunning evasion which made no concession with regard to taxes, but made no mention of them either. It left intact in the minds of many members the impression that a distinction had been drawn between "external" and "internal" taxes, and that impression would have fateful consequences for the future. For the moment, however, the Declaratory Act seemed little if anything more than a gesture to save face. Amid the rejoicing and relief on both sides of the Atlantic there were no omens that the quarrel would be reopened within a year. To be sure, the Sugar Act remained on the books, but Rockingham reduced the molasses tax from three pence to a penny a gallon, less than the cost of a bribe.

## Fanning the Flames

But the king continued to have his ministers play musical chairs. Rockingham fell for the same reasons as Grenville, a quarrel over appointments, and the king invited Pitt to form a ministry including the major factions of Parliament and rewarded him with the title of earl of Chatham. Burke compared the coalition to pigs gathered at a trough. The ill-matched combination would have been hard to manage even if Pitt had remained in charge, but the old warlord began to slip over the fine line between genius and madness, leaving direction to the indolent duke of Grafton, who headed the cabinet after Pitt resigned in 1768. For a time in 1767 the guiding force in the ministry was Charles Townshend, chancellor of the Exchequer, whose "abilities were superior to those of all men," according to Horace Walpole, "and his judgement below that of any man." The erratic Townshend took advantage of Pitt's absence to reopen the question of colonial taxation and seized upon the notion that "external" taxes were tolerable to the colonies—not that he believed it for a moment.

THE TOWNSHEND ACTS    In May and June 1767 Townshend put his plan through the House of Commons and in September he died, leaving behind a bitter legacy: the Townshend Acts. First, he set out to bring the New York assembly to its senses. That body had defied the Quartering Act and refused to provide billets or supplies for the king's troops. Parliament, at Townshend's behest, suspended all acts of the assembly until it yielded. New York protested but finally caved in, inadvertently confirming the suspicion that too much indulgence had encouraged colonial bad manners. Townshend followed up with the Revenue Act of 1767, which levied duties ("external taxes") on colonial imports of glass, lead, paints, paper, and tea. Third, he set up a Board of Customs Commissioners at Boston, the colonial headquarters of smuggling. Finally, he reorganized the vice-admiralty courts, providing four in the continental colonies—at Halifax, Boston, Philadelphia, and Charleston.

The Townshend duties were something of a success on the ledger books, bringing in revenues of £31,000 at a cost of about £13,000. But the intangible costs were greater. For one thing the duties taxed goods exported from England, indirectly hurting British manufacturers, and had to be collected in colonial ports, increasing collection costs. But the greater cost was a new drift into ever-greater conflict. The Revenue Act of 1767 posed a more severe threat to colonial assemblies than Grenville's taxes, for Townshend proposed to apply these moneys to pay governors and other officers and release them from dependence on the assemblies.

DICKINSON'S *LETTERS*   The Townshend Acts took the colonists by surprise, and the storm gathered more slowly than it had two years before. But once again citizens resolved to resist, to boy-

*John Dickinson, the Philadelphia lawyer who wrote the influential* Letters of a Pennsylvania Farmer.

cott British goods, to wear homespun, to develop their own manufactures. Once again the colonial press spewed out expressions
of protest, most notably the essays of John Dickinson, a Philadelphia lawyer who hoped to resolve the dispute by persuasion. Late in 1767 his twelve *Letters of a Pennsylvania Farmer* (as
he chose to style himself) began to appear in the *Pennsylvania
Chronicle*, from which they were copied in other papers and in
pamphlet form. His argument simply repeated with greater detail and more elegance what Daniel Dulany and the Stamp Act
Congress had already said. The colonists held that Parliament
might regulate commerce and collect duties incidental to that
purpose, but it had no right to levy taxes for revenue whether
they were internal or external. Dickinson used the language of
moderation throughout. "The cause of Liberty is a cause of too
much dignity to be sullied by turbulence and tumult," he argued. The colonial complaints should "speak at the same time
the language of affliction and veneration."

SAMUEL ADAMS AND THE SONS OF LIBERTY   But the affliction grew
and the veneration waned. British ministers could neither concil-
iate moderates like Dickinson nor cope with firebrands like Samuel Adams of Boston, who was now emerging as the supreme
genius of revolutionary agitation. Adams, a Harvard graduate,
son of a moderately well-off family, had run down the family
brewery and failed at everything else except politics. At Harvard
he had chosen as the subject for his master's degree "whether it
be lawful to resist the Supreme Magistrate, if the Commonwealth be otherwise preserved." Now he was obsessed with the

*Samuel Adams, an organizer of the
Sons of Liberty.*

conviction that Parliament had no right to legislate at all for the colonies, that Massachusetts must return to the spirit of its Puritan founders and defend itself from a new design against its liberties.

While other men tended their private affairs, Adams was whipping up the Sons of Liberty and organizing protests in the Boston town meeting and the provincial assembly. Early in 1768 he and James Otis formulated another Massachusetts Circular Letter, which the assembly dispatched to the other colonies. The letter restated the illegality of parliamentary taxation, warned that the new duties would be used to pay colonial officials, and invited the support of other colonies. In London the earl of Hillsborough, just appointed to the new office of secretary of state for the colonies, only made bad matters worse. He ordered the assembly to withdraw the letter. The assembly refused and was dissolved. The consequence was simply more discussion of the need for colonial cooperation.

Among Townshend's legacies the new Board of Customs Commissioners at Boston further confirmed Adams's suspicions of British intentions. Customs officers had been unwelcome in Boston since the arrival of Edward Randolph a century before. But the irascible Randolph at least had the virtue of honesty. His successors cultivated the fine art of what one historian has called "customs racketeering." Under the Sugar Act, collectors profited from illegal cargoes and exploited technicalities. One ploy was to neglect certain requirements, then suddenly insist on a strict adherence. In May 1768 they set a trap for Sam Adams's friend and patron John Hancock, a well-to-do merchant. On the narrow ground that Hancock had failed to post a bond before loading his sloop *Liberty* (always before he had posted bond after loading) they seized the ship. A mob gathered to prevent its unloading. The commissioners towed the ship to Castle William in the harbor and called for the protection of British troops. In September 1768 two regiments of redcoats arrived in Boston. Clearly they were not there to protect the frontiers. On the day the soldiers arrived, a convention of delegates from Massachusetts towns declared their "aversion to an unnecessary Standing Army, which they look upon as dangerous to their Civil Liberty."

To members of Parliament the illegal convention smacked of treason, but it gave them little reason to believe that any colonial jury would ever convict the likes of Sam Adams. Consequently by formal resolution Parliament recommended that the king get information on "all treasons, or misprision of treason" committed in Massachusetts and appoint a special commission to judge the evidence under a forgotten act passed during the reign of Henry VIII by which the accused could be taken to England for trial. The king never acted on the suggestion, but the threat was unmistakable. In mid-May 1769 the Virginia assembly passed a new set of resolves reasserting its exclusive right to tax Virginians, challenging the constitutionality of an act that would take a man across the ocean for trial, and calling upon the colonies to unite in the cause. Virginia's governor promptly dissolved the assembly, but the members met independently, dubbed themselves a "convention" after Boston's example, and adopted a new set of non-importation agreements. Once again, as with the Virginia Resolves against the Stamp Act, most of the other assemblies followed the example.

In London events across the Atlantic still evoked only marginal interest. The king's long effort to reorder British politics to his liking was coming to fulfillment, and that was the big news. In 1769 new elections for Parliament finally produced a majority of the "King's Friends," held to his cause by pelf and patronage. And George III found a minister to his taste in Frederick, Lord North, the plodding chancellor of the Exchequer who had replaced Townshend. In 1770 the king dismissed the Grafton coalition and installed a cabinet of the King's Friends, with North as first minister. North, who venerated the traditions of Parliament, was no stooge for the king, but the two worked in harmony.

THE BOSTON MASSACRE    The impact of colonial boycotts on English commerce had persuaded Lord North to modify the Townshend Acts, just in time to halt a perilous escalation of conflict. The presence of soldiers in Boston had been a constant provocation. Bostonians copied the example of the customs officers and indicted soldiers on technical violations of local law. Crowds heckled and ridiculed the "lobster backs." On March 5, 1770, in the square before the customs house, a group began taunting and snowballing the sentry on duty. His call for help brought Capt. Robert Preston with reinforcements. Then somebody rang the town firebell, drawing a larger crowd to the scene. At their head was Crispus Attucks, a runaway mulatto slave who had worked for some years on ships out of Boston. Finally one soldier was knocked down, rose to his feet, and fired into the crowd. When the smoke cleared away five people lay on the ground dead or dying and eight more were wounded. The cause of resistance now had its first martyrs, and the first to die was the runaway slave, Crispus Attucks. Gov. Thomas Hutchinson, at the insistence of a mass meeting in Faneuil Hall, moved the soldiers out

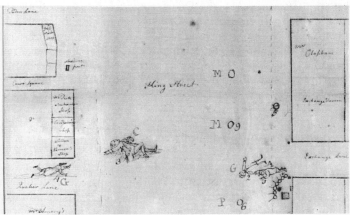

*Paul Revere's engraving of the Boston Massacre (top). Revere drew a plan of the Massacre (bottom) for use at the trial of the British soldiers. It shows the places where four of the dead fell.*

of town to avoid another incident. Those involved in the shooting were indicted for murder, but they were defended by John Adams, Sam's cousin, who thought they were the victims of circumstance, provoked, he said, by a "motley rabble of saucy boys,

negroes and mulattoes, Irish teagues and outlandish Jack tars."
All were acquitted except two, who got light punishment for
manslaughter.

News of the Boston Massacre sent shock waves up and down
the colonies. "No previous outrage had given a general alarm,"
wrote Mercy Otis Warren in her *History of the American Revolution* (1805). The incident "created a resentment which emboldened the timid" and "determined the wavering." But late in
April news arrived that Parliament had repealed all the Townshend duties save one. The cabinet, by a fateful vote of five to
four, had advised keeping the tea tax as a token of parliamentary
authority. Colonial diehards insisted that pressure should be
kept on British merchants until Parliament gave in altogether,
but the non-importation movement soon faded. Parliament, after
all, had given up the substance of the taxes, with one exception,
and much of the colonists' tea was smuggled in from Holland
anyway.

For two years little more was done to disturb relations. Discontent simmered down and suspicions began to fade on both
sides of the ocean. The Stamp Act was gone, as were all the
Townshend duties except that on tea, and Lord Hillsborough
disclaimed any intent to seek further revenues. But most of the
Grenville-Townshend innovations remained in effect: the Sugar
Act, the Currency Act, the Quartering Act, the vice-admiralty
courts, the Boards of Customs Commissioners. The redcoats had
left Boston but they remained nearby, and the British navy still
patrolled the coast. Each remained a source of irritation and the
cause of occasional incidents. There was still tinder await-
ing a spark, and colonial patriots remained alert to resist new
impositions.

### DISCONTENT ON THE FRONTIER

Through the years of agitation, parts of the backcountry
had stirred with quarrels that had nothing to do with the Stamp
and Townshend Acts. Rival land claims to the east of Lake
Champlain pitted New York against New Hampshire, and the
Green Mountain Boys led by Ethan Allen against both. Eventually the denizens of the area would simply set up shop on their
own, as the state of Vermont, created in 1777 although not recognized as a member of the Union until 1791. In Pennsylvania
sporadic quarrels broke out with land claimants who held grants
from Virginia and Connecticut, whose boundaries under their

charters overlapped those granted to William Penn, or so they claimed. A more dangerous division in Pennsylvania arose when a group of frontier ruffians took the law into their own hands. Outraged at the lack of frontier protection during Pontiac's rebellion because of Quaker influence in the assembly, a group called the "Paxton Boys" took revenge by the massacre of peaceful Conestoga Indians in Lancaster County, then threatened the so-called Moravian Indians, a group of Moravian converts near Bethlehem. When the Moravian Indians took refuge in Philadelphia, some 1,500 Paxton Boys marched on the capital, where Benjamin Franklin talked them into returning home by promising that more protection would be forthcoming.

Farther south, frontiersmen of South Carolina had similar complaints about the lack of settled government and the need for protection against horse thieves, cattle rustlers, and Indians. The backcountrymen organized societies called "Regulators" to administer vigilante justice in the region and refused to pay taxes until they got effective government. In 1769 the assembly finally set up six new circuit courts in the region and revised the fees, but still did not respond to the backcountry's demand for representation.

In North Carolina the protest was less over the lack of government than over the abuses and extortion inflicted by appointees from the eastern part of the colony. Farmers felt especially oppressed at the refusal either to issue paper money or to accept produce in payment of taxes, and in 1768 organized as Regulators to resist. Efforts to stop seizures of property and other court proceedings led to more disorders and an enactment, the Johnston Bill, which made the rioters guilty of treason. In the spring of 1771 Gov. William Tryon led 1,200 militiamen into the Piedmont center of Regulator activity. There he met and defeated some 2,000 ill-organized Regulators in the Battle of Alamance, which cost eight killed on each side. One insurgent was executed on the battlefield. Twelve others were convicted of treason and six hanged. While this went on, Tryon's men ranged through the backcountry forcing some 6,500 Piedmont settlers to sign an oath of allegiance.

In South Carolina, while Regulators protested in the interior, tensions between the colony and the imperial authorities never quite broke. There, in 1769, the very year the assembly was responding to the backcountry demands, it also voted £1,500 for the radical Bill of Rights Society in England to pay the debts of the government's outspoken critic, John Wilkes. When the king's ministers instructed the governor and council to assert themselves in the matter, royal government in South Carolina reached an impasse. The assembly passed its last annual tax law in 1769, and after 1771 passed no legislation at all.

### A WORSENING CRISIS

Two events in June 1772 broke the period of quiescence in the quarrels with the mother country. Near Providence, Rhode Island, a British schooner, the *Gaspee,* patrolling for smugglers, accidentally ran aground. Under cover of darkness a crowd from the town boarded the ship, removed the crew, and set fire to the vessel. A commission of inquiry was formed with authority to hold suspects (for trial in England, it was rumored, under that old statute of Henry VIII), but nobody in Rhode Island seemed to know anything about the affair. Four days after the burning, on June 13, 1772, Gov. Thomas Hutchinson told the Massachusetts assembly that his salary thenceforth would come out of the customs revenues. Soon afterward word came that judges of the Superior Court would be paid from the same source, and no longer be dependent on the assembly for their income. The assembly expressed a fear that this portended "a despotic administration of government."

The existence of the *Gaspee* commission, which bypassed the courts of Rhode Island, and the independent salaries for royal officials in Massachusetts both suggested to the residents of other colonies that the same might be in store for them. The discussion

*Massachusetts Gov. Thomas Hutchinson found himself at the center of the imperial crisis in 1772 and 1773.*

of colonial rights and parliamentary encroachments gained momentum once again. To keep the pot boiling, in November 1772 Sam Adams got the Boston Town Meeting to form a committee of correspondence which issued a statement of rights and grievances and invited other towns to do the same. Committees of correspondence sprang up across Massachusetts and spread into other colonies. In March 1773 the Virginia assembly proposed the formation of such committees on an intercolonial basis, and a network of the committees spread across the colonies, keeping in touch, mobilizing public opinion, and keeping colonial resentments at a simmer. In unwitting tribute to their effectiveness, a Massachusetts loyalist, called the committees "the foulest, subtlest, and most venomous serpent ever issued from the egg of sedition."

THE BOSTON TEA PARTY   Lord North soon provided them with the occasion to bring resentment from a simmer to a boil. In May 1773 he undertook to help some friends through a little difficulty. North's scheme was a clever contrivance, perhaps too clever, designed to bail out the East India Company which was foundering in a spell of bad business. The company had in its British warehouses some 17 million pounds of tea. Under the Tea Act of 1773 the government would refund the British duty of twelve pence per pound on all that was shipped to the colonies and collect only the existing three-pence duty payable at the colonial port. By this arrangement colonists could get tea more cheaply than Englishmen could, for less even than the black-market Dutch tea. North, however, miscalculated in assuming that price alone would govern colonial reaction. And he erred even worse by permitting the East India Company to serve retailers directly though its own agents or consignees, bypassing the wholesalers who had handled it before. Once that kind of monopoly was established, colonial merchants began to wonder, how soon would the precedent apply to other commodities?

The committees of correspondence, with strong support from colonial merchants, alerted people to the new danger. The government was trying to purchase acquiescence with cheap tea. Before the end of the year large consignments went out to major colonial ports. In New York and Philadelphia popular hostility forced company agents to resign. With no one to receive the tea, it went back to England. In Charleston it was unloaded into warehouses—and later sold to finance the Revolution. In Boston, however, Governor Hutchinson and Sam Adams resolved upon a test of will. The ships' captains, alarmed by the radical opposition, proposed to turn back. Hutchinson, two of whose sons were

Americans throwing the Cargoes of the Tea Ships into the River, at Boston, 1773.

among the consignees, refused permission until the tea was landed and the duty paid. On November 30, gathered in Old South Church, the Boston Town Meeting warned officials not to assist the landing, although they were legally bound to seize the cargo after twenty days in port, which expired on December 16. On that night a group of men hastened from the hall to Griffin's Wharf where, thinly disguised as Mohawk Indians, they boarded the three ships and threw the tea overboard—cheered on by a crowd along the shore. Like those who had burned the *Gaspee*, they remained parties unknown—except to hundreds of Bostonians. One participant later testified that Sam Adams and John Hancock were there—he had exchanged the countersign with Hancock: an Indian grunt followed by "me know you." About £15,000 worth of tea went to the fishes.

Given a more deft response from London the Boston Tea Party might easily have undermined the radicals' credibility. Many people, especially merchants, were aghast at the wanton destruction of property. A town meeting in Bristol, Massachusetts, condemned the action. Ben Franklin called on his native city to pay for the tea and hasten into sackcloth and ashes. But the British authorities had reached the end of patience. "The colonists must either submit or triumph," George III wrote to Lord North, and North hastened to make the king's judgment a self-fulfilling prophecy.

THE COERCIVE ACTS  In March 1774 North laid before Parliament four measures to discipline Boston, and Parliament enacted them in April. The Boston Port Act closed the port from June 1, 1774, until the tea was paid for. An Act for the Impartial Administration of Justice let the governor transfer to England the trial of any official accused of committing an offense in the line of duty—no more redcoats would be tried on technicalities. A new Quartering Act directed local authorities to provide lodging for soldiers, in private homes if necessary. Finally, the Massachusetts Government Act made the colony's council and law-enforcement officers all appointive; sheriffs would select jurors and no town meeting could be held without the governor's consent, except for the annual election of town officers. In May, Gen. Thomas Gage replaced Hutchinson as governor and assumed command of British forces. Massachusetts now had a military governor.

The actions were designed to isolate Boston and make an example of the colony. Instead they hastened development of a movement for colonial unity. "Your scheme yields no revenue," Edmund Burke had warned Parliament; "it yields nothing but discontent, disorder, disobedience. . . ." At last, it seemed to colonists, their worst fears were being confirmed. If these "Intolerable Acts," as the colonists labeled the Coercive Acts, were not resisted, the same thing would be in store for the other colonies. Still further confirmation of British designs came with news

The Able Doctor, or America Swallowing the Bitter Draught. *This 1774 engraving shows Lord North, with the Boston Port Bill in his pocket, pouring tea down America's throat. America spits it back.*

of the Quebec Act, passed in June. The Quebec Act set up a totally unrepresentative government to the north under an appointed governor and council, and gave a privileged position to the Catholic church. The measure was actually designed to deal with the peculiar milieu of a colony peopled mainly by Frenchmen, unused to representative assemblies, but it seemed merely another indicator of designs for the rest of the colonies. What was more, the act placed within the boundaries of Quebec the western lands north of the Ohio River, lands in which Pennsylvania, Virginia, and Connecticut had charter claims. Soon afterward came an announcement of new regulations which restricted sale of ungranted lands in the colonies and provided for relatively high quitrents on such lands.

Meanwhile colonists rallied to the cause of Boston, taking up collections and sending provisions. In Williamsburg, when the Virginia assembly met in May, a young member of the Committee of Correspondence, Thomas Jefferson, proposed to set aside June 1, the effective date of the Boston Port Act, as a day of fasting and prayer in Virginia. The governor immediately dissolved the assembly, whose members retired down Duke of Gloucester Street to the Raleigh Tavern and drew up a resolution for a "Continental Congress" to make representations on behalf of all the colonies. Similar calls were coming from Providence, New York, Philadelphia, and elsewhere, and in June the Massachusetts assembly suggested a meeting at Philadelphia, in September. Shortly before George Washington left to represent Virginia at the meeting, he wrote to a friend: " . . . the crisis is arrived when we must assert our rights, or submit to every imposition, that can be heaped upon us, till custom and use shall make us as tame and abject slaves, as the blacks we rule over with such arbitrary sway."

THE CONTINENTAL CONGRESS  On September 5, 1774, the First Continental Congress assembled in Philadelphia's Carpenter's Hall. The Congress members numbered fifty-five in all, elected by provincial congresses or irregular conventions, and representing twelve continental colonies, all but Georgia, Quebec, Nova Scotia, and the Floridas. Peyton Randolph of Virginia was elected president and Charles Thomson, "the Sam Adams of Philadelphia," became secretary, but not a member. The Congress agreed to vote by colonies, although Patrick Henry urged the members to vote as individuals on the grounds that they were not Virginians or New Yorkers or whatever, but Americans. In effect the delegates functioned as a congress of ambassadors, gathered to concert forces on common policies and neither to govern nor to rebel but to adopt and issue a series of resolutions and protests.

The Congress gave serious consideration to a plan of union introduced by Joseph Galloway of Pennsylvania. His proposal followed closely the plan of the Albany Congress twenty years before: to set up a central administration of a governor-general appointed by the crown and a grand council chosen by the assemblies to regulate "general affairs." All measures dealing with America would require approval of both this body and Parliament. The plan was defeated only by a vote of six to five. Meanwhile a silversmith from Boston, Paul Revere, had come riding in from Massachusetts with the radical Suffolk Resolves, which Congress proceeded to endorse. Drawn up by Joseph Warren and adopted by a convention in Suffolk County, the resolutions declared the Intolerable Acts null and void, called upon Massachusetts to arm for defense, and called for economic sanctions against British commerce.

In place of Galloway's plan the Congress adopted a Declaration of American Rights which conceded only Parliament's right to regulate commerce and those matters which were strictly imperial affairs. It proclaimed once again the rights of Englishmen, denied Parliament's authority with respect to internal colonial affairs, and proclaimed the right of each assembly to determine the need for troops within its own province. In addition Congress sent the king a petition for relief and issued addresses to the people of Great Britain and the colonies. Finally it adopted the Continental Association of 1774 which recommended that every county, town, and city form committees to enforce a boycott on all British goods. In taking its stand Congress had adopted what later would be called the dominion theory of the British Empire, a theory long implicit in the assemblies' claim to independent authority but more recently formulated in two widely circulated pamphlets by James Wilson of Pennsylvania (*Considerations on the Nature and Extent of the Legislative Authority of the British Parliament*) and Thomas Jefferson of Virginia (*Summary View of the Rights of British America*). Each had argued that the colonies were not subject to Parliament but merely to the crown; each, like England itself, was a separate realm, a point further argued after Congress adjourned in the *Novanglus Letters* of John Adams, published in Massachusetts. Another congress was called for May 1775.

The State Black-
smiths, Forging Fet-
ters for the Ameri-
cans. *A cartoon
attacking Parliamen-
tary measures of 1775
and 1776.*

In London few members of Parliament were ready to compre-
hend, much less accept, such "liberal and expanded thought," as
Jefferson called it. In the House of Lords, William Pitt, earl of
Chatham, did urge acceptance of the American view on taxation,
however, and suggested a compromise under which the Continental Congress might vote a revenue for the crown. In the
Commons, Edmund Burke, in a brilliant speech on conciliation,
urged merely an acceptance of the American view on taxation as
consonant with English principles. The real question, he argued,
was "not whether you have the right to render your people miserable; but whether it is not your interest to make them happy."

But neither house was in a mood for such points. Instead they
declared Massachusetts in rebellion, forbade the New England
colonies to trade with any nation outside the empire, and excluded New Englanders from the North Atlantic fisheries. Lord
North's Conciliatory Resolution, adopted February 27, 1775,
was as far as they would go. Under its terms, Parliament would
refrain from any but taxes to regulate trade and would grant to
each colony the duties collected within its boundaries provided
the colonies would contribute voluntarily to a quota for defense
of the empire. It was a formula, Burke said, not for peace but for
new quarrels.

## SHIFTING AUTHORITY

But events were already moving beyond conciliation. All through the later months of 1774 and early 1775 the patriot defenders of American rights were seizing the initiative. The uncertain and unorganized Loyalists, if they did not submit to non-importation agreements, found themselves confronted with persuasive committees of "Whigs," with tar and feathers at the ready. In October 1774 the Massachusetts House of Representatives, meeting in defiance of Governor Gage, restyled itself the Provincial Congress and named John Hancock head of a Committee of Safety with power to call up the militia. The militia, as much a social as a military organization in the past, now took to serious drill in formations, tactics, and marksmanship, and organized special units of Minute Men ready for quick mobilization. Everywhere royal officials were losing control as provincial congresses assumed authority and colonial militias organized, raided military stores, gathered arms and gunpowder. In Massachusetts the authority of General Gage scarcely extended beyond Boston.

LEXINGTON AND CONCORD    On April 14, 1775, Gage received secret orders from the earl of Dartmouth, who had replaced Hillsborough as colonial secretary, to proceed against the "open rebellion" that existed in the colony, even at the risk of conflict. Leaders of the provincial congress, whom Gage was directed to arrest, were mostly beyond his reach, but Gage decided to move

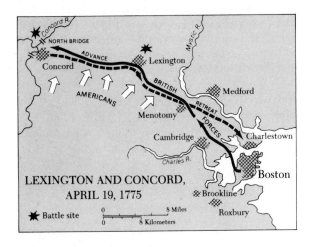

LEXINGTON AND CONCORD,
APRIL 19, 1775

quickly against the militia's supply depot at Concord, about twenty miles away. On the night of April 18 Lt.-Col. Francis Smith and Maj. John Pitcairn of the marines gathered 700 men on Boston Common and set out by way of Lexington. But local patriots got wind of the plan, and Boston's Committee of Safety sent Paul Revere and William Dawes by separate routes on their famous ride to spread the alarm. Revere reached Lexington about midnight and alerted John Hancock and Sam Adams, who were hiding there. Joined by Dawes and Dr. Samuel Prescott, who had been visiting in Lexington, he rode on toward Concord. A British patrol intercepted the trio, but Prescott got through with the warning.

At dawn on the morning of April 19 the British advance guard found Capt. John Parker and about seventy Minute Men lined up on the village green at Lexington. Parker, lacking specific orders, had left the road to Concord unobstructed, and apparently intended only a silent protest, but Pitcairn rode onto the green ordering the militia to disperse. The Americans had already begun quietly backing away when somebody fired a shot and the British soldiers loosed a volley into the Minute Men, leaving eight dead and ten wounded. The British officers hastily got their men under control and back on the road to Concord. There the Americans already had carried off most of their stores, but the British destroyed what they could—including a Liberty Pole. At Concord's North Bridge the growing American forces inflicted fourteen casualties on a British platoon, and about noon Smith began marching his forces back to Boston. The road back had turned into a gauntlet as the embattled farmers from "every Middlesex village and farm" sniped from behind stone walls, trees, barns, houses, all the way back to Charlestown peninsula. By nightfall the survivors were safe under the protection of the fleet and army at Boston, having lost 273 men along the way, while the Americans lost 95.

THE SPREADING CONFLICT   When the Second Continental Congress convened at Philadelphia on May 10, 1775, Boston was under siege by the Massachusetts militia, commanded by Gen. Artemus Ward. On the very day that Congress met, Fort Ticonderoga in New York was surprised and taken by a force of "Green Mountain Boys" under Ethan Allen of Vermont and Massachusetts volunteers under Benedict Arnold of Connecticut, who held a commission from the Massachusetts Committee of Safety. The British yielded, Allen said, to his demand "in the name of the great Jehovah and the Continental Congress." Two days later the force took Crown Point, north of Ticonderoga.

(Above) *This 1775 engraving shows Major Pitcairn directing the fire of British troops on the Minute Men at Lexington.* (Below) *American farmers fire on the British as they retreat to Boston.*

The Continental Congress, with no legal authority and no re-sources, met amid reports of spreading warfare and had little choice but to assume the de facto role of a revolutionary govern-ment. The Congress accepted a request that it "adopt" the mot-

*The Battle of Bunker Hill, and the burning of Charles Town.*

ley army gathered around Boston and on June 15 named George Washington to be general and commander-in-chief of a Continental Army. In the original organizational plan, four major-generals and eight brigadiers were commissioned. To support the enterprise Congress resorted to a familiar colonial expedient, paper money, and voted to issue $2 million with the colonies pledged to redemption in proportion to their population.

On June 17, the very day that Washington got his commission, the colonials and British forces engaged in their first major fight, the Battle of Bunker Hill. While Congress deliberated, both American and British forces in and around Boston had grown. Militiamen from Rhode Island, Connecticut, and New Hampshire joined in the siege. British reinforcements included three major-generals—Sir William Howe, Sir Henry Clinton, and John Burgoyne—who brought Gage belated orders to proceed against Concord. On the day before the battle American forces began to fortify the high ground of Charlestown peninsula, overlooking Boston. Breed's Hill was the battle location, nearer to Boston than Bunker Hill, the site first chosen (and the source of the battle's erroneous name). Gage, at the urging of Henry Clinton, ordered a frontal assault, with British forces moving in formation against murderously accurate fire from the militiamen.

On the third attempt, when the colonials began to run out of gunpowder, a bayonet charge ousted them. The British took the high ground, but at the cost of 1,054 casualties among about 2,000 men. The colonials lost about 400 in casualties and prisoners.

When Washington arrived to take charge things had again reached a stalemate, and so remained through the winter, until early March. At that time American forces occupied Dorchester Heights to the south and brought the city under threat of bombardment with cannon and mortars. Gen. William Howe, who had long since replaced Gage as British commander, reasoned that discretion was the better part of valor and retreated by water to Halifax, Nova Scotia. The last British forces, along with fearful American Loyalists, embarked on March 17, 1776, which Boston afterward celebrated as Evacuation Day—a double holiday for the Boston Irish. By that time British power had collapsed nearly everywhere, and the British forces faced not the suppression of a rebellion but the reconquest of a continent.

While Boston remained under siege the Continental Congress held to the dimming hope that compromise was still possible. On July 5 and 6, 1775, the delegates issued two major documents: an appeal to the king thereafter known as the Olive Branch Petition, and a Declaration of the Causes and Necessity of Taking Up Arms. The Olive Branch Petition, written by John Dickinson, professed continued loyalty to George III and begged him to restrain further hostilities pending a reconciliation. The Declaration, also largely Dickinson's work, traced the controversy, denounced the British for the unprovoked assault at Lexington, and rejected independence but affirmed the colonists' purpose to fight for their rights rather than submit to slavery. When the Olive Branch Petition reached London the outraged king refused even to look at it. On August 22 he ordered the army at Boston to regard the colonists "as open and avowed enemies." The next day he issued a proclamation of rebellion.

Before the end of July 1775 the Congress authorized an attack on Québec in the vain hope of rallying support from the French inhabitants. One force, under Richard Montgomery, advanced by way of Lake Champlain; another, under Benedict Arnold, struggled through the Maine woods. Together they held Québec under siege from mid-September until their final attack was repulsed on December 30, 1775. Montgomery was killed in the battle and Arnold wounded.

In the South, Virginia's Governor Dunmore raised a Loyalist force, including slaves recruited on promise of freedom, but met defeat in December 1775. After leaving Norfolk he returned on January 1, 1776, and burned most of the town. In North Carolina, Loyalist Scottish Highlanders, joined by some former Regulators, were dispersed by a Patriot force at Moore's Creek Bridge. The Loyalists had set out for Wilmington to join an expeditionary force under Lord Cornwallis and Sir Henry Clinton. That plan frustrated, the British commanders decided to attack Charleston instead, but the Patriot militia there had partially finished a palmetto log fort on Sullivan's Island (later named in honor of its commander, Col. William Moultrie). When the British fleet attacked on June 28, 1776, the spongy palmetto logs absorbed the naval fire and Fort Moultrie's cannon returned it with devastating effect. The fleet, with over 200 casualties and every ship damaged, was forced to retire. South Carolina honored the palmetto by putting it on the state flag.

As the fighting spread north into Canada and south into Virginia and the Carolinas, the Continental Congress assumed, one after another, the functions of government. As early as July 1775 it appointed commissioners to negotiate treaties of peace with Indian tribes and organized a Post Office Department with Benjamin Franklin as postmaster-general. In October it authorized formation of a navy, in November a marine corps. A committee appointed in November began to explore the possibility of foreign aid. In March 1776 the Continental Navy raided Nassau in the Bahamas, and Congress further authorized privateering operations against British vessels. But the delegates continued to hold back from the seeming abyss of independence. Yet through late 1775 and early 1776 word came of one British action after another that proclaimed rebellion and war. In December 1775 a Prohibitory Act declared the colonies closed to all commerce, and word came that the king and cabinet were seeking mercenaries in Europe, and getting them in Germany. Eventually almost 30,000 Germans served, about 17,000 of them from the principality of Hesse-Kassel, and "Hessian" became the name applied to them all. Parliament remained deaf to the warnings of Burke, Pitt, John Wilkes, Charles James Fox, and other members that reconquest would not only be costly in itself but that the effort might lead to another great war with France and Spain.

COMMON SENSE   In January 1776 Thomas Paine's pamphlet *Common Sense* was published anonymously in Philadelphia. Paine had arrived there thirteen months before. Coming from a humble Quaker background, Paine had distinguished himself chiefly as a drifter, a failure in marriage and business. At age thirty-

*Thomas Paine, whose* Common Sense *helped spark a revolution.*

seven he set sail for America with a letter of introduction from Benjamin Franklin and the purpose of setting up a school for young ladies. When that did not work out, he moved into the political controversy as a freelance writer, and with *Common Sense* proved himself the consummate revolutionary rhetorician. Until his pamphlet appeared the squabble had been mainly with Parliament. Paine directly attacked allegiance to the monarchy which had remained the last frayed connection to Britain, and refocused the hostility previously vented on Parliament. The common sense of the matter, it seemed, was that King George III and the King's Friends bore the responsibility for the malevolence toward the colonies. Monarchy, Paine boldly proclaimed, rested upon usurpation; its origins would not bear looking into. One honest man, he said, was worth more "than all the crowned ruffians that ever lived." Americans should consult their own interests, abandon George III, and declare their independence: "The blood of the slain, the weeping voice of nature cries,'TIS TIME TO PART."

### INDEPENDENCE

Within three months more than 100,000 copies were in circulation. "*Common Sense* is working a powerful change in the minds of men," George Washington said. "A few more flaming arguments as Falmouth and Norfolk and the principles of *Common Sense* will not leave many in doubt." A visitor to North Carolina's Provincal Congress could "hear nothing praised but

*The Continental Congress votes Independence, July 2, 1776.*

*Common Sense* and independence." One by one the provincial governments authorized their delegates in Congress to take the final step: Massachusetts in January, South Carolina in March, Georgia and North Carolina in April, Virginia in May. On June 7 Richard Henry Lee of Virginia moved a resolution "that these United Colonies are, and of right ought to be, free and independent states. . . ." Lee's resolution passed on July 2, a date that "will be the most memorable epoch in the history of America," John Adams wrote to his wife Abigail. The memorable date, however, became July 4, 1776, when Congress adopted Thomas Jefferson's Declaration of Independence, a statement of political philosophy which remains a dynamic force to the present day.

JEFFERSON'S *DECLARATION*   Jefferson's summary of the prevailing political sentiment, prepared on behalf of a committee of John Adams, Benjamin Franklin, Roger Sherman, and Robert R. Livingston, was an eloquent restatement of John Locke's contract theory of government, the theory in Jefferson's words that governments derived "their just Powers from the consent of the people," who were entitled to "alter or abolish" those which denied their "unalienable rights" to "life, Liberty, and the pursuit of Happiness." The appeal was no longer simply to "the rights of Englishmen" but to the broader "laws of Nature and Nature's God." But at the same time the Declaration implicitly suported the theory that the British Empire was a federation united only through the crown. Parliament, which had no proper authority over the colonies, was never mentioned by name. The enemy was a king who had "combined with others to subject us to a jurisdiction foreign to our constitution, and unacknowledged by our laws. . . ." The document set forth "a history of repeated injuries and usurpations, all having in direct object the establishment of an absolute Tyranny over these States." The "Representatives of the United States of America," therefore, declared the thirteen "United Colonies" to be "Free and Independent States."

"WE ALWAYS HAD GOVERNED OURSELVES"  So it had come to this, thirteen years after Britain acquired domination of North America. Historians have been fruitful in advancing theories and explanations: trade regulation, the restrictions on western lands, the tax burden, the burden of debts to British merchants, the fear of an Anglican bishop, the growth of a national consciousness, the lack of representation in Parliament, ideologies of Whiggery and the Enlightenment, the evangelistic impulse, Scottish moral philosophy, the abrupt shift from a mercantile to an "imperial" policy after 1763, class conflict, revolutionary conspiracy. Each of them separately and all of them together are subject to challenge, but each contributed something to collective grievances

*Thomas Jefferson's draft of the Declaration of Independence.*

that rose to a climax in a gigantic failure of British statesmanship. A conflict between British sovereignty and American rights had come to a point of confrontation that adroit statesmanship might have avoided, sidestepped, or outflanked. Irresolution and vacillation in the British ministry finally gave way to the stubborn determination to force an issue long permitted to drift. The colonists, conditioned by the Whig interpretation of history, saw these developments as the conspiracy of a corrupted oligarchy —and finally, they decided, of a despotic king—to impose an "absolute Tyranny."

Perhaps the last word on how it came about should belong to an obscure participant, Levi Preston, a Minute Man of Danvers, Massachusetts. Asked sixty-seven years after Lexington and Concord about British oppressions, he responded, as his young interviewer reported later: " 'What were they? Oppressions? I didn't feel them.' 'What, were you not oppressed by the Stamp Act?' 'I never saw one of those stamps, and always understood that Governor Bernard put them all in Castle William. I am certain I never paid a penny for one of them.' 'Well, what then about the tea-tax?' 'Tea-tax! I never drank a drop of the stuff; the boys threw it all overboard.' 'Then I suppose you had been reading Harrington or Sidney and Locke about the eternal principles of liberty.' 'Never heard of 'em. We read only the Bible, the Catechism, Watts's Psalms and Hymns, and the Almanack.' 'Well, then, what was the matter? and what did you mean in going to the fight?' 'Young man, what we meant in going for those redcoats was this: we always had governed ourselves, and we always meant to. They didn't mean we should.' "

## Further Reading

For a narrative survey of the events leading to the Revolution, see Edmund S. Morgan's *The Birth of the Republic, 1763–1789* (rev. ed., 1977),° Robert Middlekauff's *The Glorious Cause: The American Revolution, 1763–1789* (1982),° and Edward Countryman's *The American Revolution* (1985).°

For the perspective of Great Britain on the imperial conflict, see Sir Lewis Namier's *England in the Age of the American Revolution* (2nd ed., 1961) and Ian Christie, *Crisis of Empire* (1966).

The intellectual foundations for revolt are traced in Bernard Bailyn's *The Ideological Origins of the American Revolution* (1967)° and in the opening chapters of Gordon S. Wood's *The Creation of the American Re-*

°These books are available in paperback editions.

*public, 1776–1787* (1969).° To understand how these views were connected to organized protest, see Pauline Maier's *From Resistance to Revolution: Colonial Radicals and the Development of American Opposition to Great Britain, 1765–1776* (1972).° Profiles of the revolutionary generation can be found in Maier's *The Old Revolutionaries: Political Lives in the Age of Samuel Adams* (1980).° Other biographies include Merrill D. Peterson's *Thomas Jefferson and the New Nation* (1970), Dumas Malone's *Jefferson, the Virginian* (1948), Peter Shaw's *The Character of John Adams* (1976), and Eric Foner's *Tom Paine and Revolutionary America* (1976).° Jay Fliegelman's *Prodigals and Pilgrims* (1982) shows how changes in family structure predisposed colonists to revolution.

A number of books deal with specific events in the chain of crisis. Oliver M. Dickerson's *The Navigation Acts and the American Revolution* (1951) stresses the change from trade regulation to taxation in 1764. Edmund S. Morgan and Helen M. Morgan's *The Stamp Act Crisis* (rev. ed., 1962)° gives the colonial perspective on that crucial event, while P. D. G. Thomas's *British Politics and the Stamp Act Crisis* (1975) emphasizes imperial motives. Also valuable are Hiller B. Zobel's *The Boston Massacre* (1970), Benjamin W. Labaree's *The Boston Tea Party* (1964), and David Ammerman's *In the Common Cause* (1974), on the Coercive Acts. Thomas Doerflinger's *A Vigorous Spirit of Enterprise: Merchants and Economic Development in Revolutionary Philadelphia* (1986)° describes the role of that influential group in the imperial crisis. Carl L. Becker's *The Declaration of Independence* (1922)° remains the best introduction to the framing of that document. More interpretive on the contents of the Declaration is Garry Wills's *Inventing America: Jefferson's Declaration of Independence* (1978).°

For accounts of the imperial controversy at the colony level, see Patricia U. Bonomi's *A Factious People: Politics and Society in Colonial New York* (1971)° and Edward Countryman's *A People in Revolution* (1981),° both on New York; Richard D. Brown's *Revolutionary Politics in Massachusetts* (1970)° and Richard L. Bushman's *King and People in Provincial Massachusetts* (1985); James H. Hutson's *Pennsylvania Politics, 1746–1770* (1972); Rhys Isaac's *The Transformation of Virginia, 1740–1790* (1982);° and A. Roger Ekirch's *"Poor Carolina": Politics and Society in Colonial North Carolina, 1729–1776* (1981).

Events west of the Appalachians are chronicled concisely by Jack M. Sosin in *The Revolutionary Frontier, 1763–1783* (1967).

Military affairs in the early phases of the war are handled in John W. Shy's *Toward Lexington* (1965) and in other works listed in Chapter 6.

# 6 ∽

## THE AMERICAN REVOLUTION

### 1776: WASHINGTON'S NARROW ESCAPE

On July 2, 1776, the day that Congress voted for independence, British redcoats landed on the undefended Staten Island. They were the vanguard of a gigantic effort to reconquer America and the first elements of an enormous force that gathered around New York Harbor over the next month. By mid-August Gen. William Howe, with the support of a fleet under his older brother, Admiral Richard, Lord Howe, had some 32,000 men at his disposal, including 9,000 "Hessians"—the biggest single force ever mustered by the British in the eighteenth century. Washington had expected the move and transferred most of his men from Boston, but could muster only about 19,000 Continentals and militiamen. With such a force New York was indefensible, but Congress wanted it held, and in making gestures of resistance Washington exposed his men to entrapments from which they escaped more by luck and Howe's caution than by any strategic genius of the American commander. Washington was still learning his trade, and the New York campaign afforded some expensive lessons.

FIGHTING IN NEW YORK AND NEW JERSEY  The first conflicts took place on Long Island, where the Americans wanted to hold Brooklyn Heights, from which the city might be bombarded. In late August, however, Howe inflicted heavy losses in early battles and forced Washington to evacuate Long Island to reunite his dangerously divided forces. A timely rainstorm, with winds and tides, kept the British fleet out of the East River and made possible a withdrawal to Manhattan under cover of darkness.

*Gen. William Howe, commander-in-chief of His Majesty's forces in America.*

After their success on Long Island the brothers Howe sought a parley with commissioners from the Continental Congress. At the Staten Island Peace Conference on September 11 they met with Benjamin Franklin, John Adams, and Edmund Rutledge, but it soon became clear that the Howes were empowered, in effect, only to negotiate a surrender. Pardons were offered to those who returned to British allegiance and vague promises of fair treatment were advanced—but only after all "extralegal" congresses and conventions were dissolved. The Americans chose to fight on against the odds.

The odds were overwhelming, and they might have been decisive if Howe had moved quickly to pen Washington in lower Manhattan. The main American force, however, withdrew northward to the mainland and retreated slowly across New Jersey and over the Delaware River into Pennsylvania. In the retreat marched a volunteer, Thomas Paine. Having opened an eventful year with his pamphlet *Common Sense*, he composed in Newark *The American Crisis* (the first of several *Crisis* papers) which now appeared in Philadelphia:

> These are the times that try men's souls: The summer soldier and the sunshine patriot will, in this crisis, shrink from the service of his country; but he that stands it NOW deserves the love and thanks of man and woman. Tyranny, like Hell, is not easily conquered. Yet we have this consolation with us, that the harder the conflict, the more glorious the triumph.

The pamphlet, ordered read in the Revolutionary camps, resolved by its eloquence the hesitation of many and helped re-

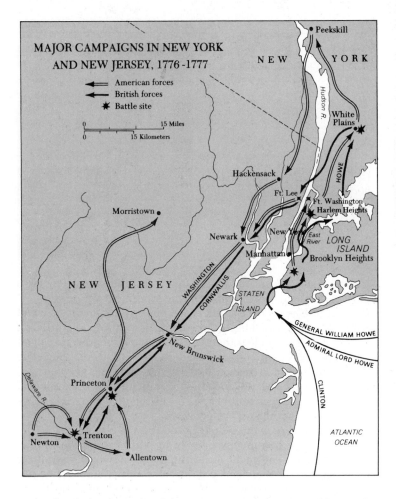

MAJOR CAMPAIGNS IN NEW YORK
AND NEW JERSEY, 1776 -1777

American forces
British forces
★ Battle site

0        15 Miles
0        15 Kilometers

N E W        Y O R K

• Peekskill

Hudson R.

White
Plains

HOWE

Hackensack

Ft. Lee

Ft. Washington
Harlem Heights

Morristown •

Newark

New York

East
River

LONG
ISLAND

Manhattan

Brooklyn Heights

N E W        J E R S E Y

WASHINGTON

CORNWALLIS

STATEN
ISLAND

GENERAL WILLIAM HOWE

ADMIRAL LORD HOWE

New Brunswick

CLINTON

Delaware R.

Princeton

ATLANTIC
OCEAN

Newton

Trenton

Allentown

store the shaken morale of the Patriots—as events would soon do
more decisively.

General Howe, firmly ensconced in New York (which the British held throughout the war), established outposts in New Jersey
and to the east at Newport, and settled down to wait out the
winter. But Washington was not yet ready to go into winter
quarters. Instead he daringly seized the initiative. On Christmas
night 1776 he slipped across the icy Delaware with some 2,400
men (an episode immortalized in the heroic and fanciful painting
of Emmanuel Leutze) and near dawn at Trenton surprised a garrison of 1,500 Hessians still befuddled from too much holiday
cheer. It was a total rout from which only 500 royal soldiers
escaped death or capture. At nearby Princeton on January 3 the

*George Washington, commander-in-chief of the Continental Army, portrayed here at the battle of Princeton.*

Americans met and drove off three regiments of British redcoats, and finally took refuge in winter quarters at Morristown, in the hills of northern Jersey. The campaigns of 1776 had ended, after repeated defeats, with two minor victories which inspirited the Patriot cause. Howe had missed his great chance, indeed several chances, to bring the rebellion to a speedy end.

## AMERICAN SOCIETY AT WAR

THE LOYALISTS Before Trenton, General Howe may have thought that Washington's army was on the verge of collapse and that he need not embitter the colonials and endanger the future restoration by inflicting needless casualties. During the summer and fall of 1776, in fact, New Jersey civilians assumed that the rebellion was collapsing and thousands hastened to sign an oath of allegiance. But the British setbacks at Trenton and Princeton reversed the outlook, and with the British withdrawal New Jersey quickly went back under insurgent control. Through most of the war, in New Jersey and in other colonies, the British would be chasing the elusive Tory majority that Loyalists kept telling them was out there waiting only for British regulars to show the flag.

Opinion concerning the war was divided three ways among Patriots or Whigs (as the revolutionaries called themselves), Tories (as Patriots called the Empire Loyalists, recalling the die-hard defenders of royal prerogative in England), and an indifferent middle swayed mostly by the better organized and more energetic radicals. That the Loyalists were numerous is evident from the departure during or after the war of roughly 100,000 of them, or more than 3 percent of the total population. But the Patriots were probably the largest of the three groups. There was a like division in British opinion. The aversion of so many Englishmen to the war was one reason for the government's hiring German mercenaries, the "Hessians."

Toryism was "a distinctly urban and seaboard phenomenon" with a clear "commercial, officeholding, and professional bias." But Tories came from all walks of life. Governors, judges, and other royal officials were almost totally loyal; colonial merchants might be tugged one way or the other, depending on how much they had benefited or suffered from mercantilist regulation; the great planters were swayed one way by dependence on British bounties, another by their debts to British merchants. In the backcountry of New York and the Carolinas many humble folk rallied to the crown. Where planter aristocrats tended to be Whig, as in North Carolina, backcountry farmers (many of them recently Regulators) leaned to the Tories. Calculations of self-interest, of course, did not always govern. Sentiment and conviction could be, and often were, the roots of loyalty.

THE MOMENTUM OF WAR    The American Revolution has ever since seemed to most Americans a fight between the Americans and the British, but the War for Independence was also very much a civil war which set brother against brother and divided such families as the Randolphs of Virginia, the Morrises of Pennsylvania, and the Otises of Massachusetts. The fratricidal hate that often goes with civil war gave rise to some of the most bloodcurdling atrocities in the backcountry of New York and Pennsylvania and in Georgia where Tory Rangers and their Indian allies went marauding against frontier Whigs. Whigs responded in kind against units of Loyalist militia or regulars. Once begun, the retaliation and counterretaliation of guerrilla warfare developed a momentum of its own.

In few places, however, were there enough Tories to assume control without the presence of British regulars, and nowhere for very long. Time and again the British forces were frustrated by both the failure of Loyalists to materialize in strength and the collapse of Loyalist militia units once regular detachments pulled out. Even more disheartening was what one British officer called "the licentiousness of the troops, who committed every species of rapine and plunder," and thereby converted potential friends into enemies. British and Hessian regulars, brought up in a hard school of warfare, tended to treat all civilians as hostile. Loyalist militiamen, at the same time, were loath to let any rebel sympathizers slip back into passivity, and so prodded them into active hostility. On the other side the Patriot militia kept springing to life whenever redcoats appeared nearby, and all adult white males, with few exceptions, were obligated under state law to serve when called. With time even the most apathetic would be pressed into a commitment, if only to turn out for drill. And sooner or later nearly every colonial county was touched by military action that would call for armed resistance. The war itself, then, whether through British and Loyalist behavior or the call of the militia, mobilized the apathetic into at least an appearance of support for the American cause. This commitment was seldom reversed once made.

MILITIA AND ARMY    Americans were engaged in the kind of fighting that had become habitual when they were colonists. To repel an attack, the militia somehow materialized; the danger past, it evaporated. There were things to take care of at home and no

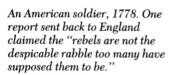

*An American soldier, 1778. One report sent back to England claimed the "rebels are not the despicable rabble too many have supposed them to be."*

time for concern about other battles over the horizon. They "come in, you cannot tell how," George Washington said in exasperation, "go, you cannot tell when, and act you cannot tell where, consume your provisions, exhaust your stores, and leave you at last at a critical moment." The militia was usually best at bushwhacking. All too often the green troops would panic in a formal line of battle, and so were commonly placed in the front ranks in the hope that they would get off a shot or two before they turned tail.

The Continental Army, by contrast, was on the whole well trained and dependable, whipped into shape by such foreign volunteers as the marquis de Lafayette and the baron von Steuben. Although some 230,000 enlistees passed through the army, many of those were repeaters who came in for tenures as brief as three months. Washington's army fluctuated in size from around 10,000 troops to as high as 20,000 and as low as 5,000. At times he could put only 2,000–3,000 in the field. Line regiments were organized, state by state, and the states were supposed to keep them filled with volunteers, or conscripts if need be, but Washington could never be sure that his requisitions would be met.

PROBLEMS OF FINANCE AND SUPPLY  The same uncertainty beset the army and Congress in their quest for supplies. None of the states came through with more than a part of its share, and Congress reluctantly let army agents take supplies directly from farmers in return for Quartermaster Certificates, which promised future payment. Congress managed to raise some $9 million from the domestic sale of bonds, some $11 million from foreign loans, and about $6 million in requisitions on the states. Since these totals fell short of the war's cost, the only recourse left was paper money. In June 1775 Congress began the issuance of Continental currency and kept the printing presses running until nearly $250 million was outstanding before the end of 1779. The states issued about another $200 million. By 1780 the Continental dollar had depreciated so badly that Congress called in the notes, taking them for payments in place of silver at a ratio of $40 in paper to $1 in silver. Over $100 million came in under that proviso, but new notes were issued in their place to the amount of about $4.5 million.

With goods scarce and money plentiful, prices in terms of "Continentals" rose sharply. During the winter of 1777–1778 Washington's men would suffer terribly, less because of actual shortages than because farmers preferred to sell their produce for British gold and silver. Congress did better at providing mu-

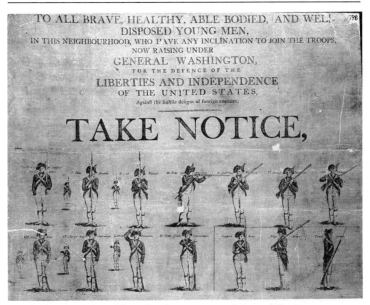

TO ALL BRAVE, HEALTHY, ABLE BODIED, AND WELL
DISPOSED YOUNG MEN,
IN THIS NEIGHBOURHOOD, WHO HAVE ANY INCLINATION TO JOIN THE TROOPS,
NOW RAISING UNDER
GENERAL WASHINGTON,
FOR THE DEFENCE OF THE
LIBERTIES AND INDEPENDENCE
OF THE UNITED STATES,
Against the hostile designs of foreign enemies,

# TAKE NOTICE,

*A poster recruiting soldiers for the Continental Army. The Congress appealed to those interested in "viewing the different parts of this beautiful continent, in the honourable and truly respectable character of a soldier," and then returning home "with his pockets FULL of money and his head COVERED with laurels."*

nitions than at providing other supplies. In 1777 Congress established a government arsenal at Springfield, Massachusetts, and during the war states offered bounties for the manufacture of guns and powder. Still, most munitions were supplied either by capture during the war or by importation from France, where the government was all too glad to help rebels against its British arch-enemy.

During the harsh winter at Morristown (1776–1777) Washington's army very nearly disintegrated as enlistments expired and deserters fled the hardships. Only about 1,000 Continentals and a few militiamen stuck it out. With the spring thaw, however, recruits began arriving to claim the bounty of $20 and 100 acres of land offered by Congress to those who would enlist for three years or for the duration of the conflict, if less. With some 9,000 regulars Washington began sparring and feinting with Howe in northern New Jersey. Howe had been maturing other plans, however, and so had other British officers.

### 1777: Setbacks for the British

Divided counsels, overconfidence, poor communications, and vacillation plagued British planning for the campaigns of 1777. After the removal of General Gage during the siege of Boston, there was no commander-in-chief. Guy Carleton held an independent command in Canada, but it transpired that he was not even in charge of plans for his own theater. Instead his subordinate, the vainglorious "Gentleman Johnny" Burgoyne, had rushed back to London at the end of 1776 with news of Carleton's cautious withdrawal from Ticonderoga. In London, Burgoyne won the ear of Lord George Germain, the secretary of state for the colonies, who endorsed Burgoyne's plan and put him in command of the northern armies. Burgoyne proposed to advance southward to the Hudson while another force moved eastward from Oswego down the Mohawk Valley. Howe, meanwhile, could lead a third force up the Hudson from New York City. This three-pronged offensive would bisect the colonies along the Hudson River line.

Howe in fact had proposed a similar plan, combined with an attack on New England, and had he stuck to it, might have cut the colonies in two and delivered them a disheartening blow. But he changed his mind and decided to move against the Patriot capital, Philadelphia, expecting that the Pennyslvania Tories would then rally to the crown and secure the colony. Germain had approved that plan too, confident that some 3,000 troops left in New York would be enough to divert Patriot strength from Burgoyne. Howe and Germain, it turned out, were both wrong in their expectations. Howe, moreover, finally decided to move on Philadelphia from the south, by way of Chesapeake Bay, and that put his forces even father away from Burgoyne.

Howe's plan succeeded, up to a point. He took Philadelphia—or as Benjamin Franklin put it, Philadelphia took him. The Tories there proved fewer than he expected. Washington, sensing Howe's purpose, withdrew most of his men from New Jersey to meet the new threat. At Brandywine Creek, south of Philadelphia, Howe pushed Washington's forces back on September 11 and eight days later occupied Philadelphia. Washington counterattacked against a British encampment at Germantown on October 4, but reinforcements from Philadelphia under General Lord Cornwallis arrived in time to repulse the attack. Washington retired into winter quarters at Valley Forge while Howe and his men remained for the winter in the relative comfort of Phila-

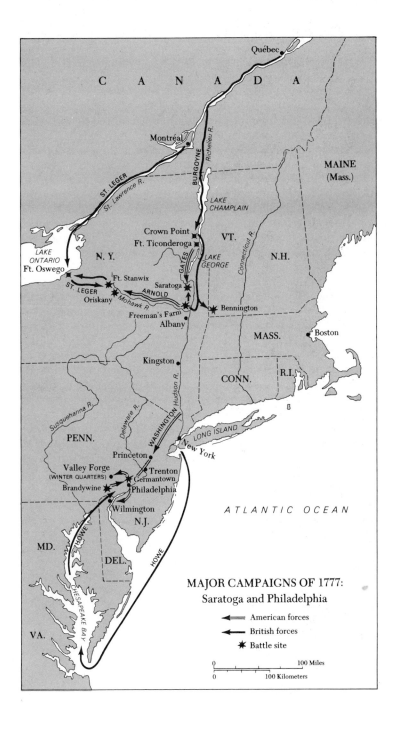

MAJOR CAMPAIGNS OF 1777:
Saratoga and Philadelphia

⇐ American forces
← British forces
✳ Battle site

0 _____ 100 Miles
0 _____ 100 Kilometers

delphia, twenty miles away. But Howe had gained a pyrrhic victory, while Burgoyne to the north was stumbling into disaster.

SARATOGA    Burgoyne moved southward along the Richelieu River toward Lake Champlain with about 9,500 men, and sent Lt.-Col. Barry St. Leger westward with a band of 900 regulars, Tories, and Canadian scouts. At Oswego they picked up nearly a thousand Iroquois allies and headed eastward for Albany. The American army in the north, like Washington's army at Morristown, had dwindled during the winter, and when Burgoyne brought cannon to Mount Defiance, overlooking Fort Ticonderoga, the Continentals prudently abandoned the fort but with substantial loss of powder and supplies. An angry Congress thereupon removed Gen. Philip Schuyler from command of the northern forces and replaced him with Horatio Gates, a favorite of the New Englanders. Fortunately for the American forces Burgoyne delayed at Ticonderoga while reinforcements of Continentals and militia arrived from the south and from New England.

Before Gates arrived, Burgoyne had already suffered two reversals. At Oriskany, New York, on August 6, a band of militia repulsed an ambush by St. Leger's Tories and Indians, and gained time for Benedict Arnold to bring a thousand Continentals to the relief of Fort Stanwix. St. Leger's Indians, convinced they faced an even greater force than they actually did, deserted him, and the Mohawk Valley was secured for the Patriot forces. To the east, at Bennington, Vermont, a body of New England militia repulsed a British foraging party with heavy losses (August 16). American reinforcements continued to gather, and after two

*The vainglorious Gen. John Burgoyne, commander of England's northern forces. Burgoyne and 5,000 British troops surrendered to the Americans at Saratoga on October 17, 1777.*

sharp battles at Freeman's Farm (September 19 and October 7) Burgoyne pulled back to Saratoga, where Gates's forces surrounded him. On October 17,1777, Burgoyne capitulated. By the terms of the surrender his 5,000 soldiers laid down their arms on their word that they would embark for England, under parole (or promise) not to participate further in the war—a genial eighteenth-century practice that saved a lot of upkeep on prisoners-of-war. American leaders, however, feared that the returned prisoners would only be replaced by others stationed in England, and reneged on this agreement. Some of the Hessians were released to assume American residence but the main forces were taken away as prisoners to Virginia. Burgoyne himself was allowed to go home.

ALLIANCE WITH FRANCE   On December 2 news of the American triumph reached London; two days later it reached Paris, where it was celebrated almost as if it were a French victory. It was a signal awaited by both French officials and American agents there, and its impact on the French made Saratoga a decisive turning point in the war. The French foreign minister, the comte de Vergennes, had watched the developing Anglo-American crisis with great anticipation. In September 1775 he had sent a special agent to Philadelphia to encourage the colonists and hint at French aid. In November of that year the Continental Congress set up a Committee of Secret Correspondence, later called the Committee for Foreign Affairs, a forerunner of the State Department. The committee employed Massachusetts colonial agent Arthur Lee as its envoy in London. Then in March 1776 it sent Silas Deane, a Connecticut merchant, to buy munitions and other supplies and inquire about French aid. In September 1776 the committee named Deane, Lee, and Benjamin Franklin its commissioners to France.

In May 1776 the French took their first step toward aiding the colonists. King Louis XVI turned over a million livres to Pierre Augustin Caron de Beaumarchais (author of *The Barber of Seville* and *The Marriage of Figaro*) for clandestine help to the Americans. Assuming the guise of a trading enterprise, Beaumarchais was soon guiding fourteen ships with war matériel to America; most of the Continental Army's powder in the first years of the war came from this source. The Spanish government added a donation, and soon established its own supply company. When the word from Saratoga arrived, Beaumarchais got so carried away in his haste to tell Louis XVI that he wrecked his carriage.

Vergennes now saw his chance to strike a sharper blow at

**The British Lion Engaging Four Powers.** *The American revolution sparked a world war, as this British cartoon suggests: "Behold the Dutch and Spanish Currs, / Perfidious Gallus in his Spurs, / And Rattlesnake, with head upright, / The British Lion join to fight; / He scorns the Bark, the Hiss, the Crow, / That he's a Lion soon they'll know."*

France's enemy and entered into serious negotiations with the American commissioners. On February 6, 1778, they signed two treaties: a Treaty of Amity and Commerce, in which France recognized the United States and offered trade concessions, including important privileges to American shipping, and a Treaty of Alliance. Under the latter both agreed, first, that if France entered the war, both countries would fight until American independence was won; second, that neither would conclude a "truce or peace" without "the formal consent of the other first obtained"; and third, that each guaranteed the other's possessions in America "from the present time and forever against all other powers." France further bound herself to seek neither Canada nor other British possessions on the mainland of North America.

Vergennes at first tried to get Spain to act with him. When Spain hesitated France took the plunge alone. By June 1778 British vessels had fired on French ships and the two nations were at war. In 1779, after extracting French promises to help her get back territories taken by the British in the previous war, including Gibraltar, Spain entered the war as an ally of France, but not of the United States. In 1780 Britain declared war on the Dutch, who persisted in a profitable trade with the French and Americans. The embattled farmers at Concord had indeed fired the "shot heard round the world." Like Washington's encounter with the French in 1754, it was the start of another world war, and the fighting now spread to the Mediterranean, Africa, India, the West Indies, and the high seas.

1778: BOTH SIDES REGROUP

After Saratoga, Lord North knew that the war was unwinable, but the king refused to let him either resign or make peace. North did propose a gesture of conciliation, but his ministry and Parliament moved in such a dilatory fashion that the Franco-American Alliance was signed before the gesture could be made. On March 16, 1778, the House of Commons finally adopted a program which in effect granted all the American demands prior to independence. Parliament repealed the Townshend tea duty, the Massachusetts Government Act, and the Prohibitory Act, which had closed the colonies to commerce. It authorized a peace commission which the earl of Carlisle was appointed to head. Further delays followed before the Carlisle Commission reached Philadelphia in June, a month after Congress had ratified the French treaties. The Congress refused to begin any negotiations until independence was recognized or British forces withdrawn, neither of which the commissioners could promise.

Unbeknownst to the Carlisle commissioners, the crown had already authorized the evacuation of Philadelphia, a withdrawal which further weakened what little bargaining power they had. After Saratoga, General Howe had resigned his command and Sir Henry Clinton had replaced him, with orders to pull out of Philadelphia, and if necessary, New York, but to keep Newport. He was to supply troops for an attack on the French island of St. Lucia and send an expedition to Georgia. In short, he was to take a defensive stand except in the South, where the government believed a latent Tory sentiment in the backcountry needed only the British presence for its release. The ministry was right, up to a point, but the sentiment turned out once again, as in other theaters of war, to be weaker than it seemed.

For Washington's army at Valley Forge the winter of 1777–1778 had been a season of suffering far worse than the previous winter at Morristown. While the great diplomatic achievement was maturing in Paris, the American force, encamped near Philadelphia, endured cold, hunger, and disease. Many deserted or resigned their commissions. Washington had to commandeer foodstuffs. The winter was marked by dissension in Congress and the army, and by an impulse to make Washington the scapegoat for the Patriots' plight. Despite rumors of a movement to replace him, there seems never to have developed any concerted effort to do so. One incident, which went down in history as the "Conway Cabal," apparently never amounted to anything more than a letter in which Gen. Thomas Conway criticized Washington and hinted at his hope that Horatio Gates would replace the commanding general. Gates disavowed any connection with the affair, except as recipient of the letter. Conway himself resigned from the service and later apologized to Washington after being wounded by another officer in a duel resulting from the affair.

As winter drew to an end the army's morale was strengthened by promises from Congress of extra pay and bonuses after the war, its spirit revived by the good news from France, and its fighting trim sharpened by the Prussian baron von Steuben who began to drill it in March. As General Clinton withdrew eastward toward New York, Washington began to move out in pursuit across New Jersey. On June 28 he caught up with the British at Monmouth Court House and engaged them in an indecisive battle, with about 300 casualties on either side. Clinton then slipped away into New York while Washington took up a position at White Plains, north of the city. From that time on the northern theater, scene of the major campaigns and battles in the first years of the war, settled into a long stalemate, interrupted by minor and mostly inconclusive engagements.

ACTIONS ON THE FRONTIER   The one major American success of 1778 occurred far from the New Jersey battlefields, out to the west where the British at Forts Niagara and Detroit had set frontier Tories and Indians to raiding western settlements. At Detroit Col. William Hamilton won the sobriquet "hair buyer" for his offers to pay for American scalps. Early in 1778 young George Rogers Clark took 175 frontiersmen and a flotilla of flatboats down the Ohio River, marched through the woods, and on the evening of July 4 took Kaskaskia by surprise. The French inhabitants, terrified at first, "fell into transports of joy" at news of the French alliance. Within a month, and without bloodshed, Clark took Cahokia (opposite St. Louis), Vincennes, and some minor outposts in what he now called the County of Illinois in the state of Virginia. After the British retook Vincennes in December, Clark marched his men (almost half French volunteers) through icy rivers and flooded prairies, sometimes in water neck deep, and laid siege to an astonished British garrison there. Then Clark, the hardened woodsman, tomahawked Indian captives in sight of the fort to show that the British afforded no protection.

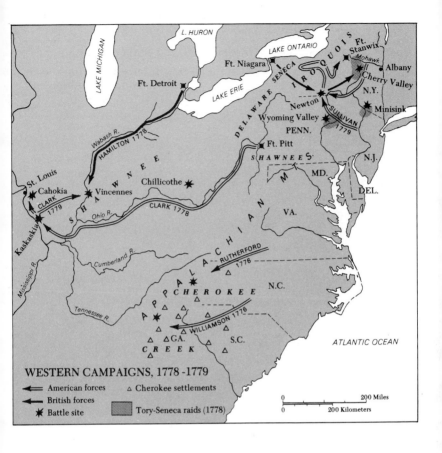

WESTERN CAMPAIGNS, 1778-1779

← American forces   △ Cherokee settlements
← British forces    ▨ Tory-Seneca raids (1778)
✳ Battle site

0        200 Miles
0        200 Kilometers

He spared the British captives when they surrendered, however, including the notorious Colonel Hamilton. Clark is often credited with having conquered the West for the new nation, but there is no evidence that the peace negotiators in 1782 knew about his exploit.

While Clark's captives traveled eastward, a much larger punitive expedition moved against the Iroquois country. On July 3, 1778, as Clark neared Kaskaskia, hundreds of Tory Rangers and Senecas (reputedly the most ferocious of the Iroquois) swept down from Fort Niagara into the Wyoming Valley of Pennsylvania, annihilated some "regular" and militia defenders, and took more than 200 scalps. The Tories and Indians continued to terrorize frontier settlements all through the summer until a climactic attack in November ravaged Cherry Valley, just fifty miles from Albany, New York. In response to the frontier outcries the Continental Congress instructed Washington to chastise the Iroquois. The task was entrusted to an expedition of 4,000 men under Gen. John Sullivan and James Clinton. At Newton (now Elmira) Sullivan met and defeated the only serious opposition on August 29, 1779, and proceeded to carry out Washington's instruction that the Iroquois country be not "merely overrun but destroyed."

The American force devastated about forty Seneca and Cayuga villages together with their orchards and food stores. So ruthless and complete was the destruction that large numbers of the Indians were thrown completely upon their British allies for scant supplies from Fort Niagara. The action broke the power of the Iroquois federation for all time, but it did not completely pacify the frontier. Sporadic encounters with various tribes of the region continued to the end of the war.

A similar fate befell the Cherokees farther south. In early 1776 a delegation of northern Indians—Shawnees, Delawares, and Mohawks—talked the Cherokees into striking at frontier settlements in Virginia and the Carolinas. Swift retaliation followed. In August, South Carolina forces burned the lower Cherokee towns and destroyed all the corn they could get their hands on. Virginia and North Carolina forces brought a similar destruction upon the middle and upper towns. Once again, in 1780, a Virginia–North Carolina force wrought destruction on Cherokee towns lest the Indians go to the aid of General Cornwallis, killing twenty-nine and burning over 1,000 towns and 50,000 bushels of corn, along with other supplies. By weakening the major Indian tribes along the frontier, the American Revolution, among its other results, cleared the way for rapid settlement of the trans-Appalachian West.

## THE WAR IN THE SOUTH

At the end of 1778 the focus of British action shifted suddenly to the south. The whole region from Virginia southward had been free from major action since 1776. Now the British would test King George's belief that a sleeping Tory power in the South needed only the presence of a few regulars to awaken it. So Lord George Germain conveyed to General Clinton His Majesty's plan to take Savannah and roll northward, gathering momentum from the Loyalist countryside. For a while the idea seemed to work, but it ran afoul of two things: first, the Loyalist strength was less than estimated; and second, the British forces behaved so harshly as to drive even loyal men into rebellion.

SAVANNAH AND CHARLESTON   In November 1778, in accord with the king's desire, Clinton dispatched 3,500 men from New York and New Jersey under Lt.-Col. Archibald Campbell to join Gen. Augustin Prevost's Florida Rangers in attacking Savannah. So small was the defending force of Continentals and militia that Campbell quickly overwhelmed the Patriots and took the town. Almost as quickly, with the help of Prevost, Campbell brushed aside opposition in the interior; Gov. James Wright returned and reestablished the royal government in Georgia. There followed a byplay of thrust and parry between Prevost and South Carolina

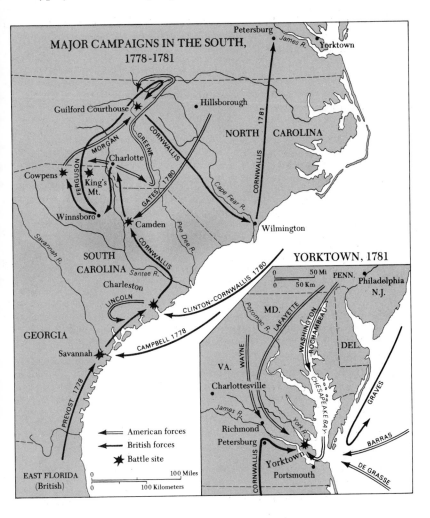

MAJOR CAMPAIGNS IN THE SOUTH, 1778-1781

YORKTOWN, 1781

forces. Prevost finally drove toward Charleston, his redcoats plundering plantation houses along the way. The pillage so delayed his army that in May 1779 Prevost fetched up against impregnable defenses on Charleston Neck and narrowly escaped entrapment by Gen. Benjamin Lincoln's Continentals.

The seesaw campaign took a major turn when General Clinton brought new naval and land forces southward to join a massive amphibious attack which bottled up General Lincoln on the Charleston peninsula. On May 12, 1780, Lincoln was compelled to surrender the city and its 5,500 defenders, the largest army surrendered since Saratoga and the greatest single American loss of the war. At this point Congress, against Washington's advice, turned to the victor of Saratoga, Horatio Gates, to take command and sent him south. Charles Lord Cornwallis, dispatched with one of three columns to subdue the Carolina interior, surprised Gates's force at Camden, South Carolina, and threw his new army into a rout, led by Gates himself all the way back to Hillsborough, North Carolina, 160 miles away. It had come to pass as Gates's friend and neighbor Charles Lee had warned after Saratoga: "Beware that your Northern laurels do not turn to Southern willows."

THE CAROLINAS   Cornwallis had South Carolina just about under control, but his cavalry leaders Banastre Tarleton and Patrick Ferguson, who mobilized Tory militiamen, overreached themselves in their effort to subdue the Whigs. "Tarleton's Quarters" became bywords for savagery, because "Bloody Tarleton" gave little quarter to vanquished foes. Ferguson sealed his own doom when he threatened to march over the mountains and hang the leaders of the Watauga country. Instead the "overmountain men" went after Ferguson and, allied with other backcountry Whigs, caught him and his Tories on Kings Mountain, just inside South Carolina. There, on October 7, 1780, they devastated his force of about 1,100. By then feelings were so strong that American irregulars continued firing on Tories trying to surrender and later inflicted indiscriminate slaughter on Tory prisoners. Kings Mountain, an unaccustomed victory, is sometimes called the turning point of the war in the South. Its effect, by proving that the British were not invincible, was to embolden small farmers to join guerrilla bands under partisan leaders like Frances Marion, "the Swamp Fox," and Thomas Sumter, "the Gamecock."

While the overmountain men were closing on Ferguson, Congress had chosen a new commander for the southern theater, Gen. Nathanael Greene, the "fighting Quaker" of Rhode Island.

A man of infinite patience, skilled at managing men and saving supplies, careful to avoid needless risks, he was suited to a war of attrition against the British forces. From Charlotte, where he arrived in December, Greene moved his army eastward toward the Pee Dee River, to a site picked by his engineer, the Polish volunteer Thaddeus Kosciuszko. As a diversion he sent Gen. Daniel Morgan with about 700 men on a sweep to the west of Cornwallis's headquarters at Winnsboro. Taking a position near Cowpens, Morgan found himself swamped by militia units joining him faster than he could provide for them. Tarleton caught Morgan and his men on January 17, 1781, with the rain-swollen Broad River at their backs—a position Morgan took deliberately to force the green militiamen to stand and fight. Once the battle was joined, Tarleton mistook a readjustment in the American line for a militia panic, and rushed his men into a destructive fire. Tarleton and a handful of cavalry escaped, but more than 100 of his men were killed and more than 700 taken prisoner.

Morgan then fell back into North Carolina, linked up with Greene's main force at Guilford Court House (now Greensboro), and then led Cornwallis on a wild goose chase up to the Dan River where, once the Americans had crossed, the British could not follow. His supplies running low, Cornwallis drew back to Hillsborough. When reinforcements of militiamen from Virginia and the Carolinas arrived, Greene returned to Guilford Court house and offered battle on March 15, 1781. There he placed his militiamen at the front of the line, asking them only to fire three shots before they drew back. As he feared, they fled the field, but in the process drew the pursuing redcoats into an enfilading fire from either side. Having inflicted heavy losses, Greene prudently withdrew to fight another day. Cornwallis was left in possession of the field, but at a cost of nearly 100 men killed and more than 400 wounded. In London, when the word arrived, parliamentary leader Charles James Fox echoed King Pyrrhus: "Another such victory and we are undone."

Cornwallis marched off toward the coast at Wilmington to lick his wounds and take on new supplies. Greene then resolved to go back into South Carolina in the hope of drawing Cornwallis after him or forcing the British to give up the state. There he joined forces with the guerrillas already active on the scene, and in a series of brilliant actions kept losing battles while winning the war: "We fight, get beat, rise, and fight again," he said. By September he had narrowed British control in the Deep South to Charleston and Savannah, although for more than a year longer Whigs and Tories slashed at each other "with savage fury" in the backcountry, where there was "nothing but murder and devastation in every quarter," Greene said.

Meanwhile Cornwallis had headed north away from Greene, reasoning that Virginia must be eliminated as a source of reinforcement before the Carolinas could be subdued. In May 1781 he marched north into Virginia. There, since December, Benedict Arnold, now a British general, was engaged in a war of maneuver with American forces under Lafayette and von Steuben. Arnold, until September 1780, had been American commander at West Point; there he nursed grievances over an official reprimand for extravagances as commander of reoccupied Philadelphia, and plotted to sell out the American stronghold to the British. The American capture of the British go-between, Maj. John André, revealed Arnold's plot. Forewarned, Arnold joined the British in New York while the hapless André was hanged as a spy.

YORKTOWN    When Cornwallis linked up with Arnold at Petersburg, their combined forces rose to 7,200, far more than the small American force there. British raiders went out deep into Virginia, and one sortie by Tarleton nearly captured Governor Jefferson and his legislature at Charlottesville. When American reinforcements arrived under Anthony Wayne, captor of Stony Point in 1779, Cornwallis moved back toward the coast to establish contact with New York. In a fatal miscalculation, he picked Yorktown as a defensible site. There seemed to be little reason to worry about a siege, with Washington's main land force attacking New York and the British navy in control of American waters.

To be sure, there was a small American navy, but it was no match for the British fleet. Washington had started it with some fishing vessels during the siege of Boston, but American privateers, acting under state or Continental authority, proved far more troublesome. Most celebrated then and after were the exploits of Capt. John Paul Jones, who crossed the Atlantic in 1778 with his sloop of war *Ranger* and gave the British navy some bad moments in its home waters. In France, Benjamin Franklin got Jones an old Indiaman which the captain named the *Bonhomme Richard* in honor of Franklin's Poor Richard. Off England's Flamborough Head on September 23, 1779, Jones won a desperate battle with the British frigate *Serapis*, which he captured and occupied before his own ship sank. This was the occasion for his stirring and oft-repeated response to a British demand for surrender: "I have not yet begun to fight."

Still, such heroics were little more than nuisances to the British. But at a critical point, thanks to the French navy, the British lost control of the Chesapeake waters. For three years Washington had waited to get some military benefit from the French alliance. In 1780 the French finally landed a force of about 6,000 at Newport, which the British had given up to concentrate on the South, but the French army under the comte de Rochambeau sat there for a year, blockaded by the British fleet. In 1781 the elements for combined action suddenly fell into place. In May, as Cornwallis moved into Virginia, Washington persuaded Rochambeau to join forces for an attack on New York. The two armies linked up in July, but before they could strike at New York, word came from the West Indies that Admiral De Grasse was bound for the Chesapeake with his entire French fleet and some 3,000 soldiers. Washington and Rochambeau immediately set out toward Yorktown, all the while preserving the semblance of a flank movement against New York.

*This French engraving shows Lord Cornwallis handing over his sword in surrender at Yorktown, October 19, 1781.*

On August 30 De Grasse's fleet reached Yorktown and landed his troops to join Lafayette's force already watching Cornwallis. On September 6, the day after a British fleet under Admiral Thomas Graves appeared, De Grasse gave battle and forced Graves to give up his effort to relieve Cornwallis, whose fate was quickly sealed. Graves departed four days later for repairs in New York. De Grasse then sent ships up the Chesapeake to ferry down Washington's and Rochambeau's armies, which brought the total American and French forces to more than 16,000, or better than double the size of Cornwallis's army. The siege began on September 28. On October 14 two major redoubts guarding the left of the British line fell to French and American attackers, the latter led by Washington's aide Alexander Hamilton. A British counterattack on October 16 failed to retake them, and later that day a squall forced Cornwallis to abandon a desperate plan to escape across the York River. On October 17, 1781, four years to the day after Saratoga, he sued for peace, and on October 19 the British force of almost 8,000 marched out, their colors cased. Gen. Benjamin Lincoln, captured at Charleston, later returned in a prisoner exchange and now Washington's second in command, directed them to the field of surrender as the band played somber tunes along with the English nursery rhyme, "The World Turned Upside Down":

> If buttercups buzzed
> after the bee;
> If boats were on land,
> churches on sea;
> If ponies rode men,
> and grass ate the cow;
> If cats should be chased,
> into holes by the mouse;
> If mammas sold their babies,
> To gypsies for half a crown;
> If summer were spring
> And the other way round;
> Then all the world would be upside down.

## NEGOTIATIONS

Whatever lingering hopes of victory the British may have harbored vanished at Yorktown. "O God, it's all over," Lord North groaned at news of the surrender. On February 27, 1782, the House of Commons voted against further prosecution of the war and on March 5 passed a bill authorizing the crown to make peace. On March 20 Lord North resigned and a new ministry was made up of the old friends of the Americans headed by the duke of Rockingham, who had brought about repeal of the Stamp Act. The new colonial minister, Lord Shelburne, became chief minister after Rockingham's death in September, and directed negotiations with American commissioners.

As early as 1779 the Continental Congress had authorized John Adams to conduct peace negotiations, but he and Vergennes were at odds almost from the beginning, and the French foreign minister used his influence in Philadelphia to get a new five-man commission with instructions to rely on Vergennes for advice. Only three members of the commission were active, however: Adams, who was on state business in the Netherlands; John Jay, minister to Spain; and Franklin, already in Paris. Thomas Jefferson stayed home because of his wife's fatal illness, and Henry Laurens, held prisoner in the Tower of London after capture on the high seas, arrived late in the negotiations. Franklin and Jay did most of the work. In April 1782 Lord Shelburne sent a special representative, Richard Oswald, to Paris for conversations with Franklin. When Jay arrived, however, he was still smarting from snubs he had received in Madrid and intensely suspicious of Vergennes.

The French commitment to Spain complicated matters. Spain and the United States were both allied with France, but not with each other. America was bound by its alliance to fight on until the French made peace, and the French were bound to help the Spanish recover Gibraltar from England. Unable to deliver Gibraltar, or so the tough-minded Jay reasoned, Vergennes might try to bargain off American land west of the Appalachians in its place. Jay's distrust quickened when Vergennes's secretary informally suggested just such a bargain and left secretly for London. Fearful that the French were angling for a separate peace with the British, Jay persuaded Franklin to play the same game. Ignoring their instructions to consult fully with the French, they agreed to further talks provided Oswald were authorized "to treat with the Commissioners appointed by the Colonys, under the title of Thirteen United States." On November 30, 1782, the talks produced a preliminary treaty with Great Britain. If it violated the spirit of the alliance, it did not violate the strict letter of the treaty with France, for Vergennes was notified the day before it was signed and final agreement still depended on a Franco-British settlement.

THE PEACE OF PARIS   Early in 1783 France and Spain gave up on Gibraltar and reached an armistice. The final signing of the Peace of Paris came on September 3, 1783. In accord with the bargain already struck, Great Britain recognized the independence of the United States and agreed to a Mississippi River boundary to the west. Both the northern and southern borders left ambiguities that would require further definition in the future. Florida, as it turned out, passed back to Spain—along with the island of Minorca in the Mediterranean. France regained Senegal in Africa and the island of Tobago in the West Indies, both of which she had lost in 1763. The British further granted Americans the "liberty" of fishing off Newfoundland and in the

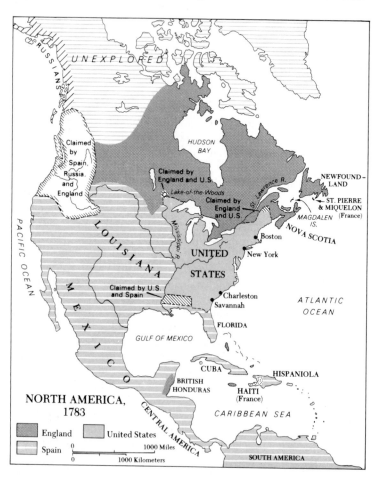

NORTH AMERICA,
1783

England   United States
Spain

St. Lawrence Gulf, and the right to dry their catches on the unsettled coasts of Labrador, Nova Scotia, and the Magdalen Islands. On the matter of debts, the best the British could get was a promise that British merchants should "meet with no legal impediment" in seeking to collect them. And on the tender point of Loyalists whose property had been confiscated, the negotiators agreed that Congress would "earnestly recommend" to the states the restoration of confiscated property. Each of the last two points was little more than a face-saving gesture for the British.

On November 24 the last British troops left New York City, and on December 4 they evacuated Staten Island and Long Island. That same day Washington took leave of his officers at Fraunces Tavern in New York. On December 23 he appeared before the Continental Congress, meeting in Annapolis, to resign his commission. Before the end of the next day he was back at Mount Vernon, home in time for Christmas.

## THE POLITICAL REVOLUTION

REPUBLICAN IDEOLOGY  The Americans had won their War for Independence. Had they undergone a political revolution as well? One answer was given years later by John Adams: "The Revolution was affected before the war commenced. The Revolution was in the minds and hearts of the people. . . . This radical change in the principles, opinions, sentiments, and affections of the people, was the real American Revolution." A movement which began as a struggle for the rights of Englishmen had become a fight for independence in which those rights found expression in governments which were new yet deeply rooted in the colonial experience and the prevailing viewpoints of Whiggery and the Enlightenment. Such ideas as the contract theory of government, the sovereignty of the people, the separation of powers, and natural rights found their way quickly, almost automatically, into the new frames of government that were devised while the fight went on—amid other urgent business.

The American Revolution was unique, Louis Hartz wrote in *The Liberal Tradition in America*, not for "the freedom to which it led, but the established feudal structure it did not have to destroy." Unlike France, Alexis de Tocqueville later said, the Americans did not have to "endure a democratic revolution." In a sense they had been born free, and they saw their revolution as in the main a defense of their liberty and property against what seemed a tyrannical and corrupt government. Still, the revolutionary controversies forced Americans to think out things once taken as a matter of course. Political thinking had to catch up with colonial institutions and practices, but once that process began it carried a momentum of its own.

The very idea of republican government was a far more radical departure in that day of kings and emperors than it would seem to later generations. The idea was rooted in that radical element of British Whiggery which a later historian labeled the eighteenth-century Commonwealthmen, a group which invoked the spirit of republican thinkers in Cromwell's England, the late Roman Republic, and classical antiquity. In the focus of republican thinking Americans began to see themselves in a new light, no longer the rustic provincials in a backwater of European culture but rather the embodiment of the virtue so long praised by intellectuals. As free citizens of a republic, unshackled by dependence on the favor of the court, Americans would cast off corruptions of the Old World and usher in a new reign of liberty and virtue, not only for themselves but for all mankind. Reality, of course, was bound to fall short of such millennial hopes, but the republican ideal served to focus and reinforce the new American vision.

NEW STATE CONSTITUTIONS    At the onset of the fighting every colony saw the departure of governors and other officials, and usually the expulsion of Loyalists from the assemblies, which then assumed power as provincial "congresses" or "conventions." But they were acting as revolutionary bodies without any legal basis for the exercise of authority. In two of the states this presented little difficulty. Connecticut and Rhode Island, which had been virtually little republics as corporate colonies, simply purged their charters of any reference to colonial ties. Massachusetts followed their example until 1780. In the other states the prevailing notions of social contract and popular sovereignty led to written constitutions which specified the framework and powers of government. One of the lessons of the Revolution, it seemed, had been that one should not rely on the vague body of law and precedent that made up the unwritten constitution of Britain. Constitution making in fact had gotten under way even before independence. In May 1776 Congress advised the colonies to set up new governments "under the authority of the people." At first the authority of the people was exercised by legislatures which simply adopted constitutions and promulgated them. But they had little more status than ordinary statutory law, it could be argued, since the people had no chance to express their wishes directly.

When the Massachusetts assembly hastily submitted a constitution to the towns for approval, however, it was rejected. Massachusetts thereupon invented what became a standard device for American constitution making: a body separate from and superior to the legislature to exercise the people's sovereignty. In 1779–1780 Massachusetts elected a special convention, chosen for the specific purpose of making a constitution. The invention of the constitutional convention was an altogether original contribution to the art of government, and one that other states copied. The resultant document went out to the town meetings with the provision that two-thirds or more would have to ratify it, which they did. The Massachusetts Constitution of 1780 declared: "The body politic is formed by a voluntary association of individuals; it is a social compact, by which the whole people covenants with each citizen, and each with the whole people that all shall be governed by certain laws for the common good."

The first state constitutions varied mainly in detail. They formed governments much like the colonial governments, with elected governors and senates instead of appointed governors and councils. Generally they embodied, sometimes explicitly, a separation of powers as a safeguard against abuses, and generally they included a Bill of Rights which protected the time-honored rights of petition, freedom of speech, trial by jury, freedom from self-incrimination, and the like. Most tended to limit the powers of governors and increase the powers of the legislatures, which had led the people in their quarrels with the colonial governors. Pennsylvania went so far as to eliminate the governor and upper house of the legislature altogether. It had an executive council of twelve, including a president, and operated until 1790 with a unicameral legislature limited only by a house of "censors" who reviewed its work every five years.

THE ARTICLES OF CONFEDERATION  The central government, like the state governments, grew out of an extralegal revolutionary body. The Continental Congress exercised governmental powers by common consent and without any constitutional sanction before March 1781. In a sense it had much the character of a diplomatic congress, composed of delegates named annually by the state legislatures. Plans for a permanent frame of government were started very early, however. Richard Henry Lee's motion for independence included a call for a plan of confederation. As early as July 12, 1776, a committee headed by John Dickinson produced a draft constitution, the "Articles of Confederation and Perpetual Union." For more than a year Congress debated the articles in between more urgent matters and finally adopted them on November 15, 1777, subject to ratification by all the states. All states ratified promptly except Maryland, which stubbornly insisted that the seven states claiming western lands should cede them to the authority of Congress. Maryland did not relent until early 1781, when Virginia gave up its claims under the old colonial charter to the vast region north of the Ohio River. New York had already given up a dubious claim based on its "jurisdiction" over the Iroquois, and the other states eventually gave up their charter claims, although Georgia did not until 1802.

When the Articles of Confederation became effective in March 1781 they did little more than legalize the status quo. "The United States in Congress Assembled" had a multitude of responsibilities but little authority to carry them out. It had full power over foreign affairs and questions of war and peace; it could decide disputes between the states; it had authority over coinage, postal service, and Indian affairs, and responsibility for the government of the western territories. But it had no power to enforce its resolutions and ordinances upon either states or individuals. And it had no power to levy taxes, but had to rely on requisitions which state legislatures could ignore at their will.

The states, after their battles with Parliament, were in no mood for a strong central government. The Congress in fact had less power than the colonists had once accepted in Parliament, since it could not regulate interstate and foreign commerce. For certain important acts, moreover, a special majority was required. Nine states had to approve measures dealing with war, privateering, treaties, coinage, finances, or the army and navy. Amendments to the articles required unanimous ratification by all the states. The Confederation had neither an executive nor a judicial branch; there was no administrative head of government (only the president of the Congress, chosen annually) and no federal courts.

## THE SOCIAL REVOLUTION

On the general frame of government there was in America a consensus—the forms grew so naturally out of experience and the prevalent theories. On other points, however, there was disagreement. As the historian J. Franklin Jameson put it, in what might be taken almost as a general law of revolutions: "The stream of revolution, once started, could not be confined within narrow banks, but spread abroad upon the land." The more conservative Patriots would have been content to replace royal officials with the rich, the well-born, and the able, and let it go at that. But more radical elements, which had been quickened by the long agitations, raised the question not only of home rule but who shall rule at home, to cite the oft-quoted phrase of the historian Carl Becker.

EQUALITY AND ITS LIMITS    The spirit of equality borne by the Revolution found outlet in several directions, one of which was simply a weakening of old habits of deference. One Colonel Randolph of Virginia told of being in a tavern when a rough group of farmers came in, spitting and pulling off their muddy boots without regard to the sensibilities of the gentlemen present: "The spirit of independence was converted into equality," Randolph wrote, "and every one who bore arms, esteems himself upon a footing with his neighbors. . . . No doubt each of these men considers himself, in every respect, my equal." No doubt each did.

What was more, participation in the army or militia activated and politicized people who had taken little interest in politics before. The large number of new political opportunities that opened up led more ordinary citizens into participation than

*Benjamin Latrobe's watercolor of a tavern in Virginia. The dress of the billiards players suggests that "the spirit of independence was converted into equality."*

ever before. The social base of the new legislatures was much broader than that of the old assemblies.

Men fighting for their liberty found it difficult to justify the denial to others of the rights of suffrage and representation. The property qualifications for voting, which already admitted an overwhelming majority of white males, were lowered still further. In Pennsylvania, Delaware, North Carolina, Georgia, and Vermont any taxpayer could vote, although commonly office-holders had to meet higher property requirements. Men who had argued against taxation without representation found it hard to justify denial of proportionate representation for the back-country, which generally enlarged its presence in the legislatures. New men thrown up by the revolutionary turmoil often replaced older men, some of whom had been Loyalists. More often than not the newcomers were men of lesser property. Some states concentrated much power in a legislature chosen by a wide suffrage, but not even Pennsylvania went quite so far as universal manhood suffrage. Others, like New York and Maryland, took a more conservative stance.

New developments in land tenure which grew out of the Revolution extended the democratic trends of suffrage requirements. Confiscations resulted in the seizure of Tory estates by all the state legislatures. Some were quite large, such as the estates of the Penn family, of Lord Fairfax in Virginia, and James DeLancey in New York. William Pepperrell of Maine lost a spread on which he could ride for thirty miles. These lands, however, were of small consequence in contrast to the unsettled lands formerly at the disposal of crown and proprietors, now in the hands of popular assemblies, much of which was used for bonuses to veterans of the war. Western lands, formerly closed by the Proclamation of 1763 and the Quebec Act of 1774, were soon thrown open for settlers.

THE PARADOX OF SLAVERY    The revolutionary principles of liberty and equality, moreover, had clear implications for the enslaved blacks. Jefferson's draft of the Declaration had indicted the king for having violated the "most sacred rights of life and liberty of a distant people, who never offended him, captivating them into slavery in another hemisphere," but the clause was struck out "in complaisance to South Carolina and Georgia." The clause was in fact inaccurate in completely ignoring the implication of American slaveholders and slavetraders in the traffic. Before the Revolution, only Rhode Island, Connecticut, and Pennsylvania had halted the importation of slaves. After independence all the states except Georgia stopped the traffic, although South Carolina later reopened it.

Black soldiers or sailors were present at most of the major battles, from Lexington to Yorktown; some were on the Loyalist side. Lord Dunmore, governor of Virginia, anticipated a general British policy in 1775 when he promised freedom to slaves, as well as indentured servants, who would bear arms for the Loyalist cause. Taking alarm at this, General Washington at the end of 1775 reversed an original policy of excluding blacks from American forces—except the few already in militia companies—and Congress quickly approved. Only two states, South Carolina and Georgia, held out completely against the policy, but by a rough estimate few if any more than about 5,000 were admitted to the American forces in a total of about 300,000, and most of those were free blacks from northern states. They served mainly in white units, although Massachusetts did organize two all-black companies and Rhode Island organized one. Slaves who served in the cause of independence got their freedom and in some cases land bounties. But the British army, which freed probably tens of thousands, was a greater instrument of emancipation than the American forces. Most of the newly freed blacks found their way to Canada or to British colonies in the Caribbean.

In the northern states, which had fewer slaves than the southern, the doctrines of liberty led swiftly to emancipation for all either during the fighting or shortly afterward. Vermont's Constitution of 1777 specifically forbade slavery. The Massachusetts Constitution of 1780 proclaimed the "inherent liberty" of all, and a court decision in 1783 freed one Quock Walker on the grounds that slavery could not legally exist under that provi-

*Elizabeth Freeman, born in Africa around 1742, was sold as a slave to a Massachusetts family. She won her freedom by claiming in court that the "inherent liberty" of all applied to slaves as well.*

sion. Elsewhere north of the Mason-Dixon line gradual emancipation became the device for freeing the slaves. Pennsylvania in 1780 provided that all children born thereafter to slave mothers would become free at age twenty-eight. In 1784 Rhode Island provided freedom for all born thereafter, at age twenty-one for males, eighteen for females. New York lagged until 1799 in granting freedom to mature slaves born after enactment, but an act of 1817 set July 4, 1827, as the date for emancipation of all remaining slaves.

South of Pennsylvania the potential consequences of emancipation were so staggering—South Carolina had a black majority—that whites refused to be stampeded by abstract philosophy. Yet even there slaveholders like Washington, Jefferson, Patrick Henry, and others were troubled. "I am not one of those . . . " Henry Laurens of South Carolina wrote his son, "who dare trust in Providence for defense and security of their own liberty while they enslave and wish to continue in slavery thousands who are as well entitled to freedom as themselves." Jefferson wrote in his *Notes on Virginia* (1785): "Indeed I tremble for my country when I reflect that God is just; that his justice cannot sleep forever." But he, like many other white southerners, was riding the tiger and did not know how to dismount. The furthest antislavery sentiment carried the southern states was to relax the manumission laws under which owners might free their slaves.

THE STATUS OF WOMEN    The logic of liberty applied to the status of women as much as to that of blacks, but wrought even less change in their sphere. Women joined in prewar campaigns to boycott British goods—in fact their support was essential to success in that cause. The war drew women at least temporarily into new pursuits. They plowed fields, kept shop, and melted down pots and pans to make shot. Esther Reed of Philadelphia organized a ladies' association which raised money to provide comforts for the troops. The fighting was man's work, but women served the armies in various support roles, such as handling supplies and serving as couriers. Wives often followed their husbands to camp, and on occasion took their places in the line, as Margaret Corbin did at Fort Washington when her husband fell at his artillery post, or Mary Ludwig Hays (better known as Molly Pitcher) did when hers collapsed of heat fatigue. An exceptional case was that of Deborah Sampson, who joined a Massachusetts regiment as Robert Shurtleff and served from 1781 to 1783 by the "artful concealment" of her sex.

Early in the struggle, on March 31, 1776, Abigail Adams wrote to her husband John: "In the new Code of Laws which I suppose

*Abigail Adams, in a portrait by Gilbert Stuart. She advised her husband, John: "Do not put such unlimited power into the hands of the Husbands."*

it will be necessary for you to make I desire you would remember the Ladies. . . . Do not put such unlimited power into the hands of the Husbands." Since men were "Naturally Tyrannical," she wrote, "why then, not put it out of the power of the vicious and the Lawless to use us with cruelty and indignity with impunity." Otherwise, "If particular care and attention is not paid to the Ladies we are determined to foment a Rebellion, and will not hold ourselves bound by any Laws in which we have no voice, or Representation." Husband John replied playfully: "We have been told that our Struggle has loosened the bands of Government every where." But Abigail's letter offered the "first Intimation that another Tribe more numerous and powerful than all the rest were grown discontented." But he continued: "Depend upon it, we know better than to repeal our Masculine systems."

And one is hard put to find evidence that the legal status of women benefited from equalitarian doctrine. There is local evidence that in parts of New England divorces were easier to get, but married women still forfeited control of their own property to their husbands, and women gained no political rights except in one state, apparently by accident. New Jersey's state constitution of 1776 defined voters as all "free inhabitants" who could meet property requirements, and some women began voting in the 1780s and continued to do so until 1807, when the state disfranchised both women and blacks. Although some limited advances were made in education, it was a slow process. The chief contribution of the Revolution seems to have been less in substantive gains for women than in a growing willingness to challenge old shibboleths, in the spirit of Abigail Adams. In an essay "On the Equality of the Sexes" (written in 1779, published in

1790), Judith Sargent Murray wrote: "We can only reason from what we know, and if an opportunity of acquiring knowledge hath been denied us, the inferiority of our sex cannot fairly be deduced from thence." Some groundwork was being laid for future battles, but meaningful victories in the cause of equality between the sexes remained in the future.

FREEDOM OF RELIGION    The Revolution also set in motion a transition from the toleration of religious dissent to a complete freedom of religion in the separation of church and state. The Anglican church, established in five colonies and parts of two others, was especially vulnerable because of its association with the crown and because dissenters outnumbered Anglicans in all the states except Virginia. And all but Virginia removed tax support for the church before the fighting was over. In 1776 the Virginia Declaration of Rights guaranteed the free exercise of religion, and in 1786 the Virginia Statute of Religious Freedom (written by Thomas Jefferson) declared that: "no man shall be compelled to frequent or support any religious worship, place or ministry whatsoever," that none should in any way suffer for his religious opinions and beliefs, "But that all men shall be free to profess, and by argument to maintain, their opinions in matters of religion."

The Congregational church developed a national body in the early nineteenth century, and Lemuel Haynes, depicted here, was its first black preacher.

New England, with its Puritan heritage, was in less haste to disestablish the Congregational church, although the rules were already being relaxed enough by the 1720s to let Quakers and Baptists assign their tax support to their own churches. New Hampshire finally discontinued tax support for its churches in 1817, Connecticut in 1818, Maine in 1820, and Massachusetts in 1833. Certain religious requirements for officeholding lingered here and there on the law books: Massachusetts and Maryland required a declaration of Christian faith; Delaware had a Trinitarian test; New Jersey and the Carolinas held that officeholders must be Protestants. But in most cases these requirements disappeared before many more years.

In churches as well as in government the Revolution set off a period of constitution making, as some of the first national church bodies emerged. In 1784 the Methodists, who at first were an offshoot of the Anglicans, came together in a general conference at Baltimore under Bishop Francis Asbury. The Anglican church, rechristened Episcopal, gathered in a series of meetings which by 1789 had united the various dioceses in a federal union under Bishop Samuel Seabury of Connecticut; in 1789 also the Presbyterians held their first general assembly in Philadelphia. The following year, 1790, the Catholic church had its first bishop in the United States when John Carroll was named bishop of Baltimore. Other churches would follow in the process of coming together on a national basis.

## EMERGENCE OF AN AMERICAN CULTURE

For all the weakness of the central government, the Revolution generated a nascent sense of common nationality. At the time of the French and Indian War an English traveler observed: "Fire and water are not more heterogeneous than the different colonies in North America. Nothing can exceed the jealousy . . . which they possess in regard to each other." But the Revolution taught Americans to think "continentally," as Alexander Hamilton put it. As early as the Stamp Act Congress of 1765, Christopher Gadsden, leader of the Charleston radicals, had said: "There ought to be no New England man, no New Yorker, known on the Continent; but all of us Americans." In the first Continental Congress Patrick Henry asserted that such a sense of identity had come to pass: "The distinctions between Virginians, Pennsylvanians, New Yorkers, and New Englanders are no more. I am not a Virginian but an American."

The concrete experience of the war reinforced the feeling. Soldiers who went to fight in other states inevitably broadened their horizons. John Marshall, future chief justice, served first in the Virginia militia and then in the Continental Army in the middle states and endured the winter of 1777–1778 at Valley Forge. He later wrote: "I found myself associated with brave men from different states who were risking life and everything valuable in a common cause. I was confirmed in the habit of considering America as my country and Congress as my government." American nationalism, like American independence, was the creation of the Revolution.

At the same time the Revolution itself marked the start of a national tradition, one that would ultimately reach back and incorporate colonial heroes in its legends. The Revolution produced symbols of unity in, for instance, the Declaration of Independence and the flag, designed by Francis Hopkinson, a Philadelphia lawyer and poet, and a pantheon of heroes whose deeds and whose stirring cries echoed down the years: Sgt. William Jasper's vaulting the palmetto fort on Sullivan's Island to retrieve the fallen flag; Patrick Henry's exhorting his countrymen to choose liberty or death; Nathan Hale's speaking his perhaps apocryphal last words before the British hanged him for a spy, "I only regret that I have but one life to lose for my country." It detracted not a bit from the effect of those cries that both paraphrased lines from Addison's *Cato* nor that William Prescott's admonition at Bunker Hill not to fire "until you see the whites of their eyes" echoed Frederick the Great. And at least some were American originals: John Parker's telling the Minute Men at Lexington, "Don't fire unless fired upon, but if they mean to have a war let it begin here!"; John Paul Jones's defiantly responding to the call for surrender, "I have not yet begun to fight!"; or Richard Henry Lee's postwar tribute to the dead Washington, "first in war, first in peace, and first in the hearts of his countrymen."

ARTS IN THE NEW NATION  The marquis de Chastellux, a French aristocrat who fought in the cause, thought the Revolution in America had generated "more heroes than she [America] has marble and artists to commemorate them." The Revolution provided the first generation of native artists with inspirational subjects. It also filled them with high expectations that individual freedom would release creative energies and vitalize both commerce and the arts. The hope that America would become the future seat of empire and the arts had excited the colonials at least since the appearance of the Anglican divine George Berkeley's celebrated "Verses on the Prospect of Planting Arts and Learning in America" (published in 1752), which included the oft-quoted line: "Westward the course of empire takes its way." Nathaniel Ames's *Almanac* for 1758 took up the theme in unmeasured terms: "The Curious have observed, that the Progress of Humane Literature (like the Sun) is from the East to the West." Soon the course of the arts and sciences would alter the face of the land. "O! Ye unborn Inhabitants of America," the *Almanac* continued, "when your Eyes behold the sun after he has rolled the seasons round for two or three centuries more, you will know that in Anno Domini 1758, we dream'd of your Times."

At the Princeton commencement in 1771 two graduating seniors and budding young authors, Philip Freneau and Hugh Henry Brackenridge, classmates of James Madison and Aaron Burr, presented "A Poem on the Rising Glory of America" in which they reviewed once again the westward transit of culture and foretold in America "the final stage . . . of high invention and wond'rous art, which not the ravages of time shall waste." The Revolution itself raised expectations yet higher. As David Ramsay put it in his *History of the American Revolution* (1789), the conflict with England "gave a spring to the active powers of the inhabitants, and set them on thinking, speaking and acting, in a line far beyond that to which they had been accustomed." The result, one historian has noted, was a sudden efflorescence of the arts: "By the time the country inaugurated its first president in 1789" it had also produced "its first novel, first epic poem, first composer, first professionally acted play, first actor and dancer, first museum, its first important painters, musical-instrument makers, magazine engravers—indeed most of the defining features of traditional high culture."

If, as it happened, no American artist of the time quite measured up to the highest expectations, many of them in the inspiration of the moment chose patriotic themes and celebrated the new nation. Ironically, the best American painters of the time spent all or most of the Revolution in England, studying with Benjamin West of Pennsylvania and John Singleton Copley of Massachusetts, both of whom had set up shop in London before the outbreak. Even John Trumbull, who had served in the siege of Boston and the Saratoga campaign, somehow managed a visit to London during the war before returning to help his brother supply the Continentals. Later he adopted patriotic themes in *The Battle of Bunker Hill*, and his four panels in the Capitol Rotunda at Washington: *The Declaration of Independence, The Sur-*

Surrender of Lord Cornwallis. *John Trumbull completed his painting of the pivotal British surrender at Yorktown in 1794.*

render of General Burgoyne, *Surrender of Lord Cornwallis,* and *The Resignation of General Washington.* Charles Willson Peale, who fought at Trenton and Princeton and survived the winter at Valley Forge, produced a virtual portrait gallery of Revolutionary War figures. Over twenty-three years he painted George Washington seven times from life and produced in all sixty portraits of him. Peale's portrait of Washington after the battle of Princeton (painted in 1779; see p. 223) is believed to be the most faithful representation of the general at the time of the War of Independence.

The poet John Trumbull (cousin of the painter) produced perhaps the most successful creative work on the Revolution in *M'Fingal* (1776), a mock heroic satire on American Tories. At the time its ironic tone suited the public temper less than *Common Sense,* but it went through many editions after the war. Joel Barlow, associated with Trumbull in a literary group called the Hartford Wits, later composed an ambitious patriotic epic, *The Vision of Columbus* (1787), enlarged and revised as *The Colum-*

*biad* (1807), designed to show America as "the noblest and most elevated part of the earth." Widely hailed at the time as an instant classic, it was pretentious and almost unreadable. Barlow is better remembered for *The Hasty Pudding* (1796), a mock epic which celebrated American simplicity in contrast to Old World sophistication. The Revolution-era poems of Philip Freneau, such as his elegy "To the Memory of Brave Americans," "Eutaw Springs," and "The Memorable Victory of Paul Jones," capture better than any others the patriotic emotions of the war.

EDUCATION   The most lasting effect of postwar nationalism may well have been its mark on education. In the colonies there had been a total of nine colleges, but once the Revolution was over, eight more sprang up in the 1780s and six in the 1790s. Several of the revolutionary state constitutions had provisions for state universities. Georgia's was the first chartered, in 1785, but the University of North Carolina (chartered in 1789) was the first to open, in 1795. An interest in general systems of public schools stirred in some of the states, especially in Pennsylvania and Virginia. Jefferson worked out an elaborate plan for a state system that would provide a rudimentary education for all, and higher levels of education for the talented, up through a state university. The movement for public education, however, would reach fruition much later. At the time, and well into the next century, no state would have a system of schools in the present-day sense.

Education played an important role in broadening and deepening the sense of nationalism, and no single element was as important, perhaps, as the spelling book, an item of almost universal use. Noah Webster of Hartford, while teaching at Goshen, New York, prepared an elementary speller published in 1783. By 1890 more than 60 million copies of his "Blue Back Speller" had been printed, and the book continued to sell well into the twentieth century. In his preface Webster issued a cultural Declaration of Independence: "The country," he wrote, "must in some future time, be as distinguished by the superiority of her literary improvements, as she already is by the liberality of her civil and ecclesiastical constitutions." Volume II of Webster's *Grammatical Institute*, a grammar, appeared in 1784, and Volume III, a reader, in 1785, crammed with selections from the speeches of Revolutionary leaders who, he said, were the equals of Cicero and Demosthenes. Other titles, *The American Spelling Book* (the "Blue Back") and *An American Selection of Lessons in Reading and Speaking*, pursued a growing fashion in textbooks of using the word American in the title: American arithmetics as well as spellers appeared. Jedediah Morse, author of *American Geography* (1789), said that the country needed its own text-books so that the people would not be affected with monarchical and aristocratic ideas.

In a special sense American nationalism was the embodiment of an idea. This first new nation, unlike the rising nations of Europe, was not rooted in antiquity. Its people, save the Indians, had not inhabited it over the centuries, nor was there any nation of a common descent. "The American national consciousness," one observer wrote, ". . . is not a voice crying out of the depth of the dark past, but is proudly a product of the enlightened present, setting its face resolutely toward the future." And American nationalism embodied a universal idea, with implications for all the world.

Many people, at least since the time of the Pilgrims, had thought America to be singled out for a special identity, a special mission. Jonathan Edwards said God had singled out America as "the glorious renovator of the world," and still later John Adams proclaimed the opening of America "a grand scheme and design in Providence for the illumination and the emancipation of the slavish part of mankind all over the earth." The mission had sub-tly changed, but it was still there. It was now a call to lead the way for all mankind toward liberty and equality. Meanwhile, however, Americans had to come to grips with more immediate problems created by their new nationhood.

## Further Reading

The Revolutionary War is the subject of many good surveys. Don Higginbotham's *The War of American Independence* (1971) and Robert Middlekauff's *The Glorious Cause: The American Revolution, 1763–1789* (1982),° are especially useful. Military history buffs will appreciate Christopher Ward's *The War of the Revolution* (2 vols., 1952) for its de-tail of maneuvers and its clear maps. For the first-person perspective provided by memoirs and reports by contemporaries, see *The Revolution Rememberd* (1980),° edited by John C. Dann. The British side of the conflict is handled well by Piers Mackesy in *The War for America, 1775–1783* (1964). Much good work has appeared recently on the social his-tory of the Revolutionary War. See John W. Shy's *A People Numerous and Armed* (1976),° Charles Royster's *A Revolutionary People at War* (1979),° Lawrence D. Cress's *Citizens in Arms* (1982), and E. Wayne Carp's *To Starve the Army at Pleasure* (1984).

° These books are available in paperback editions.

Biographical studies of the major American military figures include James T. Flexner's *George Washington in the American Revolution, 1775–1783* (1968), Samuel E. Morison's *John Paul Jones: A Sailor's Biography* (1959),° and Charles Royster's *Light-Horse Harry Lee* (1984). For the British side, see Ira D. Gruber's *The Howe Brothers and the American Revolution* (1972)° and Richard J. Hargrove's *General John Burgoyne* (1983).

Why some Americans remained loyal to the crown is the subject of Bernard Bailyn's *The Ordeal of Thomas Hutchinson* (1974),° Robert M. Calhoon's *The Loyalists in Revolutionary America, 1760–1781* (1973), and Mary Beth Norton's *The British-Americans* (1972).° Paul H. Smith's *Loyalists and Redcoats* (1964) traces the military role of the Tories, and Wallace Brown's *The King's Friends* (1965) argues that the Loyalists came from all classes of colonial society.

The effort to trace the social effects of the Revolution goes back at least to J. Franklin Jameson's *The American Revolution Considered as a Social Movement* (1926). More recently, Jackson Turner Main's *The Social Structure of Revolutionary America* (1965) looks at the quantitative evidence for the emergence of social equality, while Rhys Isaac's *The Transformation of Virginia, 1740–1790* (1982)° examines the social conflicts in that pivotal state. See also Gary Nash's *The Urban Crucible* (1984).° The question of disestablishment and religious liberty is treated in Sidney Mead's *The Lively Experiment* (1963). Relevant chapters in Winthrop D. Jordan's *White over Black* (1968) address the issue of emancipation during the Revolutionary period. One of the few recent community-level studies of Revolutionary change is Robert A. Gross's *The Minutemen and Their World* (1976). Mary Beth Norton's *Liberty's Daughters* (1980)° and Linda K. Kerber's *Women of the Republic* (1980)° document the role women played in securing independence. Joy D. Buel and Richard Buel's *The Way of Duty* (1984)° shows the impact of the Revolution on one New England family.

The standard introduction to the diplomacy of the Revolutionary era remains Samuel F. Bemis's *The Diplomacy of the American Revolution* (1935). Jonathan R. Dull's *A Diplomatic History of the American Revolution* (1985) is useful as well. Richard B. Morris's *The Peacemakers* (1965) examines more closely the negotiations for the Treaty of Paris.

# 7 &

## SHAPING A FEDERAL UNION

### The Confederation

Speaking to fellow graduates at the Harvard commencement in 1787, young John Quincy Adams lamented "this critical period" when the country was "groaning under the intolerable burden of . . . accumulated evils." More than a century later the popular writer and lecturer John Fiske used the same phrase, the "critical period," as the title for a history of the United States under the Articles of Confederation. For many years it was the fashion among historians to dwell upon the weaknesses of the Confederation and the "accumulated evils" of the time to the neglect of major achievements.

The Congress of the Confederation, to be sure, had little if any more governmental authority than the United Nations would have 200 years later. "It could ask for money but not compel payment," as one historian wrote, "it could enter into treaties but not enforce their stipulations; it could provide for raising of armies but not fill the ranks; it could borrow money but take no proper measures for repayment; it could advise and recommend but not command." The Congress was virtually helpless to cope with problems of diplomacy and postwar depression that would have challenged the resources of a much stronger government. It was not easy to find men of stature to serve in such a body, and often hard to gather a quorum of those who did. Yet in spite of its handicaps the Confederation Congress somehow managed to survive and to lay important foundations for the future. It concluded the Peace of Paris in 1783. It created the first executive departments. And it formulated principles of land distribution and territorial government which guided expansion all the way to the Pacific coast.

Throughout most of the War for Independence the Congress remained distrustful of executive power. It assigned administrative duties to its committees and thereby imposed a painful burden on conscientious members. At one time or another John Adams, for instance, served on some eighty committees. In 1781, however, anticipating ratification of the Articles of Confederation, Congress began to set up three departments: Foreign Affairs, Finance, and War, in addition to a Post Office Department which had existed since 1775. Each was to have a single head responsible to Congress. For superintendent of finance Congress chose Robert Morris, a prominent Philadelphia merchant who by virtue of his business connections and a talent for financial sleight-of-hand brought a semblance of order into federal accounts. The other departments had less success to their credit, and indeed lacked executive heads for long periods. The first secretary for foreign affairs, Robert R. Livingston, left that post in May 1783 and was not replaced by John Jay until the following summer. Given time and stability, however, Congress and the department heads might have evolved something like the parliamentary cabinet system. As it turned out, these agencies were the forerunners of the government departments that came into being later under the Constitution.

FINANCE    But as yet there was neither president nor prime minister, only the presiding officer of Congress and its secretary, Charles Thomson, who served continuously from 1774 to 1789. The closest thing to an executive head of the Confederation was Robert Morris, who as superintendent of finance in the final years of the war became the most influential figure in the government, and who had ideas of making both himself and the Confederation more powerful. He envisioned a coherent program of taxation and debt management to make the government financially stable; "a public debt supported by public revenue will prove the strongest cement to keep our confederacy together," he confided to a friend. It would wed to the support of the federal government the powerful influence of the public creditors. Morris therefore welcomed the chance to enlarge the debt by issuing new securities in settlement of wartime claims. Because of the government's precarious finances, these securities brought only ten to fifteen cents on the dollar, but with a sounder treasury—certainly with a tax power—they could be expected to rise in value, creating new capital with which to finance banks and economic development.

In 1781, as part of his plan, Morris secured a congressional charter for the Bank of North America, which would hold federal

*Robert Morris, the most influential figure in the Confederation government, in a portrait by Charles Willson Peale.*

deposits, lend money to the government, and issue banknotes that would be a stable currency. A national bank, it was in part privately owned and was expected to turn a profit for Morris and other shareholders, in addition to performing a public service. But his program depended ultimately on a secure income for the government, and foundered on the requirement of unanimous approval for amendments to the Articles of Confederation. During the war he nearly got for Congress the power to levy a 5 percent import duty, but Rhode Island's refusal to ratify the necessary amendment stood in the way. Once the war was over the spur of military need was gone. Local interests and the fear of a central authority—a fear strengthened by the recent quarrels with king and Parliament—hobbled action.

To carry their point, Morris and his nationalist friends in 1783 risked a dangerous gamble. Washington's army, encamped at Newburgh on the Hudson River, had grown restless in the final winter of the war. Their pay was in arrears as usual, and experience gave them reason to fear that claims to bounties and life pensions for officers might never be honored once their services were no longer needed. In January 1783 a delegation of officers appeared in Philadelphia with a petition for redress. Soon they found themselves drawn into a scheme to line up the army and public creditors with nationalists in Congress and confront the states with the threat of a coup d'état unless they yielded more power to Congress. Horatio Gates and other high officers were drawn into the network and endorsed an inflammatory address against any further "milk and water" petitions. Alexander Hamilton, congressman from New York and former aide to General Washington, sought to bring his old commander into the plan.

Washington sympathized with the purpose. If congressional powers were not enlarged, he had told a friend, "the band which at present holds us together, by a very feeble thread, will soon be broken, when anarchy and confusion must ensue." But Washington was just as deeply convinced that a military coup would be both dishonorable and dangerous. When he learned that some of the plotters had planned an unauthorized meeting of officers, he summoned a meeting first and confronted the issue. Drawing his spectacles from his pocket, he began: "I have grown not only gray but blind in the service of my country." When he had finished his dramatic and emotional address, his officers, with Gates in the chair, unanimously adopted resolutions denouncing the recent "infamous propositions" and the Newburgh Conspiracy came to a sudden end. By the middle of June all those who had enlisted for the duration were furloughed with three months' pay in the personal notes of Superintendent Morris. Washington awaited the British evacuation of New York with a skeleton force serving time enlistments.

A body of Pennsylvania recruits provided a sorry aftermath to the quiet dispersal. Their pay in arrears, about eighty militiamen mutinied, marched from Lancaster to Philadelphia, and with reinforcements from regiments there, conducted a threatening demonstration in front of Independence Hall. When state authorities failed to provide a guard, for fear the militia would join the mutiny, the Congress after three days fled to Princeton, later adjourned to Annapolis, then Trenton, and in 1785 finally settled in New York. Moving from place to place, often unable to muster a quorum, the Congress suffered growing futility. An amendment to give Congress power to levy duties for twenty-five years, proposed in 1783, met the same fate as the previous amendment. In 1784 Morris resigned as superintendent of finance and a committee took charge once again.

The Confederation never did put its finances in order. The Continental currency had long since become a byword for worthlessness. It was never redeemed. The debt, domestic and foreign, grew from $11 million to $28 million as Congress paid off citizens' and soldiers' claims. Each year Congress ran a deficit on its operating expenses. Since the Confederation remained unable to pay off its securities, some of the states agreed to assume the burden of their citizens. They accepted in payment of taxes and imposts the indents (certificates) which Congress issued in lieu of interest payments—and Congress then took back the indents in payment of requisitions on the states, up to a fourth of the total amount due. Some of the states accepted federal securities in payment for state securities or for land. The foreign debt alone ran up to $11 million, but in spite of everything, Congress somehow managed to find the money to pay interest on loans from Dutch bankers and kept open a line of credit at least from that source.

LAND POLICY   The one source from which Congress might hope ultimately to draw an independent income was the sale of western lands. But throughout the Confederation period that income remained more a fleeting promise than an accomplished fact. The Confederation nevertheless dealt more effectively with the western lands than with anything else. There Congress had direct authority, at least on paper. Thinly populated by Indians,

WESTERN LAND
CESSIONS, 1781-1802

Ceded by N.Y., 1781
Ceded by Va., 1784 & 1792
Ceded by S.C. to Ga., 1787
Ceded by Ga., 1802
States with no western claims

Frenchmen, and a growing number of American squatters, the region north of the Ohio River had long been the site of overlapping claims by colonies and speculators. The Revolution itself had been brought on in no small part by disagreement over western lands and British feelings that the colonies should be taxed for their administration and defense. In 1784 Virginia's cession of lands north of the Ohio was complete, and by 1786 all states had abandoned their claims in the area except for a 120-mile strip along Lake Erie, which Connecticut held until 1800 as its "Western Reserve," in return for giving up its claims in the Wyoming Valley of Pennsylvania.

As early as 1779 Congress had made a commitment in principle not to treat the western lands as colonies. The delegates resolved instead that western lands ceded by the states "shall be . . . formed into distinct Republican states," equal in all respects to other states. Between 1784 and 1787 policies for the development of the West emerged in three major ordinances of the Confederation Congress. These documents, which rank among its greatest achievements—and among the most important in American history—set precedents that the United States followed in its expansion all the way to the Pacific. Thomas Jefferson in fact was prepared to grant self-government to western states from an early stage, when settlers would meet and choose their own officials. Under Jefferson's ordinance of 1784, when the population equaled that of the smallest existing state the territory would achieve full statehood. Congress, however, rejected Jefferson's specific provision for ten future states with bizarre if melodious names like Assenisipia and Cherronesus, although three of the suggestions later turned up on the map with only slight alteration: Michigania, Illinoia, and Washington.

In the Land Ordinance of 1785 the delegates outlined a plan of land surveys and sales which would eventually stamp a rectangular pattern on much of the nation's surface, a pattern still visible from the air in many parts of the country because of the layout of roads and fields. Wherever Indian titles had been extinguished, the Northwest was to be surveyed into townships six miles square along east-west and north-south lines. Each township in turn was divided into 36 lots (or sections) one mile square (or 640 acres). The 640-acre sections were to go at auction for no less than $1 per acre or $640 total. Such terms favored land speculators, of course, since few dirt farmers had that much money or were able to work that much land. In later years new land laws would make smaller plots available at lower prices, but in 1785 Congress was faced with an empty treasury. In each township, however, Congress did reserve the income from the sixteenth

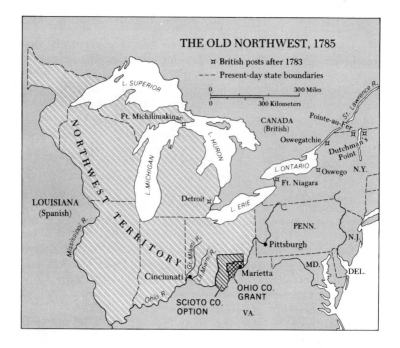

THE OLD NORTHWEST, 1785

¤ British posts after 1783
- - - Present-day state boundaries

0                300 Miles
0         300 Kilometers

section for the support of schools—a significant departure at a time when public schools were rare.

In seven ranges to the west of the Ohio River, an area in which recent treaties had voided Indian titles, surveying began. But before any land sales occurred a group of speculators from New England presented Congress a seductive offer. Organized in Boston, the group took the name of the Ohio Company and sent the Rev. Manasseh Cutler to present their plan. Cutler proved a persuasive lobbyist, and in 1787 Congress voted a grant of 1.5 million acres for about $1 million in certificates of indebtedness to Revolutionary War veterans. The arrangement had the dual merit, Cutler argued, of reducing the debt and encouraging new settlement and sales. Further, to ensure passage the lobbyist cut in several congressmen on another deal, the Scioto Company, which got an option on 5 million acres more. In April 1788 the Ohio Company's first settlers floated downstream from Pittsburgh on a flatboat aptly named the *May-flower* and established Marietta. The Scioto Company never took up its option, but that did not prevent its European agent from selling lands it did not own—with the help of an Englishman named, of all things, Playfair! In 1790 several hundred French settlers arrived only to find that they had no title to the lands they had supposedly bought. A sympathetic Congress relieved their distress by voting them a grant of land. In 1788 a New Jersey speculator got an option on lands between the Great and the Little Miami Rivers and soon had Cincinnati and several other villages under way.

THE NORTHWEST ORDINANCE    Spurred by the plans for land sales and settlement, Congress drafted a new and more specific frame of territorial government to replace Jefferson's ordinance of 1784. The new plan backed off from Jefferson's recommendation of early self-government. Because of the trouble that might be expected from squatters who were clamoring for free land, the Northwest Ordinance of 1787 required a period of colonial tutelage. At first the territory fell subject to a governor, a secretary, and three judges, all chosen by Congress. Eventually there would be three to five territories in the region, and when any one had 5,000 free male adults it could choose an assembly and Congress would name a council of five from ten names proposed by the assembly. The governor would have a veto and so would Congress. The resemblance to the old royal colonies is clear, but there were two significant differences. For one, the Ordinance anticipated statehood when any territory's population reached 60,000. For another, it included a bill of rights which guaranteed religious freedom, representation in proportion to population, trial by jury, habeas corpus, and the application of common law. And finally, the Ordinance excluded slavery permanently from the Northwest—a proviso Jefferson had failed to get accepted in his Ordinance of 1784. This proved a fateful decision. As the progress of emancipation in the existing states gradually freed all slaves above the Mason-Dixon line, the Ohio River boundary of the Old Northwest extended the line between freedom and slavery all the way to the Mississippi.

The lands south of the Ohio River followed a different line of development. Title to the western lands remained with Georgia, North Carolina, and Virginia for the time being, but settlement proceeded at a far more rapid pace during and after the Revolution, despite the Indians' fierce resentment of encroachments on their hunting grounds. Substantial centers of population grew up around Harrodsburg and Boonesboro in the Kentucky Blue Grass and along the Watauga, Holston, and Cumberland Rivers, as far west as Nashborough (Nashville). In the Southwest active movements for statehood arose early. North Carolina tentatively ceded its western claims in 1784, whereupon the Holston settlers formed the short-lived state of Franklin, which became little more than a bone of contention between rival speculators until North Carolina reasserted control in 1789, shortly before the cession of its western lands became final.

Indian claims too were being extinguished. The Iroquois and Cherokees, badly battered during the Revolution, were in no position to resist encroachments. By the Treaty of Fort Stanwix (1784) the Iroquois were forced to cede land in western New York and Pennsylvania. In the Treaty of Hopewell (1785) the Cherokees gave up all claims in South Carolina, much of western North Carolina, and large portions of present-day Kentucky and Tennessee. Also in 1785 the major Ohio tribes gave up their claim to most of Ohio, except for a chunk bordering the western part of Lake Erie. The Creeks, pressed by the state of Georgia to cede portions of their lands in 1784–1785, went to war in the summer of 1786 with covert aid from Spanish Florida. But when Spanish aid diminished, the Creek chief traveled to New York and in 1791 finally struck a bargain which gave the Creeks favorable trade arrangements with the United States, but did not restore the lost lands.

TRADE AND THE ECONOMY   In its economic life, as in planning westward expansion, the young nation dealt with difficult problems vigorously. Congress had little to do with achievements in the economy but neither could it bear the blame for a depression that wracked the country for several years during the transition to independence, the result of the war and separation from the British Empire. In New England and much of the backcountry fighting seldom interrupted the tempo of farming, and the producers of foodstuffs especially benefited from rising prices and wartime demands. The southern Tidewater suffered a loss of slave labor, much of it carried off by the British. Returns from indigo and naval stores declined with the loss of British bounties, but in the long run rice and tobacco benefited from an enlarged foreign market for their products.

Merchants suffered far more wrenching adjustments than the farmers. Cut out of the British mercantile system, they had to find new outlets for their trade. Circumstances that impoverished some enriched those who financed privateers, supplied the armies on both sides, and hoarded precious goods while demand and prices soared. By the end of the war a strong sentiment for free trade had developed in both Britain and America. In the memorable year 1776 the Scottish economist Adam Smith brought out *The Wealth of Nations*, a classic manifesto against mercantilism. Some British statesmen embraced the new gospel, but the public and Parliament still clung to the conventional wisdom of mercantilism for many years to come.

British trade with America did resume, and American ships

Wethersfield Girls Weeding Onions. *The war seldom interrupted the tempo of farming in New England, though it did heighten the need for all family members to work in the fields.*

were allowed to deliver American products and return to the United States with British goods. American ships could not carry British goods anywhere else, however. The pent-up demand for familiar goods created a vigorous market in exports to America, fueled by British credits and the hard money that had come into America from foreign aid, the expenditures of foreign armies, or wartime trade and privateering. The result was a quick cycle of boom and bust, a buying spree followed by a money shortage and economic troubles that lasted several years.

In colonial days the chronic deficit in trade with Britain could be offset by the influx of coins from trade with the West Indies. Now American ships found themselves excluded altogether from the British West Indies. But the islands still demanded wheat, fish, lumber, and other products from the mainland, and American shippers had not lost their talent for smuggling, at which the islanders connived. Already American shippers had begun exploring new outlets, and by 1787 their seaports were flourishing more than ever. Freed from colonial restraints, they now had the run of the seven seas. Trade treaties opened new markets with the Dutch (1782), Swedes (1783), Prussians (1785), and Moroccans (1787), and American shippers found new outlets on their own in Europe, Africa, and Asia. The most spectacular new development, if not the largest, was trade with China. It began in 1784–1785, when the *Empress of China* sailed from New York to Canton and back, around the tip of South America. Profits from

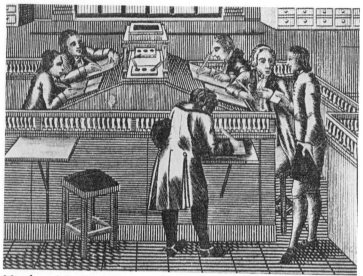

Merchants' Counting House. *Americans involved in overseas trade, such as the merchants depicted here, were sharply affected by the dislocations of war.*

its cargo of silks and tea encouraged the outfitting of other ships which carried ginseng root and other American goods to exchange for the luxury goods of the Orient.

The dislocations in trade and the need for readjustment, one historian noted, "produced bitter complaints in the newspapers and led to extravagant charges against both state and central governments, but in no case do the records of imports and exports and ship tonnages bear out the cries of havoc." By 1790 American commerce and exports had far outrun the trade of the colonies. American merchants had more ships than before the war. Farm exports were twice what they had been. Although most of the exports were the products of American forests, fields, and fisheries, during and after the war more Americans had turned to small-scale manufacturing, mainly for domestic markets. By 1787 a summary of major American enterprises included dozens of products from ships and ironwork to shoes, textiles, and soap.

DIPLOMACY  The achievements of the flourishing young nation are more visible in hindsight than they were then. Until 1787 the shortcomings and failures remained far more apparent—and the advocates of a stronger central government were extremely vocal on the subject. In diplomacy, there remained the nagging problems of relations with Great Britain and Spain, both of which still kept posts on United States soil and intrigued with Indians and white settlers in the West. The British, despite the peace treaty of 1783, held on to a string of forts from Lake Champlain to Michilimackinac. From these they kept a hand in the fur trade and a degree of influence with the Indian tribes whom they were suspected of stirring up to make sporadic attacks on the frontier. They gave as a reason for their continued occupation the failure of Americans to pay their debts, conveniently ignoring the point that the peace treaty had included only a face-saving gesture which committed Congress to recommend that the states place no legal impediment in the way of their collection. Impediments continued, nonetheless. According to one Virginian, a common question in his state was: "If we are now to pay the debts due to British merchants, what have we been fighting for all this while?"

Another major irritant was the confiscation of Loyalist property. Under the peace treaty Congress was obligated to stop confiscations, to guarantee immunity to Loyalists for twelve months during which they could return and wind up their affairs, and to recommend that the states return confiscated property. Persecutions, even lynchings, of Loyalists still occurred until after the end of the war. Some Loyalists returned unmolested, however, and once again took up their lives in their former homes. By the end of 1787, moreover, at the request of Congress all the states had rescinded the laws that were in conflict with the peace treaty.

The British refused even to dispatch an ambassador to the new nation before 1791. As early as 1785, however, the United States took the initiative by sending over that confirmed rebel, John Adams, as ambassador to the Court of St. James's. He was politely received by George III himself, but spent three years in futile efforts to settle the points at issue: mainly the forts, debts, the property rights of Loyalists, and trade concessions in the British West Indies. Unknown to Adams the British even toyed with the idea of annexing Vermont through intrigues with the Allen brothers, Ethan and Levi. Nothing came of it all, however, and Vermont became the fourteenth state in 1791.

With Spain the chief points at issue were the southern boundary and the right to navigate the Mississippi. According to the preliminary treaty with Britain the United States claimed a line as far south as the Thirty-first Parallel; Spain held out for the line running eastward from the mouth of the Yazoo River (at 32°

*John Adams, portrayed here while serving as United States ambassador to England.*

28′ N), which she claimed as the traditional boundary. The American treaty with Britain had also specified the right to navigate the Mississippi River to its mouth. Still the international boundary ran down the middle of the river most of its length and the river was entirely within Spanish Louisiana in its lower reaches. The right to navigation was a matter of importance because of the growing settlements in Kentucky and Tennessee, but in 1784 Louisiana's governor closed the river to American commerce and began to intrigue with the Creeks, Choctaws, Chickasaws, and other Indians of the Southwest against the frontiersmen, and with the frontiersmen against the United States. Gen. James Wilkinson, a Kentucky land speculator, further enriched himself with Spanish gold in return for his promise to conspire for secession of the West and perhaps its annexation by Spain. But Wilkinson was a professional slyboots, with an instinct for trouble, whose loyalties ran mainly to his own pocketbook. And he was not the only man on the make who was double-dealing with the Spaniards.

In 1785 the Spanish government sent as its ambassador to the United States Don Diego de Gardoqui, who entered into lengthy but fruitless negotiations with John Jay, the secretary for foreign affairs. Jay had instructions to get free navigation of the Mississippi and the Spanish acceptance of the 31° boundary; Gardoqui had instructions not to give them. But he did ply Jay and his wife with gifts and flattery. Finally, in hope of winning trade concessions, Jay sought permission from Congress to give up navigation of the Mississippi—an idea planted by Gardoqui in the knowledge that it would be divisive. It was granted, but only by a vote of seven to five, with the southern states holding out against such a sacrifice to the interest of northern merchants. Since ratification of a treaty required the vote of nine states, negotiations collapsed and the issues remained unsettled for nearly another decade.

THE CONFEDERATION'S PROBLEMS   The problems of trans-Appalachian settlers, however, seemed remote from the everyday concerns of most Americans. What touched them more closely were economic troubles and the currency shortage. Merchants who found themselves excluded from old channels of imperial trade began to agitate for reprisals. State governments, in response, laid special tonnage duties on British vessels and special tariffs on the goods they brought. But state action alone failed to work for lack of uniformity. British ships could be diverted to states whose duties were less restrictive. The other states tried to meet this problem by taxing British goods that flowed across state lines, creating an impression that states were involved in commercial war with each other. Although these duties seldom affected American goods, there was a clear need, it seemed to commercial interests, for a central power to regulate trade. In 1784 Congress proposed to amend the Articles of Confederation so as to permit uniform navigation acts, but Rhode Island and North Carolina objected. The amendment, like all others, failed of ratification—not for want of support but for want of unanimity.

Mechanics and artisans who were developing an infant industry with products ranging from crude iron nails to the fine silver bowls of Paul Revere wanted to go further, to take reprisals against British goods as well as British ships. They sought, and in various degrees obtained from the states, tariffs against foreign goods that competed with theirs. The country would be on its way to economic independence, they argued, if only the specie that flowed into the country had been invested in domestic manufactures instead of being paid out for foreign goods. Nearly all the states gave some preference to American goods, but again the lack of uniformity in their laws put them at cross purposes, and so urban mechanics along with merchants were drawn into the movement for a stronger central government in the interest of uniform regulation.

The shortage of cash gave rise also to some more immediate demands for paper currency as legal tender, for postponement of tax and debt payments, for laws to "stay" the foreclosure of mortgages. Farmers, who had profited during the war, found

*American craftsmen, such as this cabinetmaker, were called "mechanics" in the eighteenth century. They sought tariffs against foreign goods that competed with theirs.*

themselves squeezed by depression and mounting debts while merchants sorted out and opened up their new trade routes. Creditors demanded hard money, but it was in short supply—and paper money was almost nonexistent after the depreciation of the Continental currency. The result was an outcry for relief, and around 1785 the demand for paper money became the most divisive issue in state politics. Debtors demanded it, and in some states, most notably South Carolina, merchants supported it because there they could use the paper but did not have to take it in payment of old debts. In Pennsylvania public creditors demanded paper as a device to collect their claims against the state. Paper, they reasoned, was better than nothing. Creditors elsewhere generally opposed such action, however, because it was likely to mean payment in a depreciated currency.

In 1785–1786 seven states provided for issues of paper money. In spite of the cries of calamity at the time, the money never seriously depreciated in Pennsylvania, New York, and South Carolina. It served in five states—Pennsylvania, New York, New Jersey, South Carolina, and Rhode Island—as a means of credit to hard-pressed farmers through state loans on farm mortgages. It was variously used to fund state debts and to pay off the claims of veterans.

In Rhode Island, however, the debtor party ran wild. In 1786 the Rhode Island legislature issued £100,000 in paper, the largest issue of any state in proportion to population, and declared it legal tender in payment of all debts. Creditors fled the state to avoid being paid in worthless paper, merchants closed their doors while mobs rioted against them, and a "forcing act" denied trial by jury and levied fines against anyone who refused to take the money at face value. Eventually a test case reached the state's supreme court, and in *Trevett v. Weeden* (1787) the court ruled the law unconstitutional. The case stands as a landmark, the first in which a court exercised the doctrine of judicial review in holding a state law unconstitutional. The forcing act was then repealed and the legal tender clause finally repealed in 1789.

SHAYS'S REBELLION  Newspapers throughout the country ran accounts of developments in Rhode Island, and that little commonwealth, stubbornly cross-grained since the days of Roger Williams, became the prime example of democracy run riot—until its hotspur neighbor, Massachusetts, provided the final proof (some said) that the country was poised on the brink of anarchy: Shays's Rebellion. There the trouble was not too much paper money but too little, and too much taxation. After 1780 Massachusetts had remained in the grip of a rigidly conservative regime. Ever-larger poll and land taxes were levied to pay off a heavy debt, held mainly by wealthy creditors in Boston, and the taxes fell most heavily upon beleaguered farmers and the poor in general. When the legislature adjourned in 1786 without providing either paper money or any other relief from taxes and debts, three western counties erupted into spontaneous revolt. Armed bands closed the courts and prevented foreclosures, and a tatterdemalion "army" under Daniel Shays, a destitute farmer and war veteran, advanced upon the federal arsenal at Springfield in January 1787.

*Daniel Shays and Job Shattuck, leaders of the revolt of western Massachusetts farmers against tax and debt policy (1787).*

A small militia force, however, scattered the approaching army with a single volley of artillery which left four dead. Gen. Benjamin Lincoln, a hero of the Revolution, arrived soon after with reinforcements from Boston and routed the remaining Shaysites. The Shaysites nevertheless had a victory of sorts. The state legislature omitted direct taxes the following year, lowered court fees, and exempted clothing, household goods, and tools from the debt process. But a more important consequence was the impetus the rebellion gave to conservatism and nationalism.

Rumors, at times deliberately inflated, blew up out of all proportion a pathetic rebellion of desperate men. The rebels were linked to the conniving British and accused of seeking to pillage the wealthy. What was more, the uprising set an ominous example. "There are combustibles in every State," Washington wrote, "which a spark might set fire to." Of the disorders he asked: "Good God! Who, besides a Tory, could have foreseen, or a Briton predicted them?" The answer, of course, was nearly every political philosopher of the Whig or Enlightened persuasion who was dear to the men of the Revolution. Anarchy, they taught, was the nemesis of republics, mob rule the sequel to unchecked democracy. Shays therefore was the harbinger of greater evils to come unless the course of events were altered. Not that all the leaders of the time agreed. Jefferson was, if anything, too complacent. From his post in Paris, where one of history's great bloodbaths would soon take place, he wrote to a friend back home: "The tree of liberty must be refreshed from time to time with the blood of patriots and tyrants."

CALLS FOR A STRONGER GOVERNMENT    The advocates of a stronger central authority already had gained momentum from the adversities of the times. Public creditors, merchants, and mechanics had a self-interest in a stronger central government, and many public-spirited men saw it as the only alternative to anarchy. Gradually they were breaking down the ingrained fear of a tyrannical central authority with the evidence that tyranny might come from other quarters. And one thing readers of another century must remember, conditioned as we are to see potential conflict between human rights and property rights, is that the American of the eighteenth century considered the security of property to be the foundation stone of liberty. What the eighteenth-century American might forget, however, was that the Shaysites were fighting in defense of their property too.

Already, well before the outbreaks in New England, the nationalist movement had come to demand a convention to revise the Articles of Confederation. Such a convention had been the subject of fruitless discussions in Congress, initiated by Charles Pinckney of South Carolina, but the initiative finally came from an unexpected quarter. In March 1785 commissioners from the states of Virginia and Maryland had met at Mount Vernon upon Washington's invitation to settle outstanding questions about the navigation of the Potomac and Chesapeake Bay. Washington had a personal interest in the river flowing by his door: it was a potential route to the West, with its upper reaches close to the upper reaches of the Ohio, where his military career had begun thirty years before. The delegates agreed on interstate cooperation, and Maryland suggested a further pact with Pennsylvania and Delaware to encourage water communication between the Chesapeake and the Ohio River; the Virginia legislature agreed, and at Madison's suggestion invited all thirteen states to send delegates for a general discussion of commercial problems. Nine states named representatives, but those from only five appeared at the Annapolis Convention in September 1786—Maryland itself failed to name delegates and neither the New England states nor the Carolinas and Georgia were represented. Apparent failure was turned into success, however, by the alert Alexander Hamilton, representing New York, who presented a resolution for still another convention in Philadelphia to consider all measures necessary "to render the constitution of the Federal Government adequate to the exigencies of the Union."

## Adopting the Constitution

THE CONSTITUTIONAL CONVENTION  After stalling for several months Congress fell in line on February 21, 1787, with a resolution endorsing as "expedient" a convention "for the sole and express purpose of revising the Articles of Confederation." By then five states had already named delegates; before the meeting, called to begin on May 14, 1787, six more states had acted. New Hampshire delayed until June and its delegates arrived in July. Rhode Island kept aloof throughout. On the appointed date only the delegates from Pennsylvania and Virginia appeared, but twenty-nine delegates from nine states began work on May 25. Altogether seventy-three men were elected by the state legislatures, fifty-five attended at one time or another, and after four months thirty-nine signed the Constitution they had drafted.

The durability and flexibility of that document testify to the remarkable quality of the men who made it, an assembly of "demi-gods" according to Jefferson, who was himself absent as a diplomat in France. They were surprisingly young: forty-two was the average age, although they ranged from the twenty-seven-year-old Jonathan Dayton of New Jersey to the eighty-one-year-old Benjamin Franklin, president of the state of Pennsylvania. They were even more surprisingly mature and foresighted: many of them were widely read in history, law, and political philosophy, familiar with the writings of Locke and Montesquieu, aware of the confederacies of the ancient world, and at the same time practical men of experience, tested in the fires of the Revolution. "Experience must be our only guide," John Dickinson said. "Reason may mislead us."

Washington and Franklin were the most famous of them at the time, and both, especially Washington, lent prestige and inspired confidence. More active in the debates were James Madison, the ablest political philosopher in the group; George Mason, author of the Virginia Bill of Rights; the witty and eloquent Gouverneur Morris and James Wilson of Pennsylvania, the latter one of the ablest lawyers in the colonies and next in importance in the convention only to Washington and Madison; Roger Sherman of Connecticut; and Elbridge Gerry of Massachusetts. Conspicuous by their absence were John Adams and Thomas Jefferson, then serving in London and Paris, and during most of the convention, Alexander Hamilton, since he could not vote once his two states'-rights colleagues from New York had gone home for good.

The delegates' differences on political philosophy for the most part fell within a narrow range. On certain fundamentals they generally agreed: that government derived its just powers from the consent of the people, but that society must be protected

*James Madison was only thirty-six when he assumed a major role in the drafting of the Constitution. This miniature is by Charles Willson Peale (c. 1783).*

from the tyranny of the majority; that the people at large must have a voice in their government, but that checks and balances must be provided to keep any one group from arrogating power; that a stronger central authority was essential, but that all power was subject to abuse. They believed that even the best of men were selfish by nature, and they harbored few illusions that government could be founded altogether upon a trust in goodwill and virtue. Since governments existed to restrain men, James Madison said, their very existence was "a reflection upon human nature." Yet by a careful arrangement of checks and balances, by checking power with power, the Founding Fathers hoped to devise institutions that could somehow constrain the sinfulness of individuals.

THE VIRGINIA AND NEW JERSEY PLANS    At the outset the delegates made Washington their president by unanimous vote. One of the first decisions was to meet behind closed doors, in order to discourage outside pressures and speeches to the galleries. The secrecy of the proceedings was remarkably well kept, and knowledge of the debates comes mainly from extensive notes kept by James Madison. It was Madison, too, who drafted the proposals which set the framework of the discussions. These proposals, which came to be called the "Virginia Plan," were presented on May 29 by Edmund Randolph, governor of the state and delegate to the convention. The Virginia plan embodied a revolutionary proposal for the delegates to scrap their instructions to revise the Articles of Confederation and to submit an entirely new document to the states. The plan proposed separate legislative, executive, and judicial branches, and a truly national government to make laws binding upon individual citizens and upon states as well. Congress would be divided into two houses, a lower house chosen by popular vote and an upper house chosen by the lower house from nominees of the state legislatures. Congress could disallow state laws under the plan and would itself define the extent of its and the states' authority.

On June 15 William Paterson submitted the New Jersey or small-state plan, which proposed to keep the existing structure of Congress, but to give it power to levy taxes and regulate commerce and authority to name a plural executive (with no veto) and a Supreme Court. The different plans presented the convention with two major issues: whether to amend the Articles or draft a new document, and whether to have congressional representation by states or by population. On the first point the Convention voted, June 19, to work toward a national government as envisioned by the Virginians. On the powers of this government there was little disagreement save in detail. Experience with the Articles had persuaded the delegates that an effective government, as distinguished from a confederation, needed the power to levy taxes, to regulate commerce, to raise an army and navy, and to make laws binding upon individual citizens. The lessons of the 1780s suggested to them, moreover, that in the interest of order and uniformity the states must be denied certain powers: to issue money, to abrogate contracts, to make treaties or wage war, to levy tariffs or export duties.

Disagreement then turned less on philosophy than on geography. The first clash in the convention involved the issue of representation. Delegates from the larger states generally favored the Virginia plan, which would base representation on population; those from the smaller states rallied behind the New Jersey plan, which would preserve an equal vote to each state. In hindsight the issue was a false one, since differing interests have seldom ranged the states into blocs according to size, but at the time it was the most divisive single question to rise in the convention and one that might have wrecked the whole enterprise. The solution was the "Great Compromise," sometimes called the "Connecticut Compromise," proposed by Roger Sherman, which gave both groups their way. The larger states won apportionment by population in the House of Representatives; the smaller states got equality in the Senate, but with the vote there by individuals and not by states.

Geographic division cut another way in a struggle between northern and southern delegates which turned upon slavery and the regulation of trade, an omen of sectional controversies to come. Southerners, with slaves so numerous in their states, wanted them counted as part of the population in determining the number of their representatives. Northerners were happy enough to have slaves counted in deciding each state's share of direct taxes but not for purposes of representation. On this issue the Confederation Congress had supplied a handy precedent when it sought an amendment to make population rather than land values the standard for fiscal requisitions. The proposed amendment to the Articles would have counted three-fifths of the slaves for this purpose. The delegates, with little dissent, agreed to incorporate the same three-fifths ratio in the new Constitution as a basis for apportioning both representatives and direct taxes.

A more sensitive issue was presented by an effort to prevent the central government from stopping the foreign slave trade. Again, since slavery had not yet become the overriding issue it

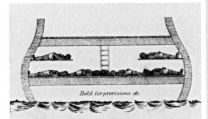

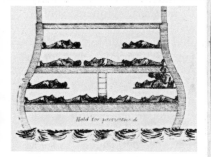

*This cross-sectional view of the British slave ship* Brookes *indicates the abominably crowded conditions the "cargo" endured in the international slave trade.*

later became, the question was fairly readily settled by establishing a time limit. "The morality or wisdom of slavery," said Oliver Ellsworth of Connecticut, "are considerations belonging to the states themselves." Congress could not forbid the foreign slave trade before 1808, but could levy a tax of $10 a head on all slaves imported. In both provisions, a sense of delicacy dictated the use of euphemisms. The Constitution spoke of "free Persons" and "all other persons," of "such persons as any of the States Now existing shall think proper to admit," and of persons "held to Service of Labor." The odious word "slavery" did not appear in the Constitution until the Thirteenth Amendment (1865) abolished the "peculiar institution" by name.

The final decision on the slave trade was linked to a compromise on the question of the broader congressional power to regulate commerce. Northern states, where the merchant and shipping interests were most influential, were prepared to give Congress unlimited powers, but the southerners feared that navigation acts favoring American shipping might work at the expense of getting southern commodities to the market by reducing foreign competition with northern shippers. Southerners therefore demanded that navigation acts be passed only by a two-thirds vote, but finally traded this demand for a prohibition on congressional power to levy export taxes and for a twenty-year, instead of a ten-year, delay on the power to prohibit the slave trade.

THE SEPARATION OF POWERS  Their essential agreement on the need for a new frame of government kept the delegates from lapsing into quarelling factions: they were determined to seek accommodation. The details of governmental structure, while causing disagreement, occasioned far less trouble than the basic issues pitting the large and small states, the northern and southern states. Existing state constitutions, which already separated powers among legislative, executive, and judicial branches, set an example which reinforced the convention's resolve to disperse power with checks and balances. The American version of checks and balances did not correspond to the old Whig model which separated powers among British commons, lords, and king, since Americans had neither lords nor a king—and the new document would specifically forbid titles of nobility—but there were parallels. The Founding Fathers expected the lower house to be closest to the people who elected it every two years. The upper house, chosen by state legislatures, was at one remove from the voters. Staggered terms of six years further isolated

Signing the Constitution, September 17, 1787. *Thomas Pritchard Rossiter's painting shows George Washington presiding over what Thomas Jefferson called "an assembly of demi-gods."*

senators from the passing fancies of public passion by preventing the choice of a majority in any given year. Senators were expected to be, if not an American House of Lords, at least something like the colonial councils, a body of dignitaries advising the president as the councils had advised the governors.

And the president was to be an almost kingly figure. The chief executive was subject to election every four years, but the executive powers corresponded to those which British theory still extended to the king; in practice these powers actually exceeded the monarch's powers. This was the sharpest departure from the recent experience in state government, where the office of governor had commonly been downgraded because of the recent memory of struggles with the colonial executives. The president had a veto over acts of Congress, subject to being overridden by a two-thirds vote in each house, although the royal veto had long since fallen into complete disuse. The president was commander-in-chief of the armed forces, and responsible for the execution of the laws. The chief executive could make treaties with the advice and consent of two-thirds of the Senate, and had the power to appoint diplomats, judges, and other officers with the consent of a Senate majority.

The president was instructed to report annually on the state of the nation and was authorized to recommend legislation, a provision which presidents eventually would take as a mandate to form and promote extensive programs. Unlike the king, however, the president could be removed for cause, by action short of revolution. The House could impeach (indict) the chief executive—and other civil officers—on charges of treason, bribery, or "other high crimes and misdemeanors," and the Senate could remove an impeached president by a two-thirds vote upon conviction. The presiding officer at the trial of a president would be the chief justice, since the usual presiding officer of the Senate (the vice-president) would have a personal stake in the outcome.

The convention's nationalists—men like Madison, James Wilson, and Hamilton—wanted to strengthen the independence of the executive by entrusting the choice to popular election. At least in this instance the nationalists, often accused of being the aristocratic party, favored a bold new departure in democracy. But an elected executive was still too far beyond the American experience. Besides, a national election would have created enormous problems of organization and voter qualification. Wilson suggested instead that the people of each state choose presidential electors equal to the number of their senators and representatives. Others proposed that the legislators make the choice. Finally, late in the convention, it was voted to let the legislature decide the method in each state. Before long nearly all the states were choosing the electors by popular vote, and the electors were acting as agents of party will, casting their votes as they had pledged before the election. This method was contrary to the original expectation that the electors would deliberate and make their own choices.

On the third branch of government, the judiciary, there was surprisingly little debate. Both the Virginia and New Jersey plans had called for a Supreme Court, which the Constitution established, providing specifically for a chief justice of the United States and leaving up to Congress the number of other justices. The only dispute was on courts "inferior" to the Supreme Court, and that too was left up to Congress. Although the Constitution nowhere authorized the courts to declare laws void when they conflicted with the Constitution, the power of judicial review was almost surely intended by the framers, and was soon exercised in cases involving both state and federal laws. Article VI declared the federal constitution, federal laws, and treaties to be the "supreme law of the land," state laws or constitutions to the contrary notwithstanding. At the time the advocates of states' rights thought this a victory, since it eliminated the proviso in the Virginia plan for Congress to settle all conflicts with state authority. As it turned out the clause became the basis for an important expansion of judicial review.

While the Constitution extended vast new powers to the national government, the delegates' mistrust of unchecked power is apparent in repeated examples of countervailing forces: the separation of the three branches of government, the president's veto, the congressional power of impeachment and removal, the Senate's power over treaties and appointments, the courts' implied right of judicial review. In addition the new frame of government specifically forbade Congress to pass bills of attainder (criminal condemnation by legislative act) or ex post facto laws (laws adopted after the event to make past deeds criminal). It also reserved to the states large areas of sovereignty—a reservation soon made explicit by the Tenth Amendment.

The most glaring defect of the Articles of Confederation, the rule of unanimity which defeated every effort to amend them, led the delegates to provide a less forbidding though still difficult method of amending the new Constitution. Amendments could be proposed either by two-thirds vote of each house or by a convention especially called upon application of two-thirds of the legislatures. Amendments could be ratified by approval of three-fourths of the states acting through their legislatures or special conventions. The national convention has never been used, however, and state conventions have been called only once—to ratify the repeal of the Eighteenth Amendment, which had established Prohibition.

THE FIGHT FOR RATIFICATION   The old rule of unanimity, if applied to ratification of the Constitution itself, would almost surely have doomed its chances at the outset. The final article of the Constitution therefore provided that it would become effective upon ratification by nine states (not quite the three-fourths majority required for amendment). Conventions were specified as the proper agency for ratification, since legislatures might be expected to boggle at giving up any of their powers. The procedure, insofar as it bypassed the existing Articles of Confederation, constituted a legal revolution, but it was one in which the Confederation Congress joined. After fighting off efforts to censure the convention for exceeding its authority, the Congress submitted its work to the states on September 28, 1787.

In the ensuing political debate, advocates of the new Constitution, who might properly have been called Nationalists because they preferred a strong central government, assumed the more reassuring name of Federalists. Opponents, who favored a more decentralized federal system, became Antifederalists. The initiative which the Federalists took in assuming their name was characteristic of the whole campaign. They got the jump on their critics. Their leaders, who had been members of the convention, were already familiar with the document and the arguments on each point. They were not only better prepared but better organized, and on the whole, made up of the more articulate elements in the community.

Much ink has been spilled by historians in debating the motivation of the advocates of the new Constitution. For more than a century the tendency prevailed to idolize the Founding Fathers who created what one nineteenth-century British statesman called "the most wonderful work ever struck off at a given time by the brain and purpose of man." In 1913, however, Charles A. Beard's book *An Economic Interpretation of the Constitution* advanced the amazing thesis that the Philadelphia "assembly of demi-gods" was made up of humans who had a selfish interest in the outcome. They held large amounts of depreciated government securities and otherwise stood to gain from the power and stability of the new order.

Beard argued that the delegates represented an economic elite of those who held mainly "personalty" against those who held mainly "realty." The first group was an upper crust of lawyers, merchants, speculators in western lands, holders of depreciated government securities, and creditors whose wealth was mostly in "paper": mortgages, stocks, bonds, and the like. The second group consisted of small farmers and planters whose wealth was mostly in land and slaves. The holders of western lands and government bonds stood to gain from a stronger government. Creditors generally stood to gain from the prohibitions against state currency issues and against the impairment of contract, provisions clearly aimed at the paper money issues and stay laws (granting stays, or postponements, on debt payments) then effective in many states.

Beard's thesis was a useful antidote to hero worship, and still contains a germ of truth, but he rested his argument too heavily on the claim that holders of personalty predominated in the convention. Most of the delegates, according to evidence unavailable to Beard, had no compelling stake in paper wealth, and most were far more involved in landholding. After doing exhaustive research into the actual holdings of the Founding Fathers, the historian Forrest McDonald announced in his book *We the People: The Economic Origins of the Constitution* that Beard's "economic interpretation of the Constitution does not work." Many prominent nationalists, including the "Father of the Constitution," James Madison himself, had no western lands, bonds, or much other personalty. Some opponents of the Constitution, on the other hand, held large blocks of personalty. McDonald did not deny that economic interests figured in the process, but they